A GUIDE TO TEACHING IN THE ACTIVE LEARNING CLASSROOM

A GUIDE TO TEACHING IN THE ACTIVE LEARNING CLASSROOM

History, Research, and Practice

Paul Baepler, J. D. Walker,
D. Christopher Brooks, Kem Saichaie,
and Christina I. Petersen

Foreword by Bradley A. Cohen

1996–2016   20TH ANNIVERSARY

Stylus
PUBLISHING, LLC.

STERLING, VIRGINIA

COPYRIGHT © 2016 BY
STYLUS PUBLISHING, LLC.

Published by Stylus Publishing, LLC.
22883 Quicksilver Drive
Sterling, Virginia 20166-2102

Library of Congress Cataloging-in-Publication Data
Names: Baepler, Paul Michel, author.
Title: A guide to teaching in the active learning classroom : history,
research, and practice / Paul Baepler, J.D. Walker, D. Christopher
Brooks, Kem Saichaie, and Christina Petersen ; foreword by Bradley
A. Cohen.
Description: First edition. | Sterling, Virginia : Stylus Publishing,
2016. | Includes bibliographical references and index.
Identifiers: LCCN 2015042806 (print) | LCCN 2016004149
(ebook) |
    ISBN 9781620362990 (cloth : alk. paper) |
    ISBN 9781620363003 (pbk. : alk. paper) |
    ISBN 9781620363010 (library networkable e-edition) |
    ISBN 9781620363027 (e-book) |
    ISBN 9781620363027 (consumer e-edition)
Subjects: LCSH: Active learning. | Classroom environment. |
Classroom management.
Classification: LCC LB1027.23 .B34 2016 (print) | LCC
LB1027.23 (ebook) | DDC 371.102--dc23
LC record available at http://lccn.loc.gov/2015042806

13-digit ISBN: 978-1-62036-299-0 (cloth)
13-digit ISBN: 978-1-62036-300-3 (paperback)
13-digit ISBN: 978-1-62036-301-0 (library networkable e-edition)
13-digit ISBN: 978-1-62036-302-7 (consumer e-edition)

Printed in the United States of America

All first editions printed on acid-free paper
that meets the American National Standards Institute
Z39-48 Standard.

Bulk Purchases

Quantity discounts are available for use in workshops and for
staff development.
Call 1-800-232-0223

First Edition, 2016

IN MEMORIAM

Kathleen O'Donovan
1945–2013

Scholar and Teacher
University of Minnesota

"I believe that teachers are like architects; that is, they design spaces, select materials, create innovative outcomes, and engender patterns of interaction that may well change not only the landscape of their students' outside world, but also the inner terrain of their bodies, minds, and hearts."

For Melanie. PB
For Valerie. JDW
For Naomi & Oliver. DCB
For Amanda, and pioneering educators everywhere. KS
For my father, Austin Petersen. CIP

CONTENTS

FOREWORD

Form follows function—that has been misunderstood. Form and function should be one,
joined in a spiritual union.

—Frank Lloyd Wright

Universities globally are engaged in a dynamic and thrilling exploration of the interplay among environment, pedagogy, and learning.
The reasons for this focus are varied, but one obvious driver is technology. Instantaneous access to nearly all human knowledge calls into question our traditional instructional practices, and the advent of fully online
degree programs (and, indeed, fully virtual universities) has given rise to
fundamental arguments as to why we have physical classrooms at all. While
reports of the death of the college campus are greatly exaggerated, they represent legitimate challenges to our traditions. More positively, new discoveries in how people learn suggest opportunities for new classroom-based
instructional methods that depart substantially from tradition. Traditional
classroom design, however, works against these pedagogies. One important
response to these challenges and opportunities is the rise of new learning
space designs like the Active Learning Classroom (ALC). As *places* where
people go to learn, universities require *spaces* that enable a powerful kind of
learning experience not easily accessed in any other way.

Higher education's traditional promise was that you went to the ivory
tower to gain the esoteric knowledge locked behind institutional walls. Once
behind the walls, the knowledge was recited to you; lecturers and lecture
halls make perfect sense in this context. That we no longer fully operate in
such a context is evident to anybody with a passing familiarity with modern
universities. The rise of the modern research university, the emergence of
student-centered and student success movements, the impact of influential
centers for teaching and learning, and persistent experimentation in curricular design and course delivery have moved us significantly forward from
traditional practice. (It is perhaps worth pausing to emphasize this obvious
but frequently overlooked fact of routine change that has been the mark of
our institutions for a very long time. Though we are inherently conserva-
tive, and traditions die hard, we are not, as some in the media would have
it, ossified replicas of medieval institutions.) Nonetheless, our classroom

designs remained largely unexamined and unchanging in their basic orienta-
tion. Lecture halls dominated, and innovation, such as it was, was in how to
build ever larger halls. While there was evolution, education as transmission
of knowledge remained steadfastly at the heart of our designs. Then along
came Google, and now, our great halls and the instructional practices that
dominate them do indeed seem, well, medieval. But—and this is the thrilling part—what to shift to in terms of both design and practice remains an
open question. We must embrace an experimental approach to finding our
way forward. Hence, the power of this book is in setting the historical context, providing a research base upon which to build, and exploring promising
instructional practices for one general design type emerging as an important
part of a larger portfolio of new learning space designs and instructional
practices that enable and support transformative learning experiences.

Importantly, new learning environments like ALCs are not merely a
response to disruptive threats. Indeed, early experiments in this form were
driven by a far more creative and positive force: a desire for better learning
outcomes and the belief that the environment had a great deal to do with
it. The fact is, we are enjoying a remarkably fertile period in the learning
sciences. Systemic and growing capacity to study brains in action and sophisticated new research methodologies in the social sciences have yielded surprising insights into how people learn. A good lecture can be a good learning
experience, but we now have irrefutable evidence revealing the limits of the
lecture-centric pedagogical tradition—especially for traditional undergraduate students—and the power of more collaborative problem-based models to
help more students learn more deeply. And we continue to learn more about
human learning with a frequency that challenges even our most dedicated
instructors to maintain awareness of critical discoveries warranting changes in
practice. New classroom designs, and practices within those spaces informed
by the science of learning, offer us the opportunity to achieve far more with
and for our students. It is a remarkable time to be a teacher, and perhaps one
that calls for renewed investment in expert pedagogical support to take full
advantage of the moment and these unique spaces.

Disruption and discovery compel us to both explore new learning space
designs on our campuses and experiment with innovative and evidence-based
instructional practices that foster deeper learning and more intimate connections between our classrooms and the physical and virtual worlds beyond.
Nevertheless, a cautionary note is in order. Students and teachers remain
wed to perhaps a more comforting and familiar view of education as the
transmission of knowledge. New learning spaces, like new teaching practices,
upset expectations and challenge both students and instructors to develop
new capacities. Building nonstandard spaces in tradition-bound institutions

is hard. Building a classroom experience that challenges deeply held beliefs about what is supposed to happen in these spaces is even harder. The authors of this book and, by proxy, the intrepid faculty and students whose experiences fill these pages bring experience and insight into why ALCs are so vital today, how to continue to study new space designs, and which practices optimize student outcomes in these spaces. If you are realizing the need for a new kind of learning space on your campus, or if you have new learning spaces but are unsure how to use them or want to know how well you are using them, you could ask for no better guide than this one.

Bradley A. Cohen
Ohio University

ACKNOWLEDGMENTS

Writing this book would not have been possible without the generous contributions of so many instructors and staff who allowed us into their classrooms, spoke with us at length, shared materials with us, commented on drafts of chapters, and otherwise generously contributed their time and insight. Much of the research and the insightful practical advice contained in this book came via their courses, their experiences, and their students. We hope this volume magnifies their hard work and helps many students and instructors who learn and teach in these rooms. And we hope they pardon us for any misrepresentation of their work.

Sue Wick, University of Minnesota
David Matthes, University of Minnesota
Michelle Driessen, University of Minnesota
Sehoya Cotner, University of Minnesota
Robin Wright, University of Minnesota
Brian Gibbens, University of Minnesota
Mark Decker, University of Minnesota
Deena Wassenberg, University of Minnesota
Anna Mosser, University of Minnesota
Anna Strain, University of Minnesota
Michael Burns, University of Minnesota
Jay Hatch, University of Minnesota
Chistopher Cramer, University of Minnesota
Leslie Schiff, University of Minnesota
Jigna Desai, University of Minnesota
Murray Jensen, University of Minnesota
Robert Poch, University of Minnesota
Lee-Ann Breuch, University of Minnesota
Catherine Solheim, University of Minnesota
Christina Clarkson, University of Minnesota
Erin Malone, University of Minnesota
Tim Kamenar, University of Minnesota
Scott Marshall, University of Minnesota
Jay Wilson, University of Minnesota
Alex Lubet, University of Minnesota

John Knowles, University of Minnesota
Jeremy Todd, University of Minnesota
Robert McMaster, University of Minnesota
Karen Hanson, University of Minnesota
Ilene Alexander, University of Minnesota
Lauren Marsh, University of Minnesota
Kimerly Wilcox, University of Minnesota
Paul Ching, University of Minnesota
Anita Gonzalez, University of Minnesota
Vanna Han, University of Minnesota
David Langley, University of Minnesota
Jeff Lindgren, University of Minnesota
Kate Martin, University of Minnesota
Colleen Meyers, University of Minnesota
Deb Wingert, University of Minnesota
Jane O'Brien, University of Minnesota
Bill Rozaitis, University of Minnesota
Mary Jetter, University of Minnesota
Elena Stetsenko, University of Minnesota
Barbara Beers, University of Minnesota
Kristi Jensen, University of Minnesota
Chris Parker, University of Minnesota
Richard G. Tiberius, University of Miami
Aimee Whiteside, University of Tampa
Robert J. Beichner, North Carolina State University
Joyce Weinsheimer, Georgia Institute of Technlogy
Sam Van Horne, University of Iowa
Jean Florman, University of Iowa
Mary Adamek, University of Iowa
Carolyn Colvin, University of Iowa
Pilar Marce, University of Iowa
David McGraw, University of Iowa
Stephen Silva, University of Iowa
Glenn Caffery, University of Massachusetts, Amherst
Adena Calden, University of Massachusetts, Amherst
Leda Cooks, University of Massachusetts, Amherst
Curtice Griffin, University of Massachusetts, Amherst
David Gross, University of Massachusetts, Amherst
Heath Hatch, University of Massachusetts, Amherst
Anita Milman, University of Massachusetts, Amherst
Jon Berndt Olsen, University of Massachusetts, Amherst
TreaAndrea Russworm, University of Massachusetts, Amherst
Kristina Stinson, University of Massachusetts, Amherst
Ludmila Tyler, University of Massachusetts, Amherst

Mei-Yau Shih, University of Massachusetts, Amherst
Bradford Wheeler, University of Massachusetts, Amherst
Nodar Kereselidze, University of Massachusetts, Amherst
Rachel Sagner Buurma, Swarthmore College
Linda Jorn, University of Wisconsin, Madison
Tanya Joosten, University of Wisconsin, Milwaukee
David A. Wicks, Seattle Pacific University
Kim Sawers, Seattle Pacific University
Jessica Knott, Michigan State University
Severin Grabski, Michigan State University
Laura A. Pasquini, University of North Texas
Marco Molinaro, University of California, Davis
Matt Steinwachs, University of California, Davis
Chris Pagliarulo, University of California, Davis
Tiffany Johnson, University of California, Davis
Kara Moloney, University of California, Davis
Jim Schaaf, University of California, Davis
Jean VanderGheynst, University of California, Davis
Diana Oblinger, EDUCAUSE
Ana Franco-Watkins Auburn University
Diane Boyd, Auburn University
Guy Rohrbaugh, Auburn University
Scott Simkins, Auburn University
Mary Deane Sorcinelli, Mount Holyoke College
Cheryl Neudaur, Minneapolis Community and Technical College

The authors would also like to thank Melanie Brown, who read the manuscript at various stages—suggesting valuable changes; reformatting the text; and, in some cases, adding new thoughts and outside perspectives. Her steady and consistent readings helped us immensely.

INTRODUCTION

*T**his could be great, or this could be a real disaster.* That's an opinion we've heard in one form or another from many students and instructors when they encounter an Active Learning Classroom (ALC) for the first time. At the very least, they're pretty certain that what's going to happen in the classroom is not business as usual, and that sense in itself can be disconcerting or exciting. Briefly, ALCs are classrooms that arrange students around tables, each table with a whiteboard mounted on the wall and often with the capacity to project the screen of a student's laptop to the rest of the class. One of our motivations for writing this book is to ease this transition into ALCs and help instructors and students find their place in them more quickly and learn how to use them to their best advantage. As we start to explore these rooms, though, let's take a moment to recognize how disorienting they can be, and try to see them from the newcomer's point of view.

Imagine the *student*. What's going through his mind when he walks into his first ALC? He's probably a little lost, trying to find his bearings by locating the front and the back of the room. Where is he supposed to look? Maybe he's wondering what's going on with all of those flat-screen TVs. Is he going to have to learn some new technology on top of everything else in this course? If not immediately upon seeing the round tables, then by the time he sits down, he knows he's going to be facing other students. People are going to be looking at him and talking to him, and that probably means group work, which, he knows from past courses, can go a lot of different ways. Maybe he has had an experience similar to that of a recent student who voiced his trepidation about working collaboratively in an ALC: "Listen, I get we are all supposed to help each other, but the world doesn't always work that way. People can be assholes."

Notwithstanding that particular student's warning, in general we know that students value ALCs and feel more engaged in classes held in them. In their survey comments, students have suggested they frequently value interactions with their peers. One student wrote, "My group members are great; they work hard on the projects." But despite her appreciation of her classmates, the same student was also critical of the way the instructor structured the work and selected the topics. The student wrote,

The projects are in depth; however, they do not measure disciplinary knowledge. This class is based on group work, and the group work simply tests group work skills; people do not learn basic disciplinary knowledge in this class, just a few oddly specific topics.

Another student in a different course commented, "The professors get so wrapped up in their classroom activities they fail to actually explain the concepts in a way that helps me learn the material." So the students' experience is mixed, and their potential for frustration is real.

Now, imagine the *instructor's* initial reactions to teaching in an ALC. Here is how one recalled her first moments in the room:

> I walked in the first day. . . . It was not baffling to me, but it was quite a shock to come in and see the setup. . . . It was a psychological adjustment the first time because I walked in expecting a new classroom but not this setup where I'm not in the center of the class. I expected to be kind of in the front of the class and have blackboards and things like that. So I have now come to really like it but the first day was not just a surprise, it was not even in my conception because I had never seen anything like it before.

To this instructor, the room itself was "not baffling"—after all, it's still a university classroom. Its arrangement was out of the ordinary, though, and took "a psychological adjustment." The ALC is a highly designed space that raises many unanswered questions for the instructor: Where is the actual front of the room? Where is the whiteboard? I see whiteboards for all the student tables, but where am I going to write *my* stuff so everyone can see it? If everyone or even every third person has a laptop, how am I ever going to get students to stop surfing the web and pay attention to what they're supposed to be doing? And what, quite frankly, are students *supposed* to be doing in here if I'm not lecturing? They say these spaces work, but I'm not sure it's going to work for me (see Image I.1).

These kinds of questions often greet the arrival of ALCs on campus. After spending some time teaching in the classrooms, though, and after plenty of trial and error, instructors have reported a more nuanced picture begins to come into focus. One cautiously optimistic instructor found it difficult to locate the sweet spot between lecture and active learning in his graduate-level, math-based course. He pruned lecture at the start of the course but found he had gone too far and needed to reincorporate some didactic material. With an advanced science course, he contends, students largely have no experience in the topic: "It doesn't do me any good to ask you to use your past background to discuss amongst yourselves the quantum mechanical harmonic oscillator when you've never heard of a quantum mechanical

Image I.1. ALC at the University of Minnesota.

oscillator. That's why I've struggled a little bit." But this same instructor tried a few new activities. For instance, one day a week, he had students analyze journal articles in teams, each team member taking on a specific role, and each team randomly chosen to report its findings. The students became so accustomed to working together that one day when he arrived late to class, they were already working on their articles. He said he never experienced a sudden epiphany about the rooms, but he acknowledged "a slow growth in my appreciation of just how amazing the effects of a round table can be."

Another instructor had a long history of incorporating active learning into her microbiology courses. For her initial virology class in the ALC, she didn't make many adjustments: "Just seeing what it was like to have students not lined up like prisoners [in auditorium rows] was enough of an experiment the first semester." This instructor had frequently incorporated active learning activities into her courses in traditional classrooms, but she found many of the students were reluctant and even a bit surly. The most resistant students would sit in the back of the class, and the more engaged people would sit toward the front, with students of various dispositions positioned in between. She called this self-selected pattern the "passive-aggressive gradient" that traditional rooms inspire by their stock seating arrangements. She expressed what many instructors have said, that the ALCs *feel* friendlier, even if the student population hasn't changed. It's a felt experience: "I'm not thinking that the nerds are in the front and the people in the back don't care. There are people who don't care, but they're sprinkled in with other people, and they're everywhere. They're *all* everywhere."

Thwarting the passive-aggressive gradient significantly alters the way instructors teach and students learn. Let's return to the first instructor in this introduction, the one who didn't have even a conception of what the room was about when she first entered it. After the semester was over, she remarked that she was pleasantly surprised by the space because students remained alert and never fell asleep. She noted that because of how they were seated, everyone was watching each other. "The surveillance level in the active learning classroom," she said, "is different than in a lecture hall where there is a more passive role that they assume that they're going to take, and so previously they haven't imagined themselves as actually being engaged." In the ALCs, the design of the space presents a set of conditions that assumes active engagement. For one thing, instructors can move closer to students as they walk through the room and speak with them face-to-face. This instructor describes the shift she notices as a subtle one: "There's still a power structure, there's still a hierarchy, there's still a *the instructor is more performative than the student* feel, but the students are part of an engaged audience. . . . They feel closer to me, and I feel less unavailable to them."

With each of these stories, derived from interviews and surveys we conducted from 2008 to 2015, we begin to see a more complete picture of teaching in the ALCs. What's more, we begin to observe that with this new potential there comes a slew of new challenges. For instance, some instructors have noted a sense of loss when they reduce the amount of time they lecture. A biology instructor rather ruefully admitted, "The big deal is the humbling deal." She was no longer the "rock star" at the podium; in fact, she had to struggle to feel relevant: "I almost have to be speaking in iambic pentameter or setting my hair on fire or something so that they will actually be listening." She came to realize that it really wasn't fair of her to first goad her students to engage in an activity at their table and then expect them to suddenly stop everything to listen to her, whipsawing between lecture and activities. The teaching role can also feel diminished to some because so much of an instructor's effort is put into designing learning activities rather than presenting material, and students don't necessarily recognize this work as formal teaching. Indeed, they may overlook the effort it takes to design a good course and instead feel part of an "educational experiment" and think that they are somehow cheated because they are teaching themselves. One student rather archly put it, "I'm not putting myself into massive debt to come here and learn from/ teach my fellow students. I'm paying thousands of dollars a year to learn from and be taught by an expert in the field." Thus, with more experience in these rooms, instructors have come to realize that part of effective teaching in the ALCs involves explaining the value and rationale of the instructional method, something that was often taken for granted in the lecture hall.

That we have to "teach the room" as well as the topic is just one of the lessons we've learned over the years through observing classes, interviewing faculty, listening to student focus groups, surveying students directly, and analyzing learning outcomes. As its title suggests, this book takes an historical, empirical, and practical look at the ALCs to give instructors informed guidance on how to gain the greatest educational advantage for their students. We began conducting the research that is presented in this volume in 2007 at the University of Minnesota, but the idea for the ALCs didn't start with us: The methods that work in these rooms have been tried and tested at many institutions. This book seeks to draw together advantageous teaching practices, some unique to the ALCs and others that make sense based on the type of instruction that the rooms' design suggests. Much of our advice in this book is based on a strong body of research; in other cases, we have relied on the suggestions of experienced instructors who have tried these techniques in a variety of classrooms. It's this combination of research and hands-on experience that we believe makes a compelling case for instructors to consider, particularly when faced with teaching in such an unfamiliar learning environment.

**

At this point, we may want to remind ourselves of the larger reason why instructors choose to teach in the room. It's not simply because the rooms are novel or that they create a sense of intimacy between the instructor and student. It's that the design of the space in which one teaches matters to learning. Over the course of nearly two decades, foundational research from North Carolina State University and the Massachusetts Institute of Technology produced strong indications that ALCs lead to positive student outcomes. Beginning around 1995, Professor Robert Beichner began to collect and analyze data from North Carolina State's ALCs—what they called their Student-Centered Active Learning Environment with Upside-down Pedagogies (SCALE-UP) initiative—using grades to measure student performance (Beichner et al., 1999). Comparing students taught in ALCs to those taught in traditional rooms, they concluded that students in ALCs performed better. Follow-up studies at many other institutions among thousands of students found similar results. The experiments, however, often compared simultaneous changes in the room and in the course design, so although the findings are suggestive that the ALCs had an impact, they were not conclusive. At this point in the research narrative, we could not be absolutely certain that the move to teaching in ALCs resulted in better learning results. Chapter 1 explores the early history of ALCs.

Starting in the fall of 2008, we began to conduct a series of quasi-experimental research studies at the University of Minnesota to isolate the effects of the space on student learning. In our comparisons between courses taught in ALCs and those taught in traditional rooms, we held as much constant as we possibly could, including instructor, time of day, syllabus, textbook and lab materials, in-class activities, assignments, assessments, and exams. We were unable to randomly assign students to each section, but in every other meaningful way we held the learning conditions constant. Our analysis of this study and its replication indicated that ALCs have an independent and statistically significant positive impact on student learning as measured by grades. We could confidently conclude that space indeed matters to learning. In subsequent experiments, we also found that how one teaches in the space also matters, and that a class can be flipped and blended using an ALC in a manner that reduces the total time a student spends in the ALC classroom and still produces superior outcomes. Chapter 2 outlines the parameters of these experiments in greater detail.

More recently, we began to investigate possible mechanisms and moderators that might explain how the ALCs make possible these beneficial results. As we have seen, instructors have noted a change in their relationships with students, describing them as more intimate and close. Students, too, have repeatedly noted the tighter connections they feel with other students. We call this classroom ethos the "social context" of the space, the network of formal and informal connections between the instructor and students as well as among the students. Drawing on student surveys, student focus groups, and long-form interviews with instructors, we developed and validated a reliable measure of social context, the SCALE (Social Context and Active Learning) survey. Our analysis shows social context expressed in four factors or dimensions and details the positive and negative implications of what students are experiencing in the ALCs as well as the contribution different elements of social context make to student learning outcomes. These findings and a fuller explanation of the four dimensions of social context are discussed in Chapter 3.

With a deeper understanding of the legacy and efficacy of ALCs, as well as of how the rooms condition learning experiences, we turn in Chapter 4 to the immediate questions of those who face teaching in these rooms for the first time. This chapter attends to key questions that instructors who are contemplating a shift into teaching in these rooms ask. We cover basic issues such as, "Where should I position myself in the room" and "How do I discuss the benefits of the room with reluctant students?"

Some challenges are simply too complex to discuss meaningfully in brief, so we devote entire chapters to these issues. For instance, instructors frequently seek ideas about what to do if not lecture in these rooms. Chapter 5 presents a range of activities and assignments that have been adopted successfully in the ALCs. We look at semester-long assignments and shorter activities, many of which call for group work or more formal team approaches. We devote Chapter 6 to a discussion of how to manage student groups effectively. Among other topics, we look at how to assemble groups, hold them accountable, and help student groups succeed outside of class.

Chapter 7 takes up the topic of conducting student assessment in the ALCs. Some students and instructors have found that conducting traditional testing in the rooms is difficult simply because, seated at round tables, students are able to look at each other and have been conditioned to work with each other but have not been allowed to take exams together. We look at how instructors can continue to conduct traditional exams in the ALCs and also how they might consider alternative assessments, such as collaborative quizzing and projects that call upon the affordances of the room, such as the projection screens or the fact that students can be assigned to tables, groups, and seats.

To this point, much of this book speaks to the relative advantage of the ALCs and how to manage the shift to them. Some students, however, may struggle in these rooms. For instance, some international students might not have experienced any form of active learning in their secondary education and find the social interaction difficult to fathom. Students with visual, auditory, and mobile disabilities may find various aspects of the classroom challenging to navigate. Chapter 8 presents strategies for supporting all students in the ALCs.

One of the principles animating this book is that instructors need some practical guidance and support to use the ALCs well. In Chapter 9, we suggest several approaches to working with instructors, including low-stakes interventions such as brown-bag series, technical trainings, and workshops, as well as more intensive efforts like faculty learning communities. We even include a catalog of stand-alone workshop topics and questions (see Appendix 9.1) and a full agenda for a comprehensive summer institute for schools that want to provide an in-depth, immersive, 3-day event (see Appendix 9.2).

Many instructors who invest energy into redesigning their courses want to know at the end of the term whether the effort was worth it. They want to know whether their own students benefit from the experience, a new activity is working, or students are generally satisfied with their time in the ALCs. Investigating these questions and the many others that ALCs pose requires a systematic approach to research and considerable planning. We provide some guidance on how to begin to think about conducting learning spaces research in Chapter 10.

**

The road to the ALCs is paved with Jeremiads decrying the state of traditional educational methods, from Dewey (1916) to Obama's President's Council of Advisors on Science and Technology (2012) *Engage to Excel* report. In 2006, Merrow put forward one of the most memorable descriptions of the state of American education by framing the situation this way:

> Many instructors and students have arrived at the equivalent of a non-aggression pact—"Don't expect too much of my time because I have research to do, and I won't ask much of you but will see that you get a decent grade." (p. 10)

His is a powerful indictment, and we do not disagree; but, as always, there is a countervailing story. Many faculty have been arguing forcefully for a changed way of teaching, swimming against the tide for decades. They have seen active learning succeed in their traditional classrooms, despite its awkward fit. They have made do, and they have made active learning work.

This book tries not to be one more polemic. Although we lay out the empirical case for ALCs, we understand that instructors will gravitate toward them *or not* as occasions arise and on their own terms. Beyond stating the case for ALCs, we hope to provide some guidance and inspiration for those who find themselves teaching in one. As we mention early on, it's natural to be wary of teaching in a new environment. In this case, however, a little experience, vicarious or actual, goes a long way to quelling that uncertainty. We hope this book opens up this world to you.

I

HISTORY AND RESEARCH ON ACTIVE LEARNING CLASSROOMS

The classic lecture hall that efficiently accommodates hundreds of students in a tiered-seating amphitheater works well for many purposes, including recitations, scientific demonstrations, media projection, and limited exchanges between presenter and audience. With some goodwill from students, an instructor can successfully, if awkwardly, engage students in collaborative exercises and peer instruction (Deslauriers, Schelew, & Wieman, 2011; Lyon & Lagowski, 2008; Mazur, 2009). There's no escaping, however, that stationary seating in rows with limited desk space and almost no access to a whiteboard restricts the possibilities for how students interact with each other and with the content of the course. It's difficult for students to navigate between seats or to rearrange themselves so they can face each other to discuss a question or work on a common problem. Instructors can find it difficult to keep track of individual groups of students or to wade into the center of the room to answer questions. It's a lecture hall, after all, and while it can be made to serve many purposes, it's optimized for lectures.

There is a growing body of evidence, however, that shows that students profit from what Russ Edgerton termed *pedagogies of engagement* (K. A. Smith, Sheppard, Johnson, & Johnson, 2005). These pedagogies have many names: process-oriented guided-inquiry learning (POGIL), peer learning, team-based learning (TBL), cooperative learning, and more. As we come to accept the value of these methods, it only makes sense that colleges and universities would invest in a new style of learning space that promotes these techniques and a user-centered design. It is also not surprising that these new and expensive classrooms would rise in prominence at a moment when online learning has dramatically expanded and inherently questioned traditional approaches to higher education. In some ways, the rise of the new classroom can be seen as a response to the virtual learning environment. These new learning spaces, after all, are an attempt to maximize the advantage of a face-to-face experience and to capture more of the benefit of direct interaction in a live environment.

Since the mid-1990s, several alternative classroom designs that support active and collaborative learning have emerged. With names like Student-Centered Active Learning Environment with Upside-down Pedagogies (SCALE-UP); technology-enabled active learning (TEAL); and Spaces to Transform, Interact, Learn, Engage (TILE), they represent a class of space that we term the *Active Learning Classroom* (ALC). The ALCs typically feature round or curved tables with moveable seating that allow students to face each other and thus support small-group work. The tables are often paired with their own whiteboards for brainstorming and diagramming. Many tables are linked to large LCD displays so students can project their computer screens to the group, and the instructor can choose a table's work to share with the entire class. Wireless Internet plays an important role in retrieving resources and linking to content management systems, and depending upon the size of the room, table microphones can be critical so that every student's voice can be broadcast across the room. Unlike the lecture hall with its clear division between front and back, the ALC is designed to even out that hierarchy and increase mobility for the instructor and students. The value of this design is to create a counterpart to the lecture hall and to realize a learning environment in support of active learning pedagogy and collaborative problem solving. These new classrooms have been adopted in both small scale and large scale. For example, the University of Minnesota has over a dozen ALCs (see Images 1.1 and 1.2), and the University of Southern California is in the process of reengineering 185 classrooms and 20 auditoriums (Demski, 2012).

History of Active Learning Classrooms

The redesign of the college classroom can in part be traced to the 1990s with the development of what J. M. Wilson (1994) termed the *studio classroom* for physics at Rensselaer Polytechnic Institute (Beichner, 2014). The studio classroom aimed to combine lecture, discussion, and lab in one space, "to reduce the emphasis on the lecture, to improve the relationship between the course and the laboratory, to scale up the amount of doing while scaling back the watching, to continue and expand the team and cooperative learning experiences" (J. M. Wilson & Jennings, 2000, p. 73). In developing the classrooms, designers experimented with various sizes and shapes of tables (six-foot long worktables, T-shaped, tulip-shaped). The concept of working

Image 1.1 Professors Sue Wick and David Matthes engage one of 19 tables of students in an introductory biology course in an ALC at the University of Minnesota.

Image 1.2 Floor plan of a 14-table (126-student) ALC at the University of Minnesota.

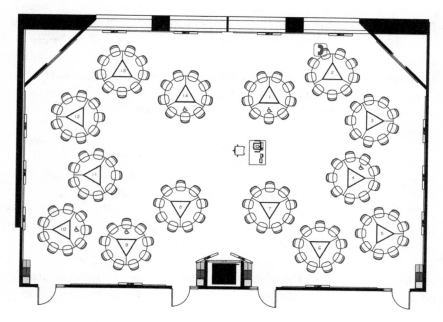

in small teams of two and larger teams of four was already implemented in these early designs.

Between 1997 and 2001, physics professor Robert Beichner and his colleagues at North Carolina State University (NCSU) designed a new series of rooms to "scale-up" the small studio learning experience for larger classes of up to 100 students (Beichner et al., 2007). The SCALE-UP approach resulted in a new space with the now-familiar seven-foot round tables and moveable seating for nine students. The configuration allowed for three teams of three students at each table and was arranged so that the instructor could circulate among all students. An emphasis was put on the development of cooperative learning through active learning and the presentation of group findings to the class and instructor. Assigned group roles and written group contracts were used to structure cooperative learning. Laptop computers provided a phenomenological focus to the design, enabling lab simulations, data collection, analysis, and mathematical modeling. By assigning reading quizzes before each topic was covered, instructors in the SCALE-UP courses kept lecture to a minimum and essentially flipped the classroom. Much of the course time was divided between what Beichner termed *tangibles* (hands-on activities) and *ponderables* (key questions on common misconceptions; Beichner et al., 2007).

Around the same time in 2000 and drawing on the work of both the studio physics movement and the SCALE-UP initiative, three faculty at the Massachusetts Institute of Technology (MIT)—John Belcher, Peter Dourmashkin, and David Litster—joined together to create the TEAL project. Targeting an electromagnetism course, the TEAL project relied less on formal cooperative learning and more on the technology aspects of the course to include advanced visualization capabilities to represent spatial relationships in complex engineering concepts. As in the SCALE-UP project, students sat nine to a round table (13 tables) and worked in groups of three, often on hands-on experiments. Personal response systems (clickers) were also added to the assessment mix.

In the wake of the classroom research and redesign efforts undertaken at Rensselaer Polytechnic Institute, NCSU, and MIT, many schools patterned classroom renovations after these innovative designs. Clemson University, for example, built several experimental rooms between 2004 and 2007 (Benson et al., 2005; Weaver, 2009). The SCALE-UP approach is used with all first-year general engineering and calculus I and II courses as well as with courses in horticulture, English, and computer science. Likewise, inspired by SCALE-UP designs, the University of Iowa in 2009 embarked on designing its new TILE classrooms. Iowa purposefully differentiated its efforts by pairing room design with faculty development support, creating the mandatory TILE Institute Seminar for faculty preparing to teach in the new rooms. Their goal was to expand the reach of the ALCs beyond primarily science, technology, engineering, and mathematics (STEM) fields and to open these learning spaces to the wider campus community (Florman, 2014; Van Horne, Murniati, Gaffney, & Jesse, 2012).

In 2007, the University of Minnesota piloted two ALCs on the Twin Cities campus in preparation for the construction of a new building (originally called Science Teaching and Student Services, now named Robert H. Bruininks Hall). The Bruininks Hall houses 10 additional ALCs of various sizes, making it one of the largest collections of such spaces in the country (Brooks, 2011; Walker, Brooks, & Baepler, 2011). With so many new classrooms, Minnesota, like the University of Iowa, opened its doors to all academic disciplines and what could originally be traced to a revolution in studio physics began to influence education, gender studies, political science, and many other fields beyond the traditional STEM disciplines. With a room renovation in 2013, Minnesota also created one of the largest ALCs with 19 round tables that can host 171 students in a single class. Such a massive ALC speaks to one of the earliest aims of SCALE-UP: to take a collaborative and active learning approach to scale.

Early Research on Active Learning Spaces

As we noted earlier, Beichner's SCALE-UP project is foundational to the study of active learning spaces and the extrapolation of a small studio environment to large lectures. Trying to comprehend an optimal room configuration as well as student social interactions and cognitive performance, Beichner and colleagues (1999) employed both qualitative and quantitative methods in a study that involved two experimental sections ($n = 35$, $n = 31$) and one control section ($n = 736$) in the 1995–96 and 1996–97 academic years. Beichner and colleagues collected over 200 hours of videotape and field notes from classroom sessions, structured and unstructured interviews, and group interviews. Using a grounded theory methodology, Beichner and colleagues determined that the most important finding of the qualitative data was the central role "that socialization played in the success of students" (p. S21). This focus on socialization was reinforced by an analysis of the second experimental group's e-mail archive. An interaction analysis of student communication patterns during class also supported the unsurprising finding that round tables with sufficient horizontal space for computing and conducting experiments facilitated student-to-student interaction. Preference for the round table scheme was also expressed through solicited feedback from students and instructors.

To assess academic performance, the researchers first used student grades of C or better as success indicators. By this measure, students in the experimental sections outperformed their counterparts in the traditional section. They also proved superior on two cognitive concept inventories (the Force Concept Inventory and the Test of Understanding Graphs in Kinematics). In follow-up studies reported nearly a decade later, Beichner and his colleagues compared data across 16,000 students in pairings of traditional and SCALE-UP studies at Coastal Carolina University, University of Central Florida, University of New Hampshire, Rochester Institute of Technology, and NCSU (Beichner et al., 2007). Using student portfolios and various conceptual learning assessments as well as student interviews and classroom recordings, the researchers found similar conceptual understanding gains as in the original study. Additionally, the comparative study suggested many positive advantages of the SCALE-UP model, including improvement in student attitudes, better attendance, and reduced failure rates (particularly for women, students of color, and at-risk students).

The work at NCSU set the groundwork for so much of the classroom redesign that was yet to happen, not only in physics and STEM but also in classrooms across the curriculum. Much of the current attention devoted to engineering intelligent learning spaces can be said to have stemmed from Beichner's instrumental early work and initial research efforts. That said, the initial studies and the broad reporting of the comparative study are limited in their ability to extend conclusions beyond their environments. Because these efforts were designed to explore outcomes of wholesale course redesign with significant curricular changes in addition to learning space alterations, it was difficult to control for confounding factors that might moderate outcomes attributed explicitly to space or methodology. The findings of the NCSU team are intriguing and suggestive, but they restrict our ability to generalize specifically about classroom space. Replication of similar course-room redesigns in many STEM fields as well as in the humanities and social sciences, however, has lent weight to the idea that altering *both the space and the curriculum* can improve learner outcomes (Beichner, 2014).

In 2000, the team of MIT researchers conducted a mixed-methods study on their first large-scale implementation of the TEAL project in a freshman electromagnetic course. The study ran over three years with two experimental sections ($n = 176$, $n = 514$) in an ALC augmented with visualization software and incorporating desktop experiments. The control group ($n = 121$) received traditional lectures. Dori and Belcher (2005) structured their analysis around how the TEAL classroom and course redesign affected students' social, cognitive, and affective outcomes.

Researchers conducted detailed classroom observations to understand the social domain and coded students' discourse along four categories: technical, sensory, affective, and cognitive. They found that social interaction was critical to the construction of knowledge and that student discourse shifted from technical and sensory types to affective and cognitive types as the semester progressed. This change was concomitant with a shift from "ambiguous, partially constructed knowledge to repaired, shared knowledge" (Dori & Belcher, 2005, p. 267). Using pre- and post-test concept inventories, the researchers determined that the students in the TEAL project made statistically significant gains across low, intermediate, and high academic levels. They concluded that "an appropriate learning environment that fosters social constructivism is instrumental in improving the achievements of students at all academic levels" (p. 270). Finally, to assess changes in the affective domain, students completed a survey and participated in focus groups. Students in the experimental section ranked problem-solving activities highest on their list of course elements that contributed to their understanding of subject material in the course. In addition to their positive reactions to the course, students in the largest section of the course (which happened also to be the section taught latest in the series) expressed some reservations about the collaborative method and the lack of live lectures.

In addition to these early and important results, the MIT study acknowledged its limitations. Like much educational research, this quasi-experiment was part of an iterative redesign process, and this larger issue introduced some uncontrollable variables in the treatment conditions. Additionally, the assessments used for the cognitive measures were incentivized differently and were made mandatory for the experimental section but were voluntary (with compensation) for the control section. Further, the control section did not have an opportunity to practice multiple-choice concept questions—as seen on the Force Concept Inventory—while the experimental section did. That the TEAL project, much like the early SCALE-UP efforts, consisted of both a course and a room redesign makes it difficult to draw conclusions on the active learning space alone or to generalize beyond the MIT environment.

Conclusion

Although not specifically addressing the college classroom, Bennett (2007) suggested this as the first critical question we should consider when planning for a new learning space: "What is it about the learning that must happen in this space that compels us to build a brick and mortar learning space, rather than rely on a virtual one?" (p. 15). His point was not to privilege the virtual over the physical, per se, but to have us think deeply about what compels us to teach and learn in a physical environment when convenience, flexibility, and cost often favor online delivery. As a start, he offers four potential reasons to select a physical space: immersion learning, the social dimension of learning, collaborative learning, and the performance aspect of teaching and learning.

The idea that learning happens as a response to an environment that offers a connection to scholars, fellow learners, and people from various disciplines is inherent in the concept of immersive learning. Naturally, this sense of immersion overlaps with the social dimension of learning that, among other things, focuses on the exposure of students to a mix of racial, ethnic, religious, and economic backgrounds that can be hidden or suppressed in a virtual world. Collaboration, of course, is not impossible online, but it remains a significant challenge without the "sensory environment" that allows for casual and frequent communication through body language and vocal inflection. To some degree, many faculty consider the classroom their performance space where they model habits of mind they wish students to follow. Depending on the course, students also view the classroom as a performance space, and this is simply difficult to replicate in a virtual environment, particularly one that is asynchronous.

As we're coming to understand more fully, the ALCs help to create a social framework that allows for the collaborative, social, and performative aspects of teaching and learning. While this is not an exhaustive list of why, in some cases, we need to consider the importance of physical space, it gives us a working rationale for concentrating our attention on how our learning spaces are designed and what they might enable.

2

WHAT WE CURRENTLY
KNOW ABOUT ACTIVE
LEARNING CLASSROOMS

cholars, instructional designers, and institutional planners have
begun to think seriously about the ways that students and instructors
might be affected by the environments in which they learn and teach.
Considerations of space have been inspired, in part, by shifts away from
lecture-based pedagogies; the physical limitations imposed by existing spaces
on innovations to classroom teaching, especially with technology; and the
willingness of institutions to experiment with innovative classroom spaces
(Savin-Baden, McFarland, & Savin-Baden, 2008). In this chapter, we present an overview of some of the most important research findings to date
on the relationship among space, teaching, and learning. Some key findings
include the following:

- Students in Active Learning Classrooms (ALCs) outperform their
  peers in traditional classrooms;
- Students in ALCs exceed their own grade expectations as predicted by
  standardized test scores;
- Using an active learning pedagogical approach in an ALC results in
  significant student learning gains over using a lecture-based approach
  in the same space; and
- Using a flipped classroom model and a blended learning approach in
  an ALC can compensate for significant reductions in face-to-face time
  in the classroom.

Important Roles of Physical Space

Following the lead of Amedeo, Golledge, and Stimson (2009), we have come to think that the importance of space to teaching and learning is manifest in at least three ways. First, although the physical classrooms lack the agency to act directly upon the individuals who learn and teach within their confines, we think that they do serve as mediators and moderators of instructor and student behavior. That is, the physical space influences, but does not determine, the behavior of its occupants by facilitating or enabling certain types of activities while inhibiting or preventing others. Second, how one uses a physical space can shape the way others think about, interact with, and use that space. For example, an instructor who adopts the posture of a "sage on the stage" expects students to react by sitting quietly, listening intently, and processing content by taking notes. Similarly, an instructor who designs and executes carefully crafted in-class problem-based activities expects students to engage one another and work together collaboratively toward a solution to the problems assigned. Third, the physical aspects of a classroom space— layout, size, and capacity—imbue a space with both meaning and expectations about how the space is to be used. A large space with tiered, fixed-row seating facing a single focal point telegraphs to both the student and the instructor that lecture is the expected approach to teaching; conversely, a space with no clear focal point filled with round tables in close proximity to wall-mounted writing surfaces and projection screens or monitors suggests strongly that collaboration and discussion are the order of the day. Learning spaces shape teaching and learning expectations (Brooks, 2012; Gaffney, Gaffney, & Beichner, 2010).

While these basic principles—space affects behavior, use of space affects how one relates to space, and space shapes expectations about teaching and learning—appeal to our intuitive, commonsense notions, these notions remained largely untested by social scientists until the early studies by researchers at North Carolina State University (NCSU) and Massachusetts Institute of Technology (MIT) mentioned in the previous chapter (Beichner et al., 1999; Beichner et al., 2007; Dori et al., 2003; Dori & Belcher, 2005). Beginning in 2007, researchers at the University of Minnesota sought to expand and improve upon these early studies by embarking on a series of systematic and progressively more sophisticated projects to understand better the impact of space on student and faculty behavior, teaching practices, and learning outcomes. In the pages that follow, we chronicle the empirical research we have conducted at the University of Minnesota from its earliest stages to the present. Additionally, we offer a glimpse at some of the empirical research that has been conducted recently at other institutions around the world and has contributed to our understanding of these classrooms.

University of Minnesota: Pilot Study

In the fall 2007 semester, the University of Minnesota gathered data in service of evaluating its efforts to retrofit two of its existing classrooms in the style of the NCSU SCALE-UP and MIT TEAL models. Despite variation in size (one room had a capacity of 117; the other held only 45), the two pilot classrooms adhered to the material guidelines of their ALC predecessors. They featured round tables that could each seat nine students, 360° wall-mounted glass marker-boards, microphones, laptop connections (for power, Internet, and projection), flat-screen monitors at each table, a centralized control panel for the instructor, and dual whole-room projection screens. As with any pilot study of an innovative project in education, the primary goal was to gauge the experiences and perceptions of students and faculty to understand what they liked and did not like, to pinpoint what worked and did not work, and to identify additional topics for future research.

The pilot research was conducted using a mixed-methods approach in which students ($n = 51$) were asked to evaluate the ALCs and their experiences in them via a survey, instructors ($n = 4$) filled out a questionnaire and participated in interviews, and researchers conducted class observations. The responses received from participants were overwhelmingly positive. Students emphasized that the space seemed to have been designed with students in mind: They reported that it provided a comfortable atmosphere in which to collaborate with each other on projects and assignments and that the configuration of the space helped them to feel more connected to not only one another but also their instructors. Changes in classroom relationships were also observed by the faculty in the study, who indicated that they felt more deeply connected to their students due to the configuration of the space and that students also appeared to be more engaged with one another than they typically are in a lecture hall setting. Moreover, instructors reported that being in the space had a transformative effect on their approach to teaching; they could no longer rely exclusively or predominantly on lecturing but felt compelled to approach their classes more as learning coaches or facilitators than as disseminators of knowledge. In terms of the mechanisms believed to be responsible for these changes in self-reported perceptions and behaviors, the digital technologies appeared to be secondary to the furniture and space design. Specifically, the round tables that forced students to face one another were cited frequently by both faculty and students as the factor most responsible for these changes.

Although the data and anecdotes collected in the pilot study supported the original decision to build the rooms, provided useful information with which to make general recommendations for using the new spaces, and may have contributed to the inspiration to later build a new classroom building comprising almost entirely ALCs, there was still very little empirical evidence that teaching and learning in these innovative formal learning environments had a significant, or even positive, impact on student learning outcomes. If advocates of active learning pedagogies wanted to see an increase in the numbers and types of spaces[1] in which their approaches to teaching could be implemented, evidence beyond measures of student and instructor satisfaction and anecdotal conjecture would be required to make the case.

University of Minnesota: Quasi-Experimental Studies

Following our pilot evaluation, we embarked upon the more ambitious research project that involved testing a series of hypotheses related to (a) the impact of space on behavior and outcomes, (b) the intentional use of space in different ways to assess the interaction between space and activity, and (c) how the attributes of spaces impact perceptions and outcomes. To isolate the impact of space, pedagogy, or any other variable, we needed to design a research project that would systematically and rigorously control for potentially confounding factors that might obfuscate our findings. Specifically, we needed to figure out ways to measure the impact of space independent of pedagogical approach as well as the impact of pedagogical approach independent of spatial constraints.

We used a 2×2 matrix to visualize the theoretical research designs we needed to consider while planning to tackle these complex research questions (see Table 2.1). This dichotomous typology provided a useful qualitative heuristic with which to categorize existing research, identify gaps, and conceptualize new projects. Specifically, we used it to identify four basic combinations of classroom space and pedagogical approach:

- Traditional classroom with primarily lecture (I),
- ALC with primarily lecture (II),
- Traditional classroom with primarily active learning (III), and
- ALC with primarily active learning (IV).

Of these four possibilities, two were not inherently of interest to us, as they either represent the combination on which most educational research has been conducted historically (I) or have been researched enough to have a solid understanding of their singular impact (III). Moreover, we were not really interested in direct and controlled comparisons of I and III, as we think that this is a research question that has been settled largely in favor of the superiority of active learning techniques over lecture-based ones for improving student learning outcomes (Freeman et al., 2014; Michael, 2006; Springer, Stanne, & Donovan, 1999).

TABLE 2.1
Research Design Typology: Learning Spaces Versus Pedagogical Approach

		Learning Space	
Pedagogical Approach	I. Traditional classroom with primarily lecture		II. ALC with primarily lecture
	III. Traditional classroom with primarily active learning		IV. ALC with primarily active learning

The intersection in which we were all ultimately interested was the one in which active learning teaching techniques are used in an ALC (IV). In fact, the early studies by the NCSU SCALE-UP and MIT TEAL researchers can be situated squarely within the matrix's lower-right quadrant. Their findings of improved student interactions and learning gains (Beichner et al., 1999); significant learning gains and improved self-reported problem-solving skills (Dori & Belcher, 2005; Dori et al., 2003); and improvements in student attendance, passing rates, and attitudes (Beichner et al., 2007) made the early case for the advantages of coupling ALC with active learning teaching methods. Beyond the aforementioned methodological issues related to a lack of controls to limit the number and type of potential confounds (see Chapter 1), the comprehensive course redesigns these projects featured lacked the systematic comparison groups with which to isolate the impact of the space on student learning outcomes. That is, based on the research designs of these early studies, we know that the combination of ALC with active learning pedagogies produced desirable effects, but we do not really know whether or not the space actually contributed to the improvements beyond those expected from the active learning pedagogy alone. To isolate the impact of space, a systematic comparison of outcomes between courses that used active learning in a traditional classroom (III) and active learning in an ALC (IV) was required.

The Original Study: ALCs Versus Traditional Classrooms

In the fall 2008 semester, we were presented with the opportunity to conduct the first systematic comparison between the conditions outlined in quadrants III and IV of Table 2.1. Professor Jay Hatch in the College of

Education and Human Development at the University of Minnesota had just completed a TBL overhaul of his Postsecondary Teaching and Learning (PSTL) 1131: Principles of Biological Sciences course and was offering one section in a traditional classroom with rows of chairs and tables and a second one in an ALC. Everything that could be held constant across these two sections of PSTL 1131 was held constant, including the instructor, time of day (one section on Mondays and Wednesdays; one section on Tuesdays and Thursdays), syllabus, textbook and lab materials, in-class activities, assignments, assessments, and exams. Although we were unable to assign students to each section randomly, thereby not achieving experimental conditions, students enrolled in the two sections without knowledge of the type of classroom in which each would be held, thus excluding intentional student self-selection. Further, our post-hoc analysis of student demographic characteristics revealed no significant differences on any key characteristics with the exception of composite ACT scores: Students in the ALC (n = 41) had ACT scores that were significantly lower ($p < .05$)[2] than their peers in the traditional classroom setting (n = 42; Brooks, 2011). The instructor also made every attempt to teach the course in exactly the same manner, although he was not entirely successful in his efforts (a point that will be discussed later). The only condition that was allowed to systematically vary across the sections was the type of space, thereby achieving the quasi-experimental conditions necessary for a comparison of the conditions present in quadrants III and IV.

Although the significantly higher average ACT scores predicted that the students in the traditional classroom would have earned significantly higher grades[3] in the PSTL 1131 course than their peers in the experimental space, students in the ALC earned raw grades that were not significantly different from those of students in the traditional classroom (p = .26; Brooks, 2011). PSTL 1131 students who took the course in an ALC both exceeded grade expectations and learned at a rate higher than their traditional classroom counterparts (see Figure 2.1). Given the controls built into this study, the most likely thing remaining that explains systematically the variation in outcomes are factors associated with the environment provided by the ALC. That is, *ALCs have an independent and statistically significant positive impact on student learning as measured by grades* (Brooks, 2011).

The identification of a clear association between the type of classroom in which students learn and the student learning outcomes observed does not, of course, suggest agency. Being in an ALC does not automatically make students smarter, help them earn higher grades, or guarantee that they learn more because the room simply does not have the capacity to act directly upon individuals who occupy it. Instead, as we suggested earlier, the affordances

Figure 2.1 Expected versus actual grades in three quasi-experimental research projects. Comparing ALCs to traditional classrooms.

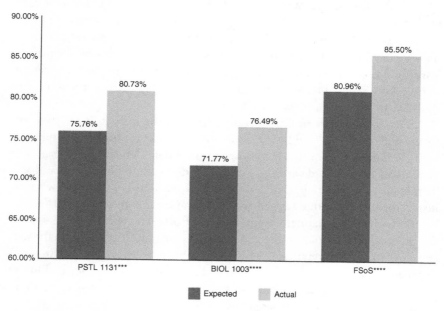

Note: ***p < .001, ****p < .0001

of the classroom serve as antecedents that may facilitate or constrain certain types of behaviors and enhance or undermine various kinds of classroom activities. Here, student perceptions of the impact of the rooms and independent classroom observations might inform our understanding of how the differences in rooms elicited different outcomes.

To understand the impact of physical learning environments on students' perceptions, we developed a set of survey-based scales designed to measure various aspects of their experiences in the classroom. In the first iteration of our survey, we measured students' perceptions of the degrees to which a classroom (a) promotes engagement, (b) enhances learning experiences, (c) presents flexibility in regard to learning opportunities, (d) is a good fit to the subject matter and course, and (e) is used well by an instructor; in later versions, we also included scales that measured students' perceptions of the impact of classrooms on university-defined student learning outcomes and confidence levels. In this first quasi-experimental study, students who took PSTL 1131 in the ALC reported significantly higher levels of engagement, enrichment, and flexibility than did the PSTL 1131 students in the traditional classroom; they also thought that the instructor used the ALC and its technology better than he used the traditional room with its technology and thought that the subject matter and course design (e.g., a problem-based approach) were a better fit to the ALC than the traditional classroom (Whiteside, Brooks, & Walker, 2010). These systematically and comparatively high ratings of the ALC are suggestive that part of the reason we might have observed the significantly larger learning gains in that space is due to the manner in which it shaped student experiences. However, it was not just the learning side of the teaching–learning curve that was affected by the variation in classroom types: The teaching side of the curve experienced the impact of the ALC in significant ways as well.

We also were able to isolate and understand the impact of the different spaces with data collected by the following methods: (a) biweekly interviews with the instructor and (b) course observation data derived from a series of systematic, randomized classroom visits that documented instructor and student behavior and activities in 5-minute intervals. During the interviews the instructor expressed the ways in which he was unable to teach each section in exactly the same manner despite his best efforts. He repeatedly mentioned the physical constraints on his ability to move around the traditional room and interact with students and how many of his problem-based activities did not seem to work as well in the traditional classroom space as they had in the ALC. He also frequently noted the ways that the ALC seemed to be more conducive to the new team-based approach to teaching that he was employing. According to the instructor, the ALC encouraged student and instructor behavior, classroom activities, and daily classroom outcomes different from those he and his students were experiencing in the traditional classroom.

Data that we collected from the classroom observations confirmed the instructor's suspicions of the impact of the space on him and his students. The instructor lectured more ($p < .001$) and remained at or near the podium more ($p < .0001$) in the traditional classroom than he did in the ALC. Conversely, classroom discussion occurred more frequently ($p < .001$), the instructor was away from the podium more ($p < .0001$), and he consulted with students more ($p < .001$) in the ALC than he did in the traditional classroom. These differences in classroom activity and instructor behavior also had a significant effect on the students in each classroom. Using sophisticated modeling techniques, we were able to demonstrate that not only were instructor behavior and classroom activities directly shaped by the type of room in which they occurred, but also, in turn, these activities shaped student behavior. Specifically, in the traditional classroom setting, the only variable that predicted that students would respond with high levels of on-task behavior was when the instructor lectured; in the ALC, the group activities and classrooms discussions were responsible for high levels of on-task student behavior (Brooks, 2012).

Do Demographic Characteristics Impact Results?

One somewhat surprising finding of our research on ALCs is the lack of any enduring differences in how students of various demographics experience the environment offered by these spaces. In our initial research from 2008, we found moderate but statistically significant differences between how students from rural Minnesota counties perceived the ALCs compared to their metropolitan peers ($p < .01$): Urban students rated the ALCs much more favorably than did rural students. We hypothesized that those differences were due primarily to differences in value systems students have resulting from the environment of their upbringing. This hypothesis was confirmed by qualitative data in which students from rural Minnesota said that the technology was unnecessary, that the expense was not worth it, and that more can and should be done with less. Metropolitan students, conversely, expressed a great deal of satisfaction with the ALCs, noting that the high-tech and collaborative environment was a familiar, exciting, and welcomed one. However, over the course of the next couple of years, both the qualitative and quantitative differences between these groups disappeared completely with the rural students' evaluations converging with those of the metropolitan ones. We think that with ALCs being such a central and ubiquitous classroom type (over 37% of all degree-seeking students at the University of Minnesota have had at least one class in an ALC) eventually students of all stripes and backgrounds simply embraced them as normal. The lack of importance of demographic characteristics like urban/rural, male/female, and ethnicity suggests that they can be used as criteria by which to assign groups without being concerned about how differences might manifest in student learning experiences and outcomes. However, results may vary at other institutions around the world, especially given that the University of Minnesota has a comparatively low level of ethnic diversity. Colleges and universities conducting research on the impact of ALCs that have different levels and different types of social divisions might be able to better answer questions related to the impact of ALCs on various demographic groups than we have.

Given the controls built into this quasi-experimental research study, the strength of the results demonstrates that ALCs not only have a positive impact on learning outcomes, classroom activities, instructor behavior, and student perceptions, but also are comparatively superior to results obtained in traditional classrooms when using active learning teaching techniques. Moreover, they serve well to support the initial hypotheses that we advanced regarding the importance of space; that is, (a) spaces act upon people by facilitating and constraining certain behaviors, attitudes, and activities; (b) how one uses spaces matters, especially in conjunction with others; and (c) the physical attributes of spaces set expectations, which, in turn, shape outcomes.

One outcome this line of research does not demonstrate is that traditional learning spaces are inherently bad; to the contrary, our findings suggest that they are quite well suited to the pedagogical approach for which they were designed—lecturing. Traditional learning spaces do not seem to undermine learning per se, although they might impede full manifestation of the benefits of active learning. This conclusion suggests that certain types of spaces are more conducive to certain teaching practices than others.

The major limitation of this research project is that the generalizability of the results may be somewhat limited, not by the data we analyzed but by the scope of the project itself. Our results are derived from one course taught by one professor in one semester at a single research university. While the evidence we have marshaled makes a compelling case, considerably more research would be required to convince institutions to make the significant investments of resources required to build ALCs on their campuses. One approach would be to expand the number of courses, instructors, and students included in the research projects, an approach that we gradually adopted over time. Another, more compelling approach was to replicate the original research project with another course taught by another instructor taken by another group of students.

The Replication Study

In the spring 2011 semester, the opportunity to replicate the original experiment using a similar quasi-experimental design with larger groups of students presented itself when Professor Sehoya Cotner in the College of Biological Sciences at the University of Minnesota invited us to conduct research on her Biology (BIOL) 1003: The Evolution and Biology of Sex course. Again, quasi-experimental conditions were obtained for this scenario: single instructor and course; same syllabus, in-class activities, assignments, exams, and assessments; two sections with non–randomly assigned students—one in a traditional lecture classroom ($n = 162$) and one in an ALC ($n = 102$). Two minor differences were present in this second study. First, the classes did not meet at the exact same time of day on different days but were held back-to-back in the middle of the same day; and, second, both the traditional classroom and the ALC were housed in the new Bruininks Hall.

ALCs and the Student Learning Experience Over Time

Since the beginning of our research in 2008, students have rated their perceptions of the impact of the ALCs on their learning experiences at significantly high levels. ALC skeptics frequently pointed out that these exceptional results simply might be an artifact of a novelty effect, or a tendency to react positively to the "something new" solely because it is new and not because of any actual benefit. Our data, however, belie that hypothesis. If the observed effects of ALCs could be attributed solely to a novelty effect, then the student perceptions of their impact would decline over time. Instead, the opposite has occurred. The data related to our theoretical constructs (e.g., engagement, enrichment, flexibility, room and course fit, and effective use) demonstrate clearly a positive trend over time that has only recently leveled off, perhaps with the inclusion of data from the newest and largest ALCs (see Figure 2.2). Our data also showed that ALCs continue to outperform traditional classrooms on each of the constructs, providing further evidence that the novelty effect is simply not applicable to the ALCs.

As with the original PSTL 1131 study, students enrolled in the two sections without knowledge of the type of classroom in which each section was being held. We again conducted post-hoc comparisons of a number of potentially relevant demographic variables (e.g., age, sex, ethnicity, year, urban/rural) and found that, despite a lack of randomization, student populations were equivalent. Once more, the only variable for which there was a major difference was the composite ACT score; students in the traditional classroom had a slightly higher, but statistically significant, average test score ($p < .05$). Despite this difference, students in the ALC section significantly outperformed grade expectations (see Figure 2.2; $p < .0001$) and earned statistically the same grade as their peers in the traditional classroom (Cotner,

Figure 2.2 Student perceptions of ALC impact on five theoretical constructs.

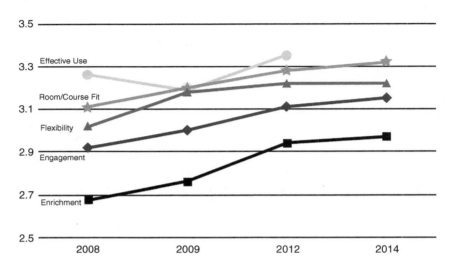

Loper, Walker, & Brooks, 2013; Walker, Brooks, & Baepler, 2011). These results are nearly identical to those obtained in the first quasi-experimental study, suggesting that the original findings are both valid and reliable. When combined with the original results, *the evidence derived from the replication offers extraordinarily strong evidence that ALCs have an independent and significantly positive impact on student learning.*

Although we were able to confirm that teaching and learning in an ALC using active learning approaches is superior to active learning in a traditional classroom (III versus IV), we still lacked evidence to support the hypothesis that lecturing is less effective than active learning approaches in an ALC (II versus IV). The next section attends to this gap by considering another quasi-experimental project that explicitly addressed this comparison.

The Effect of Pedagogy and Space

In the fall 2008 semester, at the same time we were conducting our original study of the traditional classroom versus the ALC, we began working with Professor Catherine Solheim in the Department of Family Social Science at the University of Minnesota. Solheim received an 18-month Faculty Fellowship Program grant to revise her regularly taught Family Social Science (FSoS) 3101: Personal and Family Finances course in preparation for offering it in an ALC. During the same semester, Solheim taught the course in the same manner as she had in previous semesters (i.e., instructor-centered, lecture-based, structured discussion, controlled small-group work), but instead of holding class in a lecture hall, all sessions were held in an ALC classroom.

During spring and summer 2009, Solheim overhauled the course so that the technological and spatial affordances of the ALC could be harnessed to improve learning. While the course description, rationale, and objectives remained the same, the fall 2009 version of the course was altered in the following ways: (a) attendance and participation were required and became graded components of the course; (b) all course materials (e.g., readings, videos) were to be completed *before* class; (c) the textbook was replaced with freely available online materials and articles made available through the learning management system; (d) the midterm exam was eliminated; and (e) more in-class time was designated to work on the semester-long, team-based project. Moreover, the instructor jettisoned her traditional, lengthy lectures in favor of micro-lectures to introduce and scaffold the many in-class, active learning assignments she developed. The structure of the project, then, reflects a longitudinal, quasi-experimental design in which the instructor, course, and room are held constant, but the pedagogical approach was allowed to systematically vary from a primarily lecture-based one to an approach that was more student-centered and took advantage of what the ALC had to offer (Brooks & Solheim, 2014).

Because the courses were held one year apart and because we lacked the ability to randomly assign students to one version of the course or another, we conducted the necessary post-hoc analyses of the student populations and found that on all of the relevant demographic factors (e.g., age, sex, ethnicity, year, urban/rural), including the aptitude measure of composite ACT scores, the students in the 2008 lecture-based version of the course were nearly identical to those in the 2009 active learning version (Brooks & Solheim, 2014, p. 56). In fact, they were so similar that their responses to our surveys regarding the impact of the ALC on their learning experiences were statistically identical on *every single item* except one: "The classroom in which I am taking this course encourages my active participation." On this one item, the students in the 2009 active learning version of the course agreed with the statement at significantly higher levels than did their 2008 peers who received lectures in the ALC ($p < .05$; Brooks & Solheim, 2014, p. 59).

To assess the impact of changing one's pedagogical approach to a course in order to better fit the space in which it is being held, we once again turned to students' final grades. Our null hypothesis that there was no significant difference between the students' learning outcomes in the 2008 lecture version of the course and the 2009 active learning version of the course was rejected; since the classroom was constant, the students who took the active learning version of the course earned significantly higher grades than did the students who took the lecture-based course and exceeded grade expectations (see Figure 2.2; $p < .0001$; Brooks & Solheim, 2014, p. 56).

Having conducted a series of quasi-experimental research projects on the impact of ALCs on teaching practices and learning outcomes, we have been able to demonstrate clearly the efficacy of ALCs. On the one hand, we have shown that holding all other factors constant, ALCs provide significant positive enhancements to student learning experiences; on the other, we have demonstrated that lecturing in an ALC is not nearly as effective as using active learning techniques in terms of on-task student behavior and student learning outcomes. In the following sections, we will discuss some of our other important findings germane to teaching in ALCs, beginning with a longitudinal perspective.

How Big Is Too Big? The Impact of Room Size on Student Experiences

With the construction of Bruininks Hall, the University of Minnesota became the home of the largest collection of ALCs in the world. Although the basic design principle remained largely the same, there were 7 sizes of ALCs with capacities of 27, 45, 54, 63, 90, 117, and 126 students. In 2013, 2 of the larger rooms were reconfigured to hold 171 students, making it one of the largest ALCs in the world at that time. This event prompted questions in regard to how big an ALC can be before it stops having the positive and significant impact on student learning that our research had discovered.

Following a large-scale survey project that collected data on 723 undergraduate students in 22 courses, we were in a position to shed light on this issue. We performed a series of statistical tests to investigate the relationship between the size of the room and our theoretical constructs (e.g., engagement, enrichment, flexibility, room and course fit, effective use, confidence, and student learning outcomes). Statistical modeling confirmed our general suspicions that the student experience suffers as the size of the room increases. As size of the room increases, levels of student engagement, confidence, enrichment, learning outcomes and perceptions of classroom flexibility, room and course fit, and effective use all decline significantly. The adverse effects of size, however, do not appear to have surpassed the threshold at which the positive gains contributed by the ALC environment are overshadowed. In fact, 2013–14 survey data showed that students who have taken courses in the largest of the University of Minnesota ALCs have comparable experiences to those of students in other large ALCs.

Flipping and Blending the ALC

In an era of scarce resources, college and university administrators are constantly looking for methods of increasing revenue and reducing costs. The price tag associated with ALCs and the reduced number of students who can be served by an ALC based on square footage suggests that designing, building, and maintaining such facilities may be counterproductive to their current needs. Given that we know more and better learning occurs in an ALC setting, we partnered with Professor Michelle Driessen from the Department of Chemistry at the University of Minnesota to understand how the ALC might be leveraged to address the issues of costs associated with a reduction in the number of students served (and, therefore, tuition dollars collected) in these classrooms.

Following a successful transformation of her introductory chemistry lab from a cookbook model to an active learning model, Driessen began making plans to move the lecture portion of her class from a traditional classroom into an ALC. Specifically, the plan involved putting a 350-student class that met in a lecture hall three times per week for 50 minutes each session into a 126-seat ALC with three sections that met only once per week for 50 minutes each. To do so, the instructor would have to both flip and blend[4] the class, the parameters of which are featured in Table 2.2.

Using a quasi-experimental longitudinal design, we collected data in a baseline section of the chemistry course (spring 2012) and two experimental sections (fall 2012 and spring 2013). The data collected for this project included established student surveys to measure perceptions of classroom experiences, standardized multiple-choice exams to measure subject matter learning, and various demographic measures to control for exogenous confounding variables. Again, the results demonstrated that ALCs have a significant positive impact on student learning experiences.

TABLE 2.2
Parameters for Flipping, Blending, and Moving a Lecture Course Into an ALC

Traditional Classroom/Lecture Section	ALC/Flipped and Blended
150 minutes of face-to-face time per week	50 minutes of face-to-face time per week
In-class lectures	Online lectures/materials
Random, self-selected seating	Assigned, permanent seating
Problem solving outside of class	Problem solving and clicker questions in class
No participation credit	Participation credit
Online homework	Online homework
Lab	Lab
3 midterms + final	3 midterms + final

First, students in the blended and flipped ALC reported significantly higher levels of engagement ($p < .001$), flexibility ($p < .001$), student learning outcomes ($p < .001$), and confidence ($p < .001$) than did their peers in the lecture-based traditional classroom (Baepler, Walker, & Driessen, 2014). Statistically, the degree to which the room was an appropriate fit for the course was equivalent between the control and experimental sections, suggesting that the methods by which the courses were taught aligned well with the spaces in which they were taught.

Second, student learning as measured by standardized chemistry exams improved significantly between the spring 2012 baseline semester and fall 2012 experimental semester ($p < .01$), and learning improved between the baseline and replication in spring 2013 but not at statistically significant levels ($p = .613$). Similar nominal but nonsignificant improvements in student learning were visible across all four quartiles of student aptitude as measured by grade point average (GPA), showing that this course revision did not differentially advantage or disadvantage particular ability groups. Third, controlling for a host of demographic (age, sex, major, and ethnicity) and aptitude (ACT scores, GPA) measures, taking the introductory chemistry course in the blended and flipped model held in an ALC confirmed our prediction that students would learn significantly more than (in the case of the initial experiment) or at least as much as (in the replication) students in the lecture version of the course in the traditional classroom.

This line of research is important for several reasons. First, it further emphasizes that an ALC had an effect on student learning experiences that is superior to that of traditional classrooms. Second, it demonstrates that using flipped and blended approaches to teaching is compatible with an ALC. Third, in contrast to almost everything we know about the impact of class time on student performance, it shows that using a blended and flipped approach in an ALC is such a powerful combination that students can learn as much as and more than students who spend three times the amount of class time in a traditional space receiving lectures. And, fourth, if students can learn as much and more under these conditions, the investment in ALCs and pedagogical training seems to be an excellent educational bargain for colleges and universities.

Emerging Research

The global interest in the impact of learning spaces on student learning experiences and instructor teaching approaches has been steadily increasing over the past decade. And despite the nascent character of the field, enough research has been produced already to warrant a handful of literature reviews. Two of the more prominent reviews focus on the need for new and better forms of empirical research on formal learning environments (Bligh & Pearhouse, 2011; Germany, 2014). Bligh and Pearhouse (2011) were skeptical of the possibility of linking learning outcomes directly to learning spaces and argued that changes in instructor behavior resulting from teaching in a new learning environment is a confounding variable that obscures too much. Furthermore, the authors were dismissive of the empirical techniques used in the research discussed previously on the ground that those techniques are too difficult to execute regularly, a notion that we attempt to dispel in Chapter 11. Meanwhile, noting the dearth of good evaluation techniques in the field of learning spaces, Germany (2014) made a very strong, practical case for designing robust research protocols that cover the duration of learning-spaces projects. An additional literature review of selected empirical works advocates for mixed-methods approaches that focus on multiple targets so as to triangulate results (Gierdowski, 2013).

Despite the significant advances in empirical research on the impact of learning spaces, some researchers continue to conduct theoretical and evaluative studies. Although ALCs are still relatively new, several scholars are theorizing about the next generation of learning spaces in order to think about what new spaces should emerge to complement shifts away from lecture-based pedagogies (see Fraser, 2014). Specifically, the drivers and the limitations of different modes of learning, technology, student participation, and outcome expectations all suggest that a range of types of spaces, not just ALCs, should be under consideration (Brooks, 2012; Ling & Fraser, 2014). Other scholars are engaged in empirically grounded evaluative work in seeking to understand how innovative buildings and classroom environments are received by students (Choi, Guerin, Kim, Brigham, & Bauer, 2013–14), what sorts of furniture might be more or less conducive to active learning (Harvey & Kenyon, 2013), and how classroom furniture layouts and arrangements impact the interactions among students and among students and instructors (Henshaw, Edwards, & Bagley, 2011).

One popular vein of empirical research that has emerged recently includes direct comparisons between active learning and traditional classroom spaces. Although the research designs, methodologies, and outcomes measured may vary, the underlying research questions parallel our studies. Robertson (2013) employed action research methods to explore the manner in which spaces support and encourage pedagogical innovations and found that ALCs were associated with higher levels of engagement, learning, and satisfaction. Using a more rigorous quasi-experimental design, Hill and Epps (2010) compared technologically enhanced spaces to traditional ones and found that students perceived clear differences in the spaces and preferred the upgraded classrooms. Students also experienced higher levels of enjoyment and self-reported learning and rated instructor organization at higher levels in the active learning space; instructors reported greater levels of satisfaction and better teaching evaluations in the new spaces. In a similar study, Byers, Imms, and Hartnell-Young (2014) used a standardized instrument to demonstrate that student perceptions of what they call "next-generation learning spaces" were significantly more positive than student perceptions of traditional spaces.

Beyond the basic comparisons of traditional classrooms to ALCs, some researchers have taken innovative approaches, testing new ideas and hypotheses. Alvarado, Dominguez, Rodriguez, and Zavala (2012) used an instrument called the Pedagogical Expectancy Violation Assessment (PEVA) in conducting a semester-long comparative study of how space affects student expectations. They found that students experienced significant shifts in their expectations about group work and class discussion in an ALC environment, but experienced no changes in expectations about interacting with their instructors. At the University of Minnesota–Rochester, Muthyala and Wei (2013) carried out a quasi-experimental project that compared the impact of *two different types of ALCs* on student learning outcomes. They found no significant differences between the spaces, suggesting that various shapes, layouts, and sizes of ALCs can promote the gains found at the University of Minnesota–Twin Cities campus. Beigi and Shirmohammadi (2012) took a broader view in their cross-institutional analysis of the perceptions of university environmental characteristics in Iran. Using structural equation modeling techniques, they found that spaces do, in fact, have a significant and positive effect on student attitudes toward teamwork.

Although many early studies have focused primarily on student experiences and outcomes, more recently researchers have been exploring the impact that classroom environments have on instructors and their approaches to teaching. Ahmad and Rao (2012) explored the impact of environment on teaching methods using a between-subjects comparison of instructors at a university with technologically enhanced classrooms and institutions with poorer quality facilities. In the enhanced environment not only did the students have better attitudes toward learning than their peers at the other institution, but also the instructors used a more "communicative approach" to their teaching than did their peers. DeBeck and Demaree (2012) recorded a series of teaching assistant interactions with students in a modified SCALE-UP classroom to understand how variations in levels of teaching experience played out in an active learning environment. They found the most experienced teaching assistant was the most efficient instructor with the lowest levels of interaction time but the smallest amount of variation in approach, while the least experienced instructor had the longest average interaction times and the widest variation in dealing with student issues. Van Horne and colleagues (2014) found that the space provided incentive for instructors to redesign activities supported by ALC environments, that flipping the classroom so that students complete work in advance of class works best, and that students benefit the most when faculty scaffold but do not micromanage student learning.

One of the most sophisticated of the studies of the impact of student-centered classrooms on faculty experiences was conducted by Lasry, Charles, and Whittaker (2014), the results of which echo our findings about the alignment of space and pedagogy (Brooks & Solheim, 2014). Using the Force Concept Inventory (FCI) and the Approaches to Teaching Inventory (ATI), the researchers employed a quasi-experimental design that tested the impact of four possible combinations of instructor approaches and classroom spaces on outcomes: student-centered pedagogy and space, student-centered pedagogy and teacher-centered space, teacher-centered pedagogy and student-centered space, and teacher-centered pedagogy and space. The following key findings emerged from this design: (a) The combination of student-centered pedagogy and a student-centered space is the most effective, (b) combining teacher-centered pedagogy and student-centered space is not effective and may very well produce negative results, (c) self-reported student-centeredness correlates positively with learning gains, and (d) some instructors become more student-centered after using student-centered spaces.

Conclusion

A host of new directions for research on the impact of space on teaching and learning remains to be pursued and is only now beginning to be considered. Ridenour, Feldman, Teodorescu, Medsker, and Benmouna (2013) have begun to take on the difficult task of measuring the impact of such spaces on problem-solving skills with an eye to matching instructional tools to the spaces in which they are used. Baepler and Walker (2014) have begun to theorize and unpack the manners in which the relationships among students and among students and instructors are fundamentally altered by ALCs. In their evaluation of faculty development and faculty usage of new spaces, Salter, Thomson, Fox, and Lam (2013) found that innovative spaces appear to stimulate new practices, and the experience of teaching in innovative spaces is transitive to future courses. However, we still do not understand the mechanisms that trigger the matching of skills to space or change pedagogical approaches. Morrone, Ouimet, Siering, and Arthur (2014) found that instructors utilizing new spaces frequently do not significantly change their teaching practices. That is, instructors who tend to lecture continue to do so, but faculty who self-select into ALCs are using active learning teaching techniques already. Carr and Fraser (2014) have observed that faculty confronted with new spaces for the first time frequently teach as they were taught and as they have taught themselves. Carr and Fraser argued that colleges and universities need to explore the mechanisms that can facilitate the transition to teaching in ALCs. Similarly, Van Horne and colleagues (2014) argued that faculty development programs designed to help faculty learn how to harness the affordances of ALC spaces are essential to those faculty's success. We hope that this book, with its attention to research-based methods and approaches to teaching in what Byers and colleagues (2014) termed *next-generation learning spaces*, can facilitate those transitions and foment a deeper understanding about how these processes take shape.

Notes

1. Peter Ling and Kym Fraser also advocate for a diversity of spaces in their 2014 theoretical work, "Pedagogies for next generation learning spaces: Theory, context, action," in K. Fraser (Ed.), *The future of learning and teaching in next generation learning spaces: International perspectives on higher education research* (Vol. 12, pp. 65–84). Bingley, UK: Emerald Group.
2. A p value is a statistic that indicates the probability that an event occurred by chance. In this example, $p < .05$ indicates that if we replicated this study 100 times, we would get the same result in over 95 of those instances. Or, to put it another way, there is less than a 5% probability that the observed phenomenon occurred by chance or accident.

3. For more information on the connections between ACT composite scores and college grades, see ACT (1998, 2007), Noble and Sawyer (2002), and Pascarella and Terenzini (2005).

4. In the flipped classroom model, work traditionally conducted inside the classroom (e.g., didactic exchange of content) is done outside of the classroom, and the work traditionally done outside of the classroom (e.g., hands-on, problem solving, applied learning) takes place inside the classroom. The blended component comes into play in that the instructor creates and integrates instructional videos and interactive lessons for students and makes these resources available online, thereby blending the digital learning environment with the face-to-face environment. For more on blended learning, see Picciano and Dziuban (2007) and Picciano, Dziuban, and Graham (2013).

3

THE SOCIAL CONTEXT OF TEACHING AND LEARNING

From the earliest implementations of Active Learning Classrooms (ALCs), instructors, students, and researchers have noticed that the character of relationships in ALCs seemed to be different from what they experienced in more traditional rooms. In 2007 at the University of Minnesota when we were first piloting two ALC rooms, an instructor put her finger on it: "The main thing the room does—it changes the relationship that faculty have with students, and the relationship that students have with one another." Although it would take some time to establish the efficacy of the ALCs empirically, there was almost immediately a great sense that the rooms seemed to be working, if only because we could see people behaving differently. Instructors walked up to and spoke with students all over the room, a feat that was impossible in the theater-style room. Students faced each other at tables and clustered in groups at whiteboards. Sometimes the noise level ramped up. To anyone observing the class, the environment simply felt different, even exciting. For those studying the rooms, this change in how people interacted seemed significant and was, perhaps, a possible explanation for how the ALCs improved learning outcomes. In this chapter, we explore the possibility that this network of relationships within the classroom that together constitute the "social context" of teaching and learning is a key mechanism for how ALCs produce the positive effects on the student experience and on student learning outcomes that were documented in Chapter 2.

Among our key findings are the following:

- The social context in a learning environment such as an ALC can be measured by means of four aggregated, survey-based variables. These variables describe different aspects of student–student and student–instructor relations.

- These variables predict student learning outcomes in different ways:
  - The variables we describe as "Student as Instructor" and "Student–Instructor Formal Relations" positively predict student learning outcomes, while controlling for numerous other possible influences.
  - The variable we call "Student–Instructor Informal Relations" is neutral with respect to student learning outcomes.
  - The variable we label "Student–Student General Relations" negatively predicts learning outcomes.
- The social context scores are higher in a large ALC than in a large traditional classroom.

In the previous two chapters, we provided a comprehensive review of the history and current research into the effects of the ALCs. In this chapter, we focus on a single issue and explore it in greater detail. Our intention is not only to highlight this new line of thought but also to build a bridge from research to instruction as we progress in subsequent chapters to the practical matters of teaching in these rooms.

Social Context as Mechanism

The body of research described in Chapter 2 indicates that teaching a class in an ALC can have positive effects on the student learning experience as well as on student learning outcomes. But this research does not answer the question of *how*, or in virtue of what, ALCs achieve these good effects. This is a question about the mechanisms that underlie the effectiveness of ALCs, and it is important to not only answer for theoretical reasons but also inform the design and construction of new types of learning spaces and to guide instructors toward the optimal use of ALCs.

Beginning with our first investigations of ALCs in 2007, anecdotal evidence from students and faculty pointed toward changes in classroom relationships as an important effect of moving a class from a traditional room to an ALC. In addition, there are indications in empirical research and educational theory that classroom relationships are an important mechanism that moderates the student experience and student outcomes (Amedeo, Golledge, & Stimson, 2009; Billson & Tiberius, 1991; Meyers, 2008; Pascarella & Terenzini, 2005; Tiberius & Billson, 1991; Tinto, 1997).

For these reasons, we focused on the network of interpersonal relationships in the classroom, which Tiberius and Billson (1991) called "the social context of teaching and learning," as a potential mechanism underlying the effectiveness of ALCs. In spring semester 2013 we set out to investigate social context in a systematic way. The first step in studying social context was to develop a valid and reliable measure of it. Through an iterative process spanning 5 semesters, 40 courses, and over 3,000 students at 3 institutions of higher learning,[1] we piloted, tested, and ultimately produced a survey-based measure of social context that focused on different aspects of the relationships between students and instructors and among students themselves.

The resulting instrument is called the Social Context and Learning Environments (SCALE) survey. Available on the University of Minnesota's Learning Spaces Research page (http://z.umn.edu/LSR), this survey contains 35 questions of which 25 are closed-ended social context questions answered by students on a 4-point rating scale from *strongly agree* to *strongly disagree*. (The remaining 10 questions include 8 closed-ended questions that do not directly concern social context and 2 open-ended questions that do.) From the 25 closed-ended questions on the SCALE survey, we were able to identify four valid and reliable aggregated dimensions or "factors." These factors were validated by means of exploratory principal components analysis, and the 25 closed-ended questions broke out into 4 aggregated dimensions or factors that together explained 57.05% of the variance in the data set. These factors, along with 2 representative questions from each factor, are described in the following text box.

- **Factor 1: Student–Student General Relations.** This factor contained questions that all had to do with how well students in the class knew one another, how comfortable they were with each other, and how much they learned from each other.
  - I've learned something from my classmates.
  - The students sitting near me rely on each other for help in learning class material.
- **Factor 2: Student–Instructor Formal Relations.** This dimension drew together questions that bore on the more formal aspects of the instructor–student relationship, especially those having to do with testing, grading, and fairness.
  - My instructor wants me to do well on the tests and assignments in this class.

> - Sometimes I feel like my instructor and I are on opposing teams in this class.
> - **Factor 3: Student–Instructor Informal Relations.** The questions that composed this factor concerned instructors and students being acquainted with one another in informal ways.
>   - I am acquainted with the instructor.
>   - I've spoken informally with the instructor before, during, or after class.
> - **Factor 4: Student as Instructor.** This dimension comprised questions that focused on a specific aspect of student–student relations, namely the degree to which a student occupied an instructor-like role with respect to his or her fellow students.
>   - The people sitting near me have learned something from me this semester.
>   - I can clearly explain new concepts I've learned to others in class.

Findings: Social Context and Outcomes

The development and validation of the SCALE instrument was the first part of our research and indicated that we could validly and reliably measure certain aspects of classroom social context, and the content of the SCALE dimensions told us something about the nature of what we were measuring. The second part of our research examined the importance of these dimensions. In particular, we wanted to answer two questions:

1. Is social context stronger or better in ALCs than in traditional classrooms?
2. Is social context associated with student learning outcomes?

Our hypotheses were that all dimensions of social context would be positively associated with student learning outcomes, and that social context would indeed be found to be stronger in ALCs than in traditional rooms.

We based these expectations, in the first place, on our examination of existing data from earlier research conducted in ALCs at the University of Minnesota. These "found data"—that is, data that were not collected for the purpose of investigating social context—showed that classes held in ALCs were consistently associated with a higher degree of interaction than those held in traditional rooms, and that this interaction was valued by students and by instructors (Baepler & Walker, 2014).

In the second place, we believed that much contemporary educational theory and research inclined toward the view that interactivity during the teaching–learning process was generally a good thing—for instance, the literature on student–faculty contact and rapport (Endo & Harpel, 1982; Pascarella & Terenzini, 2005) or on cooperative learning among students (Johnson, Johnson, & Smith, 1998).

Social Context and Type of Learning Space

To address both of the aformentioned questions, in spring semester 2015 we administered the SCALE survey to students in six different classes, five of which were taught in ALCs and one in a traditional classroom ($N = 612$, with 311 students in the traditional class). We also collected demographic, background, and academic aptitude information about the respondents (including age, sex, year in school, ethnicity, major, ACT score, and GPA).

To address our first question, we compared data from classes held in ALCs to data from our one traditional class. The results indicated that there was indeed a difference across different types of learning spaces in regard to the level of social context experienced by students in those spaces. The mean level of every dimension of social context was higher in the combined ALC classes than in the traditional class (see Figure 3.1).

This finding must be considered preliminary, however, because we measured social context in only a single class held in a traditional classroom. In its size and content, that large introductory chemistry class was very similar to the ALC classes we measured, and analyses of demographic and background variables indicated that the students in the traditional class were not significantly different from the students in the ALC classes. Nonetheless, we cannot exclude the possibility that this class was unusual in some way that affected its social context, independently of the classroom in which it was taught, so further research and data collection must be done to reach reliable conclusions about social context across different sorts of learning spaces.

Social Context and Learning Outcomes

To answer our second question, we conducted a multivariate analysis to examine the role played by the different aspects of social context in the determination of student learning outcomes. For our analysis we used the four dimensions of social context as predictor variables, and we included background, demographic, and aptitude information about students to control for any possible effects of those variables. We included data only from students in ALC classes ($N = 301$) in this part of our study, because we had data only from a single traditional class.

Figure 3.1 Mean scores for the four factors of social context.

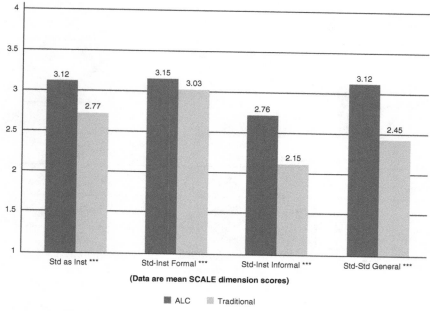

(Data are mean **SCALE** dimension scores)

■ ALC   ▨ Traditional

Note: ***p* < .001, ****p* < .0001

Our analysis found that the different aspects of social context predicted student learning outcomes—measured either by course final grades or by a standardized final exam—in different ways (see Figure 3.2). First, the more formal aspects of classroom relationships—the Student as Instructor and Student–Instructor Formal dimensions of the SCALE survey—were strong, positive predictors of learning outcomes. Second, the more informal aspects of social context were either neutral with respect to learning outcomes (Student–Instructor Informal) or detrimental (Student–Student General). These findings indicated that some types of classroom social context supported student learning, and others, contrary to our initial hypothesis, did not.

We found it unsurprising that the Student as Instructor dimension of social context was positively predictive of student learning. The extensive literature on reciprocal teaching (Pascarella & Terenzini, 2005) supports the idea that students learn when they stand in the role of the instructor with respect to their fellow students, as does research into the benefits of peer instruction (Crouch & Mazur, 2001).

We interpreted the Student–Instructor Formal dimension of social context as a reflection of instructor enthusiasm and perceived instructor fairness with respect to testing and grading practices. Seen in this way, the support

Figure 3.2 Social context dimensions and learning outcomes.

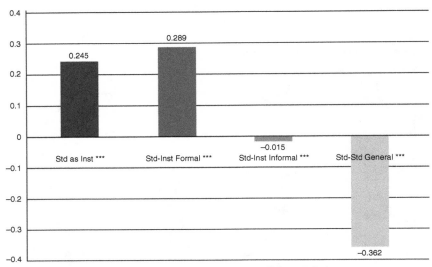

(Data are standardized beta weights from OLS regression)

Note: ***$p < .001$, ****$p < .0001$

for student learning provided by this construct was not surprising, given the connections between various perceived teacher behaviors and learning outcomes (see the literature cited in Pascarella & Terenzini, 2005).

The lack of a connection between the Student–Instructor Informal construct and student outcomes was somewhat perplexing, in light of the many sources of pedagogical advice that recommend developing good informal rapport with students (Buskist & Saville, 2001; Granitz, Koernig, & Harich, 2009). It should be noted, however, that this dimension of social context was the weakest in the sense that it comprised only three questions; thus, its ability to capture everything we might mean with the phrase "instructor–student rapport" was necessarily limited. Additionally, informal relations between instructors and students might have an impact on outcomes other than the ones we measured (e.g., student motivation, persistence, affect).

The strong negative relationship between Student–Student General Relations and student learning outcomes may have been the most counterintuitive finding from our study, because it seems in tension with the large body of literature recommending teaching techniques that have students interacting with one another—cooperative learning, collaborative learning, and so on (Johnson et al., 1998; Prince, 2004). The surprising nature of this result is particularly evident when one realizes that, while several of the questions that compose this dimension of social context have to do with whether students are acquainted or comfortable with one another, other questions focus on more specifically academic aspects of inter-student relations, such as the following:

- In general, people sitting near me in class work well together on class assignments, questions, and so on.
- During class, I often have a chance to discuss material with some of my classmates.

We formulated two hypotheses in an effort to explain this finding. First, we thought it possible that, by virtue of the sheer volume of interaction that tends to occur in ALCs, in some cases students may *mislead* one another in the course of studying course material. Second, we supposed that when students have cordial informal relations with one another, they may be hesitant to criticize one another's ideas and hence may produce *overconfidence* in their fellow students. As a test of these hypotheses, we included two questions about whether students misled each other, and we asked students to estimate what grade they would receive in the course, comparing their answers to their actual grades as a measure of overconfidence. However, neither of these measures was significantly correlated with the Student–Student General dimension of social context, so our attempts to explain that dimension's surprising negative association with student learning remain unsupported.

Finally, we should note that our study was not experimental, so we cannot draw strong causal conclusions about the relationship between social context and learning outcomes. Nonetheless, our analysis did control for a wide range of student aptitude, background, and demographic variables, so we can exclude many possible explanations for our findings. For example, because we included GPA and ACT scores in our analyses, we know that the explanation for the negative association between Student–Student General Relations and learning outcomes is *not* that academically weaker students simply had stronger relations with their fellow students.

Discussion and Pedagogical Recommendations

Social context, of course, is not an immutable property of a classroom. Indeed, the findings of our research point to several pedagogical recommendations that might help shape social context in ways that could positively influence learning. For instance, our results on the Student–Student General Relations dimension suggest that students who seem to value these aspects of the classroom dynamic may not be doing so for their actual learning value.

That is, students may enjoy each other's company or the general esprit de corps of their table. There is nothing essentially wrong with this approach, and indeed one might imagine that making friends and social contacts in college has positive learning benefits (Pascarella & Terenzini, 2005).

We also know, however, that these same informal conversations that do such a good job of building rapport can also be distracting and easily veer off topic for extended periods; indeed, numerous faculty members have suggested in anecdotal remarks that the "buzz" in ALCs is not always on topic. As they are building casual relationships, students may not be attending to their classwork to the extent necessary to perform effectively on major assessments. Nobody wants to play the scold, but students might need to be reminded that despite what might seem like an informal learning environment, they need to be vigilant about how they apportion their time and to remain on task. Collaboration can quickly devolve if groups do not self-discipline or reward those who keep conversations productive and relevant to the material. It might also be advisable to administer a digital distraction policy that asks students to be more aware of the interruptive role that phones and laptops can play in the classroom. (See our suggestion for a digital distraction policy in Chapter 4.)

Another explanation for these results might implicate the manner in which students learn when they agree with the statement, "I have learned something from my classmates." As we mentioned, it might be the case that they overestimate what they have accomplished when simply listening to a fellow classmate. Research suggests that people in general commonly judge their abilities more favorably than objective tests would estimate (Atir, Rosenzweig, & Dunning, 2015; Moore & Healy, 2008). Passively listening to an explanation of a process or solution, if that is what they are doing, is not the same as rehearsing it for oneself or teaching it to someone else. In addition to reminding students of their tendency to overestimate their knowledge, instructors may want to create additional opportunities for students to check their understanding so they don't grow complacent and overconfident about the knowledge that they believe they have learned. To help students grasp what they understand and what they do not, instructors might want to assign "exam wrappers," a metacognition activity in which students complete a worksheet before and after an exam that compels them to analyze their performance and reflect on their learning process so that they can adjust their approach to preparation (Ambrose, Bridges, DiPietro, Lovett, & Norman, 2010; Sandall, Mamo, Speth, Lee, & Kettler, 2014).

Our finding that the Student as Instructor dimension positively predicts performance suggests that instructors should consider taking advantage of opportunities to design experiences that call for this strategy. All students should be compelled to actively teach each other, such as when they practice reciprocal teaching (Larson & Dansereau, 1986; Palinscar & Brown, 1984), engage in peer learning (Crouch & Mazur, 2001), or participate in a simple jigsaw activity (see Image 3.1). In a jigsaw assignment, students become experts on a topic, frequently by reading and preparing to teach an assigned article, and present the salient features of the article to the rest of the group. This method works particularly well for upper-division courses that cover complex material. When time does not allow for peer teaching, homework assignments that call for students to fully explain their solutions would be advisable. During activities, instructors should circulate in the room, informally polling students so that they are prepared to answer questions and explain concepts. As we suggest in Chapter 5, creating assignments and activities for which students develop their answers visibly on the whiteboards around the room also compels them to express their reasoning.

At its essence, the Student–Instructor Formal dimension describes a sense of trust between the student and the instructor and a belief that the instructor is allied with the student in pursuit of learning. This trust might be expressed as a general sense of empathy, and to some degree it may resemble the psychological construct of professor–student "rapport" that has also

Image 3.1 A student uses the projection screen to make a point about using genetically modified organisms to capture carbon in the atmosphere. Students frequently use the projection screens and whiteboards to teach each other.

been associated with student learning and other behaviors that may help students succeed (Benson et al., 2005; J. H. Wilson, Ryan, & Pugh, 2010). This might help to explain why students would agree with the statement, "My instructor wants me to do well on the tests and assignments in this class" or disagree with the statement, "Sometimes I feel like my instructor and I are on opposing teams in this class." It might also help to explain why a student in an ALC would make the comment, "Working in an open, encouraging environment like this allowed me to feel more comfortable and prepared when it came to working with my team and the professor."

The positive predictive ability of the Student–Instructor Formal dimension reinforces several good teaching practices. It should come as no shock that students dislike surprises on exams and quizzes. This is a matter of perceived fairness that hearkens back to the development of student–instructor trust and clear communication. We recommend that instructors frequently revisit the goals of the course with students and make every effort to prepare students to succeed on exams. Eliminate any possibility that the mechanism of the assessment (e.g., "tricky" or overly ambiguous questions) interferes with an accurate estimation of a student's performance. Allowing students to see practice questions or even contribute questions to an exam would help create this sense of fairness. Leading a practice session, such as the "circuit training" activity we describe in Chapter 7, can telegraph to students that you're on their side and are providing them with multiple ways to prepare for exams.

We know that students appreciate classes in which they are encouraged to ask questions and classes that they perceive as enjoyable. Indeed, students enter college and choose a major (or switch majors) expecting to enjoy their coursework (Zafar, 2011). We've already noted that students often have preconceived conceptions of what it is like to learn in groups, and many have had poor experiences that they did not enjoy. A student in the middle of a set of good group learning exercises, however, described her experience this way, recognizing that the instructor had a role in how the groups functioned: "Our instructor enforces group work so that me and my group members feel comfortable working together. The instructor is super smart and engaging." An instructor who shapes the experience well so that the assignments are relevant, who presents a complex problem with significant challenges worthy of a group approach, and who helps organize group formation and group behavior is likely to create the conditions for an enjoyable class. We provide ideas and advice on creating engaging assignments in Chapter 5 and managing groups in Chapter 6.

Lastly, our finding that the Student–Instructor Informal dimension is not predictive of learning outcomes is perhaps not as surprising as it immediately seems. There is a strong body of literature that suggests that working with instructors outside of the classroom can improve retention and engagement (Pascarella & Terenzini, 2005). Our findings do not dispute this. Nor do we discount the value of many informal aspects of teaching, such as exhibiting a sense of humor, smiling, or demonstrating expressiveness, that we also know contribute to a positive classroom atmosphere and content learning (Pascarella & Terenzini, 2005). Our finding with this dimension is much narrower and simply suggests that casual acquaintanceships and other informal discussions do not predict learning, and this finding is consistent with research on interactions with faculty (Pascarella & Terenzini, 2005). They might, however, improve end-of-course teaching evaluations, as might a sense of humor and a genial demeanor, and thus should not be altogether ignored (Benton & Cashin, 2014; Erdle, Murray, & Rushton, 1985). Rather than producing a practical suggestion, knowing these results may simply help to reduce anxiety among some instructors who do not naturally tend toward informality. In other words, if an instructor maintains good formal practice with students, which includes making the class enjoyable and relevant, then the informal aspect of casual, perhaps off-topic conversations and connections may not matter to their current learning (see Table 3.1).

Conclusion

This study gives us confidence that our original anecdotal evidence revealing the importance of relationships among students and between instructor and student is accurate and potentially meaningful for teaching practice. Of course, our findings must be viewed within our own educational context and extrapolated to those that are similar. For instance, our research was conducted primarily with large STEM courses, and the demographic characteristics of our student population were typical for large universities in the upper Midwest—mostly White students and mostly native English speakers.

That said, however, our main finding can be relied on: *Relationships, or what we have posited as the "social context," seem to matter.* We have outlined some ideas about *how* social context matters to teaching, focusing on ways in which instructors might seek to foster the aspects of social context that support student learning and minimize or circumvent the aspects that are detrimental. But as with any single study, the results of our research must be understood within the larger context of educational research and theory in this area. In the chapters that follow, we return to that larger context and draw upon it in an effort to provide broad but well-grounded recommendations for teaching practice in ALCs.

TABLE 3.1

Summary of Pedagogical Recommendations Based on Social Context

Factors	*Recommendations*
Factor 1 Student–Student General Relations	Remind students to stay on track and that the room's configuration easily invites off-topic conversations. Assign exam wrappers so that students are compelled to review how they studied and what contributed to or detracted from their exam performance. Provide additional opportunities for feedback so students know whether or not they have learned something.
Factor 2 Student–Instructor Formal Relations	Periodically remind students of the goals of the course and how the activities they are conducting are linked. Review assessments to make certain that the wording is clear and that they provide a fair estimation of student achievement. Offer exam practice sessions so students know you're helping them succeed. Regularly invite questions during class. Attend to group dynamics so students know that you're mindful of how groups are working.
Factor 3 Student–Instructor Informal Relations	Be friendly, fair-minded, and natural to the degree that it suits your personality.
Factor 4 Student as Instructor	Create opportunities for students to act as a teacher, such as reciprocal teaching and peer learning. Assign jigsaw exercises so students are compelled to teach material to each other. Require students to explain answers on homework.

Note

1. We wish to thank our colleagues Samuel Van Horne at the University of Iowa, Anne Loyle at the University of Minnesota, and Jamie Schneider at the University of Wisconsin–River Falls for their invaluable help in developing the SCALE survey.

4

COMMON TEACHING
CHALLENGES IN ACTIVE
LEARNING CLASSROOMS

This is a great classroom; I just think instructors need to be trained properly to use a space like this.

—An ALC student

I think the classroom is great, but preparation is key to successfully teaching in one.

—An ALC instructor

Maybe you lived some version of a familiar classroom technology nightmare, fumbling with some machine in front of a waiting audience of students who grow increasingly frustrated or, perhaps worse, amused by your travails. You probably even witnessed this scenario as a student. Depending upon what era you went to school, you might have watched a teacher try to outwit a reluctant film projector or DVD player, only to sigh in defeat, "Well, it worked for me the last time." Possibly he was trying to project his laptop and stumbled onto that perennially helpful error message: "Source not found." Typically what comes next is either immediate capitulation or a titanic struggle of man over machine, and the drama spools out in front of class. In some cases, though, an instructor quickly resolves the problem, or he rolls out a ready-to-go plan B. Preparation in these instances is paramount.

This tenet holds true not just for technology but also for general classroom management, particularly in Active Learning Classrooms (ALCs). Instructors need strategies; resolutions; and plans B, C, and D at the ready to shift smoothly from activity to discussion, keep students on task, and regain students' attention at far-flung tables covered with devices that promise digital distractions.

In the first three chapters of this book, we have explored the genesis and history of ALCs as well as how these rooms have been studied. We have made the case that these rooms influence how students and instructors behave by facilitating particular kinds of activities and impeding others. The rooms' design conditions what can happen in those spaces and creates expectations among students and instructors. We also know that faculty who face teaching in new spaces tend to rely, at least initially, on how they have taught in the past (Carr & Fraser, 2014). This reliance on familiar techniques, such as extensive lecturing, can create a raft of problems and make the experience of learning in this new space more difficult for the student and unpleasant for the instructor. Simply feeling comfortable moving about in the space or orienting your students to the room can feel peculiar at first. In a sense, a newly designed space calls for a new teaching design that takes into consideration student expectations and the affordances of the classroom.

Some of the challenges we'll discuss in this chapter might sound familiar to instructors accustomed to lecture halls, but ALCs offer more opportunities for your direct interaction with students, groups, and technology. Space helps instructors mitigate some familiar challenges, but it also generates new hurdles. To that end, this chapter concentrates on some of the common teaching challenges you will likely face so you can begin to prepare yourself for when you move your course into an ALC.

The challenges we discuss in this chapter commonly arose in our consultations with instructors and observations of classes taught in ALCs. Some concerns address larger, more conceptual issues, such as how to manage the flow of classroom activities and how to mitigate student resistance to the rooms. Other issues concern the everyday demands of teaching in an ALC, such as where to position yourself in the room and how to regain attention once you have tasked students with a group project. Throughout the chapter we feature the many ways instructors have managed to address and overcome these hurdles to ensure student success. We have divided the challenges into the following categories:

- Planning to teach in the space
- Teaching in the space
- Managing student resistance
- Employing technology in the space

In ALCs, preparation, indeed, is key.

Planning to Teach in the Space

When instructors first enter an ALC, they are immediately struck by how different the space is from the classrooms in which they have taught before, and the vast majority quickly realize that this new type of learning space calls for a different approach to teaching (see Image 4.1). One key to having a successful experience in an ALC is advance planning—in particular, thinking about what it is like to be in the space, how to change your course to fit the space, and how to adapt your course materials.

How Do I Get Started?

The best way to get started on preparing to teach in an ALC is to visit the ALC in which you'll be teaching. To gain a more nuanced sense for how the rooms work, it's best to observe a colleague teach in an ALC. Experienced ALC instructors we spoke with said that such observations helped relieve their concerns about how they should plan to use the space effectively. One ALC instructor said, "Observation was key for me. I saw a colleague use the space, and it allowed me to picture myself using it too." Instructors who conduct an observation can see how their colleagues teach, move, manage and implement technology, and facilitate learning in the space. Instructors who do not have colleagues to visit should consider watching videos of the spaces in use at other institutions. For example, the University of Massachusetts–Amherst has created an ALC video series called "Teaching Untethered" (see https://vimeo.com/112838051). The video shows Professor David Gross of the Department of Biochemistry and Molecular Biology working in the classroom as well as sharing ideas about his process for using an ALC (see Image 4.2). Teaching at the University of Minnesota's College of Veterinary Medicine, Professor Frank Williams and his students produced a video of their experiences working in an ALC equipped with digital microscopes and a central wet lab (see https://sites.google.com/a/umn.edu/cvm-alc/in_action).

What Takes the Place of Lecture in the ALCs?

Most instructors sense very quickly that ALCs are not configured for lecture. The lack of a central focal point for student attention means that lecturing is somewhat awkward in ALCs, and the round tables call for learning activities that engage students with one another. Research supports this perception: Studies have shown that using lectures as the dominant method of teaching in ALCs is not particularly effective (e.g., Brooks, 2012; Walker, Brooks, & Baepler, 2011). It is not popular with students, either. As one ALC instructor told us, "Students will hate it when you lecture [in the ALC]. You have

Image 4.1 A large ALC at the University of Minnesota.

Image 4.2 Students in Professor David Gross's biochemistry course at the University of Massachusetts–Amherst manipulate images to explore the double helix structure of DNA.

to give up on that idea." In a room with round tables, whiteboards, and multiple screens, students expect to be able to act, not sit still to listen to long talks.

Although lecture is not effective if used as the primary mode of instruction, many faculty who teach in ALCs still make use of *micro-lectures*—shorter lectures interspersed between periods of student activity. A biochemistry and molecular biology professor estimated that he spends 20% of the time in his ALC courses lecturing. Recognizing that there is "no need to rehash things students already know" from reading the course textbook, this instructor uses his micro-lectures to introduce new concepts, clarify misconceptions, and deal with general course administration (e.g., quiz reminders, office hours, readings for next time). He explained that ALC courses are "about students learning actively," and instructors should not think of these classes as "lecture courses."

The ALC layout typically includes a podium or console in the center of the room surrounded by round tables that ring the rest of the room. You may find lecturing from the center of the space initially feels unnatural because you will necessarily have your back to some people in the room at all times. A wireless presentation remote control can give you some freedom to move about the room. Should you need to draw a diagram or underline a point while you are away from the central console, you can use a software program, such as Doceri (see http://doceri.com), to control a presentation from your tablet or iPad. If you were teaching calculus, for example, and needed to draw an equation, you could use Doceri to do so from anywhere in the room. Similarly, if you were teaching art history, you could pass your tablet to a student and ask her to draw on a pre-loaded image to emphasize its visual composition. In this manner, you can combine micro-lecturing, the room's technology, and student participation.

Replacing lecture with group work as the dominant instructional mode poses challenges as well. Some students revealed that the frequency of small-group work leaves them feeling isolated from the rest of the students in the class with whom they do not interact. Other students also indicated that an overreliance on group work can grow tiresome. Instructors should endeavor to balance the small-group/large-class activities and discussion.[1] For example, a resource economics professor has groups report out on activities and assignments simultaneously (a by-product of the TBL methodology). He feels that this process allows the students to see that many others have arrived at similar solutions so students across the room feel like they have learned together. A music therapy professor frequently changes the groups to ensure students have a chance to interact with different individuals over the course of the semester because "it gives them a chance to learn from someone else's perspective."

How Much Effort Will It Take to Redesign My Course for the ALC?

Fully redesigning any course and its instructional activities (along with assessments, etc.) takes effort, and instructors we spoke with suggested that newcomers take what Petersen and Gorman (2014) called "small, sane steps" toward course development. Consider modifying just a single lesson, topic, or unit as a pilot before redesigning an entire course. You may initially find only an element of each lesson or class period that might work for active engagement. For example, is a topic particularly relevant? An environmental conservation instructor who was new to teaching in an ALC had student teams assume the roles of various community members and discuss how a new housing development impacts the local ecosystem. This activity permitted students to understand the issue from not only an academic perspective but also a practical and civic angles as well. In science courses, instructors may already have problems that they normally parse on the whiteboard during their lectures. Convert the worked problem into a group problem-solving activity and have the students find the solution. Another instructor recommended simply asking tables of students to compose an answer to a question on the whiteboards. Small, sane steps.

Veteran ALC instructors say early in the process they underestimated the high level of commitment they needed to fully adapt and (re)design a course for delivery in an ALC. A resource economics professor shared a response common among ALC instructors in saying he did not have as much time as he would have liked before teaching for the first time in an ALC. He estimated that he spent about 20% more time working on the materials for this first ALC course than he would in a typical course preparation. An environmental science professor said when adapting a course for an ALC space, preparing activities "took an enormous amount of time, especially compared to a traditional class." Van Horne and colleagues (2014) found that instructors frequently misjudged the time dedicated to an assignment.

How Do I Cover All the Content?

Many instructors are naturally concerned about not having enough time to cover material when they redesign their courses so heavily around group activities. Research, however, supports the value of active learning (e.g., Freeman et al., 2014; Oliver-Hoyo, 2011), and instructors who teach in ALCs tend to agree. For example, a biology professor felt that she was "freed" from having to "go over" simple material (e.g., stages of mitosis) covered elsewhere in the course materials. An environmental sciences professor said, "Less is more when [students] have a deeper understanding" of the material. He saw that sophomore students in his ALC class were learning material typically taught at the graduate level. He devoted the time saved not to reviewing textbook readings, rather to developing additional problem-solving activities, including an exercise he typically used in his graduate courses. As for coverage, one ALC instructor acknowledged, "I have covered more content than I've ever covered [in a traditional classroom] every single time I've taught in the ALC. I've actually covered more; I've never covered less." A biochemistry and molecular biology professor likewise estimated that he covered 10% to 15% more content in an ALC compared to the same course taught in a traditional classroom. The layout of the space helped him see when students were challenged. He noted that in an ALC it is easier to detect this when the students are applying what they are learning rather than passively sitting in their seats. When an instructor moves around in an ALC, he simply sees the room from different perspectives: He can see what students are writing on whiteboards, hear how they are thinking about a problem, and judge when to intervene and address a problem as students are tackling it.

Of course, there are caveats. When first teaching in the space, many instructors reported a need to revise their plans on how they would use class time as challenges arose. A math instructor said, "I had a plan, but I knew I had to be flexible. Sometimes I ended up lecturing when an activity I planned didn't fully develop." A history professor said he still lectures at length when students need clarification or when changing topics within a class period.

How Do I Manage Class Flow?

The instructors we worked with acknowledged that they had to get used to the idea of giving up some control over how students learned throughout the course. The transition from the "sage on the stage" to the "guide on the side" presents challenges to many instructors, and some of those challenges manifest in major structural changes. Plant biology professor at the University of Minnesota, Sue Wick, mentioned that she sought to achieve "a balance between really high structure for the course and then being able to go with the flow." This equilibrium means preparing to be flexible by organizing strong, diverse teams of students and developing structured activities. Within these structures, you can begin to feel comfortable about adapting to students' interests and unexpected questions. A professor of Spanish and Portuguese said that she struggled in the beginning, but once she figured out the new activities and general structure for the course, it became clearer how she was going to accomplish her goals: "I still make changes, but I am more relaxed."

Instructors who have been teaching a particular course in a traditional classroom for many years may notice a qualitative difference in the variety and depth of questions students ask them while holding the class in an ALC. A biology professor warned, "Get ready to not know everything." She was struck at how well the groups worked to filter out commonly asked questions. If someone did not know the answer to a relatively straightforward problem, students asked a neighbor at the table. This exchange allowed new and more challenging questions to emerge for which the biology instructor could not necessarily prepare:

> In the traditional classroom, again, I could predict what they would ask. I'd be sitting there talking about something, I'd see a hand go up, and I would have put $20 down on what that student was going to ask. You know what I mean? Whereas in the active learning class, whoo! And they were sophisticated questions. Sometimes with societal or legal relevance.

Teaching in the Space

This section focuses on the practical challenges associated with day-to-day teaching and classroom management in an ALC. Even instructors who visit an empty room before teaching in it for the first time might feel a bit of sensory overload on the first day when students fill the seats, begin to talk, and start to work on an activity in earnest. Instructors new to the space often call out the lack of a central focal point in the room as especially flummoxing. One ALC instructor explained, "I wasn't sure where the front was at first; it was sort of disorienting not to see all of the chairs pointed forward." Students recognize this disorientation too, with one student in an ALC noting the room's arrangement "makes it difficult to watch the professor as she is in the middle, and we focus on the screens [on the periphery] normally." Instructors new to ALCs find that it can be difficult to locate and hear students, to move through the space, and to regain attention from a new spot in the room. The lack of a central focal point means instructors need to plan for how to direct attention in the space, including defining the *front* of the room and positioning themselves to ensure students can locate the speaker. Anticipating these classroom management issues and thinking about how to cope with them can help instructors assert some control over the ALC and minimize avoidable confusion in the unfamiliar space.

Where Should I Stand?

ALCs create a situation that disrupts the eye contact and body language typical in traditional learning environments. For some part of each class period, students and instructors likely will be staring at each other's backs, an arrangement that can feel disrespectful and even rude for both speaker and listener (see Image 4.3). We suggest you address this peculiarity of the seating arrangement at the outset. You might tell students, "My back will be to some of you at different times, but that's natural for this space. Likewise, you probably won't always face me, and I promise not to be offended." If you are comfortable with an informal atmosphere, consider the approach a humanities professor takes with her students. She tells them,

> This is a different kind of classroom. I'll be moving around a lot. That's okay. At any time, you may move around; it's not rude. It's acceptable. In fact, I encourage you to do that. Think of it as more of a conference room than a classroom.

Let your students know that you intend to use the room as it was designed and that you are going to circulate to see how people are faring. Students

Image 4.3 To see the instructor, some students must repeatedly look behind themselves.

seem receptive to instructors who move about the classroom. One student remarked, "Because there is a nice flow of space, the instructor can walk around and even in a huge room she feels close, and by being face-to-face with other students I always feel engaged."

Instructors who coteach or have graduate and/or undergraduate teaching assistants in the room might consider dividing the rooms into zones to ensure they reach all the tables. Developing an adequate "coverage" plan helps instructors provide timely feedback during in-class activities so that students stay on task. Remaining physically close to students may also reduce their temptation to be digitally distracted (more on this topic later). Because it's so much easier to maneuver among students in an ALC, it's also easy to overlook the fact that even ALCs can have the equivalent of the lecture hall's back row: that place where students go unseen and unheard. One instructor mentioned that when she first taught in the ALCs, she inadvertently created "dead zones," and students at these least-visited tables grew progressively more disengaged. Once she realized this situation, she made a concerted effort to encircle every table at least once a class period and move into those tighter spaces encumbered by coats and other hurdles: "I will move backpacks, [and other items]. if necessary, and stand right behind somebody who is on Facebook until he/she redirects his/her attention. Basically, I've gotten braver and less concerned with looking nosy."

How Do I Make Certain Everyone Can Be Heard?

As in many large lecture halls, most of the instructors who teach in large ALCs use wireless microphones (e.g., lavaliere or lanyard). Many of the rooms already have microphones installed at student tables as well. A biology professor recommends introducing students to the practice of using the microphone on the first day so that they begin to become accustomed to the sound of their own voice:

> I ask them to grab a mic and say something into it, then pass it to someone else at the table. I end up with about 30 seconds of cacophony, but I feel like students are more willing to use the mics asking questions after that.

Another instructor observed, "I find that students have to get used to hearing their own voice on the speakers [throughout the classroom] a few times before they are comfortable with the mics." Allowing students to practice good microphone presence may reduce inhibitions and encourage more active participation in class activities (see Image 4.4).

How Do I Regain Attention?

The lack of a distinct "front" of the room can make reestablishing attention during an activity a challenge. To regain attention in the space, some

Image 4.4 A chemistry student glances at a monitor while preparing to speak.

instructors use a consistent phrase (e.g., "Attention, everyone") to bring the noise level down and to shift students' focus from the activity back to the instructor. Some use web-based electronic clocks (see www.online-stop-watch.com) to count down activity time and sound effects to signal a time to return attention to the instructor. Yet other instructors borrow from their primary school counterparts and raise their hand when it is time to refocus; when students see the instructor's hand raised, they raise their hands as well. By the time a majority of students have their hands raised, noise from groups in the class has diminished, and the instructor has students' attention and can shift to the next topic.

To make it easier for students to locate a student speaker, instructors can consider making use of a special light or call signal. In many rooms, the indicator lights or call signals are mounted above monitors or near tables. For example, a history professor has his students push the call button, which was originally designed to alert an instructor that assistance was needed at a particular table, to indicate either when they have completed a task or when members of the table are speaking and/or reporting out. Being able to switch smoothly between the seeming chaos of group activities to the familiar order of a whole-class discussion not only is a good classroom management practice but also helps students who may have difficulty paying attention.[2]

Managing Student Resistance

First impressions matter, and an ALC can make a memorable one: Many students enter ALCs skeptical about the space, and research confirms that this initial negative reaction, while not the most common, is still widespread. In one ALC, at least some students found the technology and furnishings (e.g., large monitors, connectivity outlets, round tables, and modern furniture) excessive (Whiteside, Brooks, & Walker, 2010). One student in that study suggested that "the technology is impressive but impractical" and that the ALCs are a "waste of money." Another student likewise found the ALC excessive, and noted "its design aesthetic [was] a waste of money and space. We don't need fancy equipment or flat screens to foster creative energy." For some students, the open design and visible technology, for whatever reason, disturb them. If instructors preparing to teach in ALCs realize that some students associate the rooms with wastefulness, then those instructors can (and should) take steps early in the course to address these concerns. Students may not be aware of the potentially positive effects the room can have on learning, especially if they have had limited exposure to similar spaces. Left unchecked, students' disregard for the technology and design of the ALC may contribute to their ongoing resistance and dissatisfaction throughout the term. As we mentioned in the introduction, it may be incumbent on the instructor, particularly in introductory courses, to "teach the room" so that students are aware of why you are teaching in an ALC and how they can benefit the most from the experience.

How Do I Convince Students ALCs Are Beneficial to Them?

Early interventions by instructors are critical to helping students understand how the layout of the room changes what will happen there. An English professor, for example, suggested giving students an opportunity on the first day of class to think about the space to make known any negative feelings: "I ask students how they feel about the room and get feedback from them and address their concerns about it. I don't assume that they're going to love it." Many ALC instructors introduce space as an important element of the course, explaining that the room's physical structure helps to facilitate student-centered or collaborative work. Some instructors talk about how the teaching role changes as a result of the space. A physics professor said, "I explain to them how my role is going to be different. My time is now focused on what they are struggling with rather than repeating what is in the book."

One technique for countering student resistance to the space is to expose students to research that informs why they are learning in these rooms. Instructors could explain, for instance, that the types of activities that take place in ALC spaces can promote problem-solving abilities (Haak, HilleRisLambers, Pitre, & Freeman, 2011). In terms of outcomes, instructors could share evidence that has demonstrated that students perform a half standard deviation better in active learning STEM courses than they do in courses delivered predominantly by lecture (Freeman et al., 2014). Walker and colleagues (2011) found that students of all abilities and levels benefit from taking courses in an ALC. Perhaps the most compelling evidence instructors could share early in the term comes from past students' perceptions of their experiences in an ALC: Students thought the space added to their ability to develop confidence working in groups, connect with classmates and the instructor, and understand varying perspectives (Walker et al., 2011).

Using institution- and/or class-specific examples is another way instructors can demonstrate the value of an ALC and manage reactions to it. To establish why the space matters, one astronomy instructor shows students anonymous exam grades of his previous students—one set from students who completed the course in an ALC and another set from those who took the same exam in a more traditional "lecture" setting. The instructor points out that those past students who participated in collaborative work in the ALC performed better on exams by about 10% compared to those who collaborated in the traditional space. He said this practice of giving current students some historical data helps reduce resistance to the space because they see it is in their best interest and has been reflected in past students' final grades.

David Matthes, a biology professor at the University of Minnesota, suggested that it was not enough to simply mention that students have been shown to learn better in these rooms. To garner student buy-in, it is critical, he suggests, to "re-inoculate" students with the evidence that ALCs and the pedagogical methods employed in them are shown to produce better student learning gains:

> Most students come into [an ALC] with the expectation that group work is bad. Many come into this room and immediately have an association of "oh no!" I think we need to remember that expectation management is the number one thing that any professor moving into these rooms needs to do to get their students on board with them. And that means you tell them they're not guinea pigs. We're not just "giving this a try." We're not just going to "see how this goes." No. You say, this is what the data shows: This is going to be a great experience for you. You're going to learn way better in this classroom. Not just as well—better! And more importantly, you'll learn different types of things.
>
> You have to believe it. Maybe I didn't at first, but now I *know*. So now I can teach in here better than I could my first semester. But believing in the space is important for you and for them. And that expectation management is what gets you their buy-in. And their buy-in gets you a lot of results.

How Do I Demonstrate the Relevance of ALCs to Students?

Providing a brief introduction in the syllabus to student-centered instructional strategies and the ALC's role in them is another way to help defuse potential student skepticism early in the course and illustrates how the ALC benefits all students. Instructors can purposely link collaborative work in the space to a general or a discipline-specific pedagogical strategy. A molecular biology instructor, for instance, has her students look for evidence of how many single-authored papers appear in the field as a way to demonstrate how collaboration extends into academia. She said students quickly realize that collaboration and teamwork are valuable components to scholarly work and "life after college in all its forms." Professors Curt Griffin and Kristina Stinson at University of Massachusetts–Amherst have each taught an environmental science course called Ecosystems, Biodiversity, and Global Change in an ALC. In their syllabi, both provide this overview about students' work in teams:

> You spend most of your class time working in teams applying what you've learned from the textbook and from in-class discussions/mini-lectures. Teams solve real-world problems and answer questions about how the world works. That's what environmental science and conservation are all about. . . . Most of our class time is spent applying what we've learned.

By aligning the work students will do in the ALC with the "real-world" problem solving expected of environmental scientists and conservationists, Griffin and Stinson present the classroom as a pre-professional space in which students will practice skills of value in the field beyond college.

Mentioning specific instructional strategies, like TBL, is another approach to consider. Associate Professor Jon Berndt Olsen, also at University of Massachusetts–Amherst, teaches History 101A: Western Thought Since 1600 and includes the following passage on the first page of his syllabus:

> This course is taught using the team-based learning pedagogy. TBL is an alternative to lecture-based learning. The main purpose of TBL is to transform the classroom experience from acquiring knowledge to applying it. In other words, students spend class time applying course content and concepts in a team format. While most of the learning occurs among students in their teams, faculty are always present and available to provide guidance over material that the teams find difficult to master. Published studies have demonstrated that students enrolled in TBL courses learn as much, and probably more content and concepts as they do in lecture-based courses. Furthermore, TBL promotes the development of teamwork skills while students learn to apply course content to "real world" situations.

In defining *TBL* as "transform[ing] the classroom experience," Olsen implicitly recasts students' familiar notion of the classroom as a place for acquisition to one for active engagement and application. In other words, in this passage Olsen has incorporated most of the strategies we have recommended in this chapter thus far to help students come to recognize the value of learning in an ALC. Making an intentional and repeated connection to evidence of improved learning gains for students can dispel some of their resistance. Including and referencing collaborative strategies in the syllabus (e.g., teamwork and problem solving) and specific methodologies (e.g., TBL) signal to students the instructor's commitment to use that strategy in the space.

In addition to helping students learn better, you might also point out that how they are learning material in the course may help them learn a practical skill set that may help them as they enter the workforce. Allowing students on the first day of the course to reflect on the types of skills valued by employers is another way to present the ALC as relevant. Instructors may ask their students to generate a list of skills on a whiteboard or in a Google doc that they think are sought by employers. Students can compare their thoughts with classmates at the table to see similarities and differences. The instructor can then have groups report what they thought would be most valued. Finally, the instructor can display data showing the preferences desired by employers.

For example, the Association of American Colleges and Universities' 2015 employer survey lists skills employers want students to have when entering the workplace. Among the top skills is the ability to work with others; in fact, 83% of employers sought an increased focus on "the ability to work effectively with others in teams" (Hart Research Associates, 2015, p. 4). Furthermore, the report stated that "fully 80% of employers say that during the hiring process it is very important to them that recent college graduates demonstrate the ability to apply learning in real-world settings" (p. 6). ALCs are designed for just this outcome. We see similar findings in a survey conducted by the National Association of Colleges and Employers (2014): The ability to work as part of a team jumped as a desired attribute among that year's respondents. Just over 71% of respondents in 2013–14 favored the ability to work in a team; a year later, almost 78% of respondents sought evidence of it (p. 32).

In the previous year, the same organization conducted a similar survey and listed the following as the top five skills employers sought at that time:

1. Ability to work in a team
2. Ability to make decisions and solve problems
3. Ability to plan, organize, and prioritize work
4. Ability to communicate verbally with people inside and outside an organization
5. Ability to obtain and process information (National Association of Colleges and Employers, 2014)

Employment data like these complement the educational research and help students come to recognize the value of working in an ALC. As a physics instructor tells his students, "This is real life. When you apply for a job—any job—after college, you are applying to a team."

Employing Technology in the Space

The amount and kind of technology in the ALC are difficult to miss. Although it is important to note that *technology* can be broadly defined (meaning that some instructors will single out the round tables as their favorite technology), the flat screens, microphones, projectors, wireless Internet, and whiteboards make an impact and shape expectations. Regardless of whether one sees the technology in the space as a boon or a distraction, instructors should carefully consider how to integrate it (or not) into their courses.

What Do I Do With All That New Technology?

When you walk into a new classroom with flat-screen monitors lining the wall and microphones on all of the tables, it is easy to assume that the class is going to use technology in a sophisticated manner. That assumption can be intimidating for everyone, and it is an expectation you should manage regardless of what you intend to do in the room. For example, if students need to bring a device to class or to use a particular software program, make them aware of that in the syllabus and call attention to your choice on the first day. Seasoned ALC instructors use technology in various ways. A math instructor uses clickers, laptops, the learning management system, and specialized software, including a program to help her students conduct peer evaluations. A humanities professor who teaches a course on "dystopia, video games, and comic books" said that technology is heavily integrated into her course. She has students bring video game consoles, and she admits that it would not be possible to conduct a class like this in many traditional classrooms. A biology professor calls the whiteboards "pure gold." They get students out of their seats to work together in a fashion public to everyone who cares to glance at their work. Especially if students begin to use whiteboards at the outset of a course, they will naturally begin to own the space communally.

Other instructors do not rely heavily on technology. A cognitive psychology professor, for instance, said her students primarily use presentation software in the room. If you do not intend to use much of the obvious technology in the room, let students know to expect that the screens will largely remain dark. After all, the ALC is used for different types of courses, and your class may not need to use every feature of the room. A Spanish and Portuguese professor said, "I believe technology has a purpose. It's perfectly fine if it is there and it is not open. I use [technology] where it can be helpful."

How Do I Manage Digital Distractions?

Regardless of the extent to which they incorporate the ALC's technology into their courses, instructors need to prepare to address the challenge of digital distractions in the classroom. Popular and scholarly attention has been focused on the prevalence of digital distractions and issues surrounding multitasking in the classroom (e.g., Fried, 2008; Junco, 2012; Sana, Weston, & Cepeda, 2013; Taneja, Fiore, & Fischer, 2015), and distraction is certainly a concern for instructors who teach in ALCs (Petersen & Gorman, 2014; Van Horne et al., 2014). Students have access to an increasing number of devices on college campuses (Dahlstrom & Bichsel, 2014), so the prospects for distraction are high. As such, instructors in ALCs need to think carefully about how the use of technology aligns with course outcomes and integrate it accordingly.

A communications professor said she lets students know when it is time to use the laptops: Students "are going to have their devices, and it's hard to tell them to turn it off, but you can set expectations about appropriate use, like for note-taking." She has found walking around the space also helps to maximize time-on-task. A music therapy instructor will simply say "laptops open" or "laptops closed" to indicate when students are to access technology in the classroom. Finally, an environmental science professor minimizes students' technology distractions by designing rigorous in-class activities; as a result, students are too busy in class to have time to "surf the net."

To help students regulate their own behavior with technology, Rachel Sagner Buurma, a faculty member at Swarthmore College, inserts a "Your Own Devices Policy" into the course syllabus, which calls students' attention to self-distraction and suggests ways of avoiding it:

> Because our class is intensively collaborative, I will expect that you will be focused on the texts and on your classmates. If it is your experience that having a screen in front of you can distract you from the work of being in class, please take measures to prevent such self-distraction. (I like StayFocused; you may like other programs or strategies.) Also because the intensively collaborative work of this class will sometimes be screen-based work, you should know that you may be requested, at very short notice, to project your device's screen for the class to view. Please plan accordingly. (Buurma, 2014, "Your Own Devices Policy")

Which Technologies Are Critical to Know?

We mentioned earlier that you have to "teach the room," and by that we mean that you need to explain to students the value and potential of the room and your methods for teaching in it as you do. It's also critical to "learn the room," and here we mean it quite literally: You should learn how to control the essential equipment within the space. The basic technology

Image 4.5 An integrated ALC control panel.

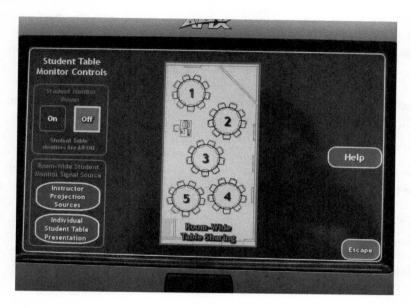

of the classroom can be daunting, particularly if the ALC you are using is equipped with the capability to project student laptops. Suddenly, you may need to know how to allow students to project their laptops onto the whiteboard or onto the table's screen. Maybe you'll want to select one table's projection to be broadcast to the entire room. Do you know how to adjust the volume of someone's video or lower the lights so more detail in a projection can be revealed? There are many permutations of what you might want to do, so knowing how to use the room's main control console and helping students learn what to do with any controls available to them is going to make everyone's life easier (see Image 4.5). Many schools will publish a quick guide on how to use the room's technology, and this is certainly worth reviewing ahead of time. Indeed, we highly recommend practicing with the technology and asking one or two colleagues to go with you to an ALC and act as students so you can get a sense of what it takes to manipulate the room's capabilities. We detail several instructional development opportunities around this topic, including possible room use scenarios you can try, in Chapter 9. Learning the room and knowing that you can orchestrate the multiple projection sources can give you the confidence you need to expand your teaching, invent new assignments, and help students work together.

Conclusion

This chapter explored the host of challenges that face instructors new to teaching in an ALC. These challenges may arise in other classrooms as well, but due to the specific purpose of ALCs, we suggest newcomers reflect upon the challenges described here as they prepare to teach in an ALC. How an instructor prioritizes these challenges depends on a number of factors (e.g., class size, course level, comfort with technology), but this chapter outlined general areas for all instructors to address or review before teaching in an ALC.

With all teaching, however, some degree of flexibility is needed to ensure the transition to teaching in an ALC is a manageable process. A cognitive psychology professor offered these words of advice to those preparing to teach in an ALC: "I planned a lot, but the learning process is dynamic, so you have to be flexible and go with the rhythm of the class." Teaching in an ALC is challenging, and it will take time to adapt, but feeling like you've prepared can give you confidence to transform your teaching and how your students learn.

Notes

1. For details about assignments in ALCs, see Chapter 5.
2. For more information on helping students with disabilities learn in ALCs, see Chapter 8.

5

ASSIGNMENTS AND
ACTIVITIES

So I think prepare like crazy. And it's not the lectures you need to prepare.
It's everything but the lectures.

—An ALC instructor

The advice of the instructor in the epigraph of this chapter to prepare *everything but the lectures* before teaching in an Active Learning Classroom (ALC) makes sense, but what exactly is the "everything" she's referring to? Is it radically—or even all that much—different from what most teachers already do?

We have already suggested what should seem by now quite obvious: ALCs, by themselves, are not a ready-to-go solution. Shared desk space, moveable seating, and the replacement of tight rows with team tables create favorable conditions for active learning. The rooms offer the opportunity to try learning activities that are uncomfortable or seemingly unnatural in a traditional space. But the *everything else* takes imagination and planning. We aim in this chapter, which describes activities instructors have used in ALCs, to give you practical ideas you can implement and adapt to prepare your own *everything else*.

The assignments (one of which has been recognized with distinction by *Science* magazine) we describe in this chapter are drawn from a broad range of disciplines and teaching approaches. Many are not unique to the ALCs. Indeed, faculty have been working wonders in traditional classrooms for years, and the literature is replete with creative examples of how instructors have practiced active learning despite the constrained conditions of the classrooms. Thus, the examples we are showcasing here might well be modified to work in a traditional classroom; however, the majority of these exercises would be challenging in a room with fixed seating, where they might engender significant student resistance.

In assembling this collection, a few common features of effective ALC activities emerged:

- Most of the information transmission in the form of lecture by the professor is significantly reduced or moved out of the classroom;
- Most activities are supported by graded pre-class reading, homework, and quizzes or post-class homework;
- Students often work in small teams on activities designed to provide them with a deeper understanding of the topic; and
- Classroom activities are typically followed by some form of whole-class synthesis facilitated by the instructor that may take the form of a discussion, a short assessment, or a mini-lecture.

Many of these activities can be traced to specific active learning teaching approaches. These approaches include team-based learning (TBL; Michaelsen, Knight, & Fink, 2004), process-oriented guided-inquiry learning (POGIL; Eberlein et al., 2008), the studio or workshop approach (Lackney, 1999), and the flipped classroom approach (EDUCAUSE Learning Initiative, 2012). Though the details of each differ, these approaches share some common elements that include moving away from a traditional passive lecture approach, increasing the responsibility students take for their own learning, using class time to allow students to work cooperatively on course-related material, and encouraging interaction among classmates and between the instructor and students. We do not address the details of these general approaches because there are excellent overviews available already (Davidson, Major, & Michaelsen, 2014; Eberlein et al., 2008; Michaelsen et al., 2004). Although the activities we describe may conform to one of these teaching approaches, in most cases they represent an eclectic combination of attributes.

In the end, the *everything else* we describe in this chapter—the activities and assignments that complement online or shortened lectures—are offered with the intent that they may be adapted to your situation. We believe most or all of these activities can be modified to support different learning outcomes and disciplinary subjects. Table 5.1 lists all of the activities described in this chapter.

TABLE 5.1
Activities Described in Chapter 5

Activities	Examples	ALC Elements Used
Semester-long projects	Team genetic engineering proposal and poster presentation project	CP, DC, MPS, OA, TPS, TT, WB
	Community partners project	CP, MPS, TPS, TT, WB
	Drug design proposal	CP, OA, TBS, TT, WB
Problem sets	Team problem sets	CP, OA, TPS, TT, WB
	Team problem sets with assigned roles	OA, TT
Structured discussions and debates	Literature analysis	CP, MPS, OA, TPS, TT, WB
	Teams write a "Frankenpaper"	CP, MPS, OA, TPS, TT
	"Ponderables"—thinking experiments	TT, WB
	Structured debates	OA, TPS, TT, WB
Experiments with manipulables	Natural selection using M&M's	OA, TT
	Laboratory experiments	CP, MPS, OA, TPS, TT, WB
	Ordered steps in a process	OA, TT, WB
Skill development activities	Teams generate and modify a hypothesis	CP, MPS, OA, TPS, TT, WB
	Teams answer subjective questions using evidence	MPS, OA, TPS, TT, WB
	Small-group discussion leading	CP, TPS, TT, WB
Topic introduction activities	Four corners topic/background questions	OA, WB
	Syllabus scavenger hunt	OA, TT

Note. Abbreviations refer to the ALC's physical aspects utilized for the activity.

CP = central spot for plug-ins; DC = document camera; MPS = main projection screen; OA = open arrangement of room; TPS = table projection screens; TT = team tables; WB = whiteboards.

Semester-Long Projects

Some classes culminate in a final project designed to synthesize many (or all) of the course learning outcomes. A team project provides students with the experience of collaborating with others to create a product that would be difficult for one person to create on her or his own. The unique challenge of a semester-long team project is moving students through the distinct phases of the project toward specific milestones. From the small tables for team discussion to the easily navigable open space for display of student work, the ALCs design features support teams as they work on project milestones.

Team Genetic Engineering Proposal and Poster Presentation Project

A poster presentation is a good way to teach students how to organize and communicate what they have learned and accomplished during the semester. Students must synthesize data and integrate multiple ideas into an accessible format that they then can present and defend in a public forum. The following is a detailed example of how a poster session concludes a semester-long investigation in an introductory biology course.[1]

Genetic engineering proposal

This project won the *Science* prize for inquiry-based instruction. For this project, students propose the development and use of genetically modified organisms to solve a societal problem. Students work nine to a team as assigned by the instructors early in the semester to distribute the students' assets, liabilities, and preferred team roles. Teams begin this exercise by choosing a challenge or question of interest as well as a gene and an organism that they propose to modify to address that challenge. Teams describe their plans in a written proposal submitted to the instructors early in the semester. Teams collect and include background information needed to explain the rationale and relevance of their proposal, create project-specific aims, and outline plans for achieving their aims. As students work on the various stages of the project in class, the instructors circulate throughout the room to answer questions and check on the project's progress. Examples of past project titles include "Glow Fish: Zebrafish as Bioindicators of Mercury," "Cracking the Peanut Allergy: Gene Silencing of Allergenic Ara h Proteins in *Arachishypogaea* to Eliminate Deadly Food Allergy," and "Edible Hepatitis B Vaccine in Bananas" (Wick, Decker, Matthes, & Wright, 2013). See Table 5.2 for an outline of the project structure. For a complete calendar of all project activities within the context of the course, see Appendix 5.1; for examples of actual student project submissions, see Appendix 5.2 with assignment instructions for each of the project subtasks.

TABLE 5.2
Genetic Engineering Proposal Project Structure

Week	Project subtask
3–5	Teams choose their project topic.
6–7	Teams create an *Annotated Bibliography*.
8	Teams write the project *Background*.
9–10	Teams write up the *Research Plan*.
10–11	Teams write up the *Discussion* and *Summary*.
12	Teams submit the poster draft for feedback from peers.
13	Teams submit final poster draft.
14	Team presentations and peer review.

Note. See Appendix 5.2 for a complete description of each of these subtasks.

The ALC space supports multiple aspects of the project well: Student teams face each other at their tables for discussion and planning, and students use their individual table projection screens to collaborate on their posters during class, allowing teams to see other groups' posters. Teams can search for electronic resources to show on their table's screen or have the resource projected to the entire room by the instructor. Students typically use the whiteboard for group outlining or drafting ideas. Most of these activities would be difficult or impossible to accomplish in a traditional classroom, particularly the poster presentation itself, which requires room for students to congregate and discuss the posters.

Related activities
To help students succeed, the project is highly structured in stages for submission of key project elements, such as the annotated bibliography, for grading and instructor feedback throughout the semester. This structure helps the students make timely progress and holds the teams accountable throughout the lengthy project. The grading of most of the subtask assignments is completed according to a grading rubric that students receive prior to turning in each milestone of their project (see Appendix 5.3).

To ensure individual accountability of all team members, students are required to submit a weekly Team Accountability Documentation Sheet (see Appendix 5.4) that asks each team member to list his or her contributions for that week. At the end of the semester, students conduct a peer evaluation of their team members that will determine a small percentage of an individual's final project grade. The Team Accountability Documentation Sheets are returned to each team prior to the peer evaluation so that team members can review their teammates' contributions.

Poster presentation

During the poster session in the ALC, student teams present their posters to their classmates and instructors (see Images 5.1 and 5.2). Posters are attached to the whiteboards around the perimeter of the room, allowing students and instructors to move among the posters and interact with the presenters. The entire class period is spent viewing and assessing posters in an atmosphere designed to simulate a professional conference poster session. During the activity, a subset of the student teams stays with the poster to present their challenge and findings and to answer participants' questions. At the same time, the remaining members of the team are assigned other posters to view and grade with a rubric (see Appendix 5.5). Halfway through the class, student teams flip roles so that all students present and assess each other's work. As an added incentive to design a creative and effective poster, a prize for best poster is determined by a group of student and faculty judges.

The instructors for this course remarked that most of the posters are of extremely high quality, and students take their role as presenter seriously. Encouraged to affect a professional appearance for the presentation, most students dress up for the event, lending it a serious tone. One indication that students are asking sophisticated questions is the fact that, as the instructors observed, "Industrial, academic, or federal labs [are] pursuing projects similar to those proposed by . . . students" (Wick et al., 2013).

Community Partners Project

Working with community partners on a long-term project gives students the experience of working with stakeholders beyond the academy and helps them explore the relevance of course content in the real world. A good example of this kind of project takes place in a writing studies usability testing course.[2] The instructor identifies different community entities, such as a county public library, with a usability testing need whose staff will work with a student team throughout the term. Four students per team work on a 10-week project that culminates in a written report and a PowerPoint presentation to the entire class and to the community partners.

In this complex and high-stakes project, teams analyze the end-user perspective of their community partner's website, generate research questions, and design and administer usability testing. One hour a week of class time in the ALC is dedicated to student team interactions. For instance, during "data analysis day" students bring to class the data they have collected from their usability testing and work with their teams to make sense of it. Teams pore

Image 5.1 Students pick up posters for poster presentation rehearsal.

over the data and gather around the whiteboards where they use sticky notes to identify and diagram themes in their data. Their work is informed by the community partner's website projected on their individual table monitor. The instructor moves around the room and checks in with each team. She asks questions and pushes students to connect their claims to evidence. At the end of this time, each team reports their initial findings to the entire group. The instructor wraps up the class by facilitating a discussion to help students synthesize what they have learned that day. The instructor shared

Image 5.2 Student teams take turns presenting their posters to other students during the poster session on the final day of the project.

that many clients make changes recommended by the student teams. Students have used their written reports as evidence of usability testing experience in job interviews and, in fact, many have been hired as interns or as usability technicians.

The instructor explained that this activity can be done in a traditional classroom, but features of these spaces make it more difficult for both her and the students. Desktops are small, and it is difficult for students to spread out their laptops and their notes. Predictably, the only whiteboard in the room is covered when the projection screen is down, precluding the use of the whiteboard and the screen at the same time. Finally, the lack of a central plug-in site as is found at the center of the ALC team tables forces students to extend computer cords from their desks across the aisle to wall outlets, creating barriers to moving easily throughout the space. In contrast, the open arrangement of the ALC allows the instructor to easily interact with student teams while they are working.

Drug Design Proposal

If working with community partners is not feasible for a course, faculty or students can role-play a particular entity. This approach requires

TABLE 5.3
Drug Design Proposal Project Structure

Week	Project Subtask
5	Teams choose their project topic.
7	Teams identify scholarly resources.
8	Teams write the project background material.
9	Teams write up the significance section.
10	Teams write up the drug target plan.
12	Teams submit a project draft.
13	Teams present their proposals.

students to assume another viewpoint to design material appropriate for that audience. An example of this adaptation takes place in an upper-level undergraduate pharmacology course in which student teams present drug development proposals to a mock panel of drug company representatives. The project is scaffolded so that intermediate assignments with instructor feedback are due throughout the term. (Intermediate assignments are listed in order in Table 5.3.) Students spend class time collaborating on each of these assignments.

Teams of four create a proposal for the development of a new drug designed to address a human disease or condition. Using a PowerPoint slideshow, students present their proposal to a fictitious drug company at the end of the semester. The role of the drug company representatives to whom the teams pitch their proposals is played by pharmacology faculty. Teams must use published literature to explain the science informing their proposals, justify the importance of their proposal based on human incidence data, and make the case that their approach is better than others currently available.

As in the preceding examples of semester-long project activities, the ALC is conducive to these in-class collaborations: Student teams engage in face-to-face conversations at the team tables, search for scholarly resources on library databases, and display electronic resources on the tables' projection screens. All of these tasks are more challenging to undertake in a traditional classroom. The features that allow for easy group discussions and sharing of resources also support a motivational component that is important for semester-long projects, during which students could lose energy and enthusiasm as the term wears on. In the ALC, students literally face their teammates on a regular basis during structured time for them to work on their project. The peer interaction in close quarters reinforces a sense of accountability students feel toward their teammates. Likewise, the in-class sessions reserved for working on clearly defined project milestones help prevent procrastination and propel students' steady, self-regulated progress.

Problem Sets

Problem sets engage students with course material by requiring them to apply foundational knowledge to new situations. In-class problem sets are often assigned in flipped classes in which the development of problem-solving skills is a major course outcome. Students listen to videotaped lectures at home and work on problems collaboratively in class. The flipped teaching approach is greatly enhanced in an ALC, because student teams can gather at small tables to work together on problems while the instructor circulates among the tables to check on student progress and answer questions.

Team Problem Sets

A general chemistry class presents a compelling example of team problem sets in a flipped classroom.[3] This course was redesigned so that instead of attending three hours of lecture per week in a traditional classroom, students interact for one hour in an ALC; the other two hours are spent outside of class watching recorded lectures online. When they come together in the ALC, student teams work on problem sets with challenging, multi-part questions. Weekly team problem sets require student groups in teams of three to collaboratively solve a series of related problems of increasing difficulty. The assignment creates structure to support students through the increasing levels of challenge and provides opportunities for rapid feedback from their peers and the instructor.

An example problem set addresses kinetic-molecular and pressure theory. Students download a worksheet with six multi-part questions from the course management system prior to coming to class (see Appendix 5.6). Initial questions ask students to make predictions based on drawings of particles in containers. The next series of questions asks students to collect "data" from an ideal gas law simulation on the website PhET (http://phet.colorado.edu). Using this simulation, students adjust the volume, temperature, and number of gas particles in a virtual container to see what happens in the vessel when, say, a single factor is held constant. Students record and graph the data generated by their simulations and return to the worksheet to answer more challenging questions. Throughout the hour, the instructor circulates through the room checking in with student teams. She has access to everybody in the room and is constantly moving from table to table, interacting with students for brief periods of time before moving on to the next table. If students have questions or are looking for the "correct" answer, she guides them to make realizations about the data they are collecting. At times during the worksheet activity, the instructor will engage the entire class in a discussion, asking for student teams to report their results and to compare and contrast their findings with neighboring teams. These discussions also present natural opportunities for her to identify and address misconceptions students may have about the topic.

The design of the ALC supports many aspects of this activity. Small tables facilitate face-to-face team discussions and easy viewing of the problem set. Whiteboards facilitate the graphing of data, and the open layout of the classroom facilitates instructor interaction with each team. It would be much more difficult to engineer this activity in a traditional classroom, and it is precisely because of this difficulty that the instructor conducting this team problem-set assignment decided to switch from a traditional classroom to an ALC.

Related activities

To prepare for their time working together in the ALC, students complete a series of out-of-class activities. They read assigned passages in the course textbook and watch the instructor's videotaped lectures posted on the course management system. Prior to each class, students are required to complete a graded pre-class activity that assesses their foundational knowledge about the topics that will be addressed in the problem set. After the class session, students complete online homework due at the end of the week. Thus, the in-class problem set is part of a cycle of activities that includes, in order, (a) pre-class reading and lecture viewing, (b) a graded pre-class activity, (c) the in-class activity and discussions, and (d) graded online homework, all related to the week's topic. This cycle repeats in subsequent weeks with each new topic, and students become accustomed to the flow of the activity.

As we detailed in Chapter 2, even though in this redesigned course students spend in the ALC only a third of the time they previously spent in the lecture hall, they perform as well as or better on the course's validated multiple-choice chemistry exam. Additionally, students' perceptions of their engagement, enrichment, and confidence also increased (Baepler, Walker, & Driessen, 2014).

Team Problem Sets With Assigned Roles

For beginning students working on problem sets in teams, it can help to assign team roles to provide more structure. These assigned roles ensure coverage of important problem-solving components. Strong use of assigned roles for team problem sets takes place in a foundational anatomy class taught in an ALC.[4] Working in teams of three, with three teams at each table, students complete problem sets throughout the term. Teams have assigned roles of reader, recorder, and reporter: A first person reads the question aloud, a second person records the work, and a third person reports the work.

An example of a problem set in this foundational anatomy class concerns epithelial tissue histology (see Appendix 5.7). Teams receive a problem set consisting of 11 questions of increasing difficulty to complete during the class period. The problem set has simplified drawings of different epithelial cell types in cartoon form to illustrate the similarities and differences between them. The worksheet asks a series of questions designed to promote critical thinking about the role of epithelial tissue in the body. The worksheet begins with simpler, lower-order concepts ("Describe the morphology of the following epithelial tissue cells") and builds to more complex, higher-order items that ask students to integrate what they know with new information ("The majority of dust is composed of human skin cells. What does this indicate about the rate of mitosis for epithelial tissue?").

Students can access material from the textbook or use their laptops to clarify concepts and facts, although, unlike the chemistry class's ideal gas law activity, experimental data are not required to complete this problem set. As in the chemistry activity, however, the instructor and the teaching assistants circulate teaching assistants throughout the room during the period to monitor progress and respond to student questions. Students completing this activity in the anatomy class are not directly given answers but are asked guiding questions designed to help them identify answers themselves. For example, if a student asks why skin cancers are so common, the instructor asks the student to define what *cancer* is and then connect this to what the student knows about how epithelial cells divide. This is a way of having students integrate existing knowledge and course resources to answer their own questions.

At the end of the activity, the instructor leads a whole-class discussion designed to help students synthesize what they have learned. After circulating among the student tables, the instructor has an approximate sense of where students are having problems. These are the areas to be addressed in this closing discussion. Correct answers are given to students during the wrap-up to provide them with feedback on how their teams performed on the problems.

Related activities

To prepare for this problem-set activity with structured team roles, students must read assigned chapters from the textbook and complete a graded homework assignment prior to coming to class. Thus, the classroom exercise is part of a larger cycle of activities consisting of, in order, (a) pre-reading, (b) homework problems, (c) in-class activity, and (d) whole-class discussion at the end of the class session. This cycle is repeated each week with a different topic.

The instructor of this anatomy course remarked that the quality of student conversations he has overheard during this assignment convinced him that students in ALCs have a deeper understanding of the topic than students he has taught using a more traditional lecture approach in a lecture auditorium.

Structured Discussions and Debates

These activities are designed for students to discuss topical questions in depth. Though dialogue can occur in any classroom, small-group discussions are easier to accomplish in an ALC where students face each other in groups. Furthermore, the open arrangement of the room allows for the instructor to approach and listen in on all of the student groups, not just those groups accessible to the aisles. In the following sections we describe three discussion activities and a structured debate activity used by instructors in ALCs.

Structured Discussion: Literature Analysis

In humanities courses, asking students questions to guide their analysis of a text helps them read and think more critically and consider different analytical perspectives. A good example of this critical and analytical reading and reflection takes place in an American literature class.[5] The instructor provides student groups with questions to discuss as a team, to arrive at a joint response, and eventually to present their findings to the rest of the class. Each group receives a different question about the class reading. An example of this structured discussion activity refers to a reading assignment of two poems by William Cullen Bryant. Group prompts include the following:

- If "Thanatopsis" is a poem that offers consolation on the subject of death, then what is it saying that could be construed as comforting?
- In what ways are Bryant's views on nature, life, and death a departure from his Puritan ancestors?
- In what ways is Bryant using nature in his poem "The Prairies"? What is he saying about the earth, spirituality, and human beings?

Teams of six students receive these prompts on the course management system at the beginning of class and spend the session discussing and preparing presentations to share at the end of that day's class. Many teams use the whiteboards near their tables to aid in outlining their discussion. Motivation and accountability are built into this activity by requiring students to present their findings to the entire class. The instructor notices lively, in-depth conversations about the prompts as he walks around the room to listen to the teams' conversations and address questions.

After each team presents, the other groups ask questions of the presenting team. The instructor provides incentive for asking questions by informing students that one of the team discussion questions will appear on their next exam. After student teams present, the instructor synthesizes the day's conversation in a wrap-up discussion with the entire class.

Related activities

Students prepare for this discussion by completing assigned reading before class. Exams include the questions that were discussed in class as well as new questions designed to determine students' ability to think critically about different perspectives on the reading. A unique feature of this activity is the instructor-prepared slide for each team presentation. Prior to class, the instructor prepares a PowerPoint slide for each team's question that includes the question itself and related visual material, which he projects during the student team presentation to the whole class. Having the slide completed ahead of time allows the presenting team to focus on their answer to the question rather than slide preparation.

Structured Discussion: Teams Write a "Frankenpaper"

Group writing can be used as an analytical tool for interpreting readings, learning to write under time pressure, and exposing students to different writing styles. An instructor created a team writing activity he calls a "Frankenpaper" that takes place in an introductory philosophy class.[6] Teams of four to five students have 50 minutes to write a complete draft of a typical paper, including its citations on course reading. Students use group-editing software (Etherpad) in their course management system to accomplish this exercise. The teams are randomly assigned, and those students work together for one major assignment before the instructor changes team membership, which occurs two or three times during a semester. Topics for the Frankenpapers are related to previously assigned reading; one topic, for example, asks students to write an essay explaining the difference between two essays they have read, one written by Carnap and the other by Quine. The writing prompt states that Carnap argues for the claim that "external questions" cannot be cognitive and then asks, "How did Quine propose to get around that argument?" Students review each other's work to see how other teams approached the same writing prompt.

A goal of this assignment is for students to practice reading and comprehending essays written by and for professional philosophers; another goal is for students to practice academic writing. The instructor says having students write as a team exposes them to the writing habits and styles of their peers, which may positively influence their own writing style. They also gain experience working collaboratively to develop arguments and organize ideas. He describes the classroom behavior during this activity as high energy, with students eagerly engaging with the material and enjoying the work. He believes this increased energy is prompted by students' having to rush to complete the essay within a single class period. The instructor makes this a low-stakes assignment by grading it as only complete or incomplete. He states that the pressure students feel to work hard comes from their "own sense of responsibility for their product and the social pressure of working in a group."

Although the instructor has led this activity in a traditional classroom, he reports that the tables at which students write and face each other in the ALC make it much easier for team members to interact. Also, because students can see the team document on the individual projection screens, everyone can participate in the process of composing and editing.

Structured Discussion: "Ponderables" — Thinking Experiments

In thinking experiments, students apply their knowledge of a subject to develop a logical solution to a particular problem. The instructor of an introductory physics class in an ALC calls it a "ponderable." Students work in teams of three to four, seated at round tables that hold up to three teams each. Student groups are chosen by the instructor according to academic background and ability to distribute resources equitably (Beichner et al., 2007).

The instructor presents problems that relate physics concepts to students' everyday lives. For example, "How would you design a car radio antenna optimized for your favorite FM station?" Students are given time to discuss the question and use the whiteboard to sketch out their solution. As in most activities in which teams interact independently, the instructor moves through the room monitoring solutions from each team and answering questions. At the end of each ponderable class session, the instructor leads a plenary activity such as a clicker question or class discussion that compares and contrasts teams' solutions. These wrap-up activities help students synthesize material and provide them with feedback on how well they demonstrated understanding of the concept.

The ALC is ideal for this activity because students can face each other during their discussions and use the whiteboards to sketch their plans. The open arrangement allows the instructor and teaching assistants to circulate around the room, checking in with each group and scanning the whiteboards for visible evidence of appropriate understanding. In fact, this assignment was one of the original activities used to shape the design of the first ALC. After class, students complete follow-up homework that asks more challenging questions than the questions they encountered in class (Beichner et al., 2007).

Structured Debates

Structured debates allow students to examine different perspectives of a controversial issue and formulate effective arguments to support a stance. An excellent example of this approach occurs in a Gender, Women, and Sexuality Studies class,[7] in which students debate questions like this one: "Does same-sex marriage provide the path to equality and liberation?" The instructor divides the class into four groups, one to develop and present the "pro" argument, one for the "anti" argument, one for the "pro" counterargument, and one for the "anti" counterargument. For large classes, she divides each group into subgroups. Groups or subgroups are instructed to use course readings and supplemental materials to help construct their arguments. They are allotted class time over three sessions to sit together at their team tables and formulate their argument. Multiple members of a group can use their laptops at the same time to contribute to a shared document visible on the table projection screen. As the different groups project their plans on a screen or detail them on a whiteboard, participants can begin to sense how the debate will unfold and determine the general level of argument that they will need to produce. The instructor walks among the groups as they are preparing, observes their work, and responds to questions. On debate day, each group has 20 minutes to make their arguments. The final group to present summarizes the entire debate. Groups are able to project PowerPoint slides or other visuals to the room to aid in their presentation.

The instructor believes that the arrangement of the ALC is amenable to this activity because teams can easily work together at a single table and also see and interact with nearby teams. In fact, the table arrangement that places students face-to-face communicates from day one that students should be working together collaboratively.

Related activities

After the debate, students are required to compose a two- to three-page write-up that asks them to (a) describe their contribution to the debate,

(b) evaluate how their team worked together, and (c) indicate where they stood personally on the issue at the end of the debate. This final graded writing assignment is written outside the classroom and helps inform subsequent discussion of and reflection on the debate process, which the instructor leads in the next class session.

Experiments With Manipulables

Students may need to work with materials (manipulables) to develop deeper understanding of course concepts. The ALCs can be used as laboratory space to conduct different experiments using objects that can be handled and rearranged. A few examples of these experiments are outlined in this section.

Natural Selection Using M&M's

Replicating a theoretical process is one way for students to render a concept more concrete and memorable. A clever example of this approach takes place in a biology class in which student groups simulate the process of natural selection.[8] The goal of the exercise is to reveal and correct student misconceptions about the mechanisms of evolution.

At the outset of the activity, each group of four or five students is given a quarter cup of M&M's and a folder that matches the color of one of the candies. Students are instructed to choose 16 M&M's at random and place them on their colored folder. In most cases there will be some M&M's that are the same color as the folder on which they are resting. Teams are then given three seconds to quickly pick off eight M&M's. This action demonstrates how color may help to conceal prey from a predator; M&M's the same color as the folder do not stand out against the background and, therefore, are less likely to be chosen. Students are then asked to produce the next generation of "progeny" by replacing each remaining M&M with another M&M of the same color. They repeat the selection activity again, followed by another round of replacing M&M's for the next generation. After several "generations," it is very likely that in some groups there is a "proliferation" of the M&M's that are the same color as the background folder, hence demonstrating how the trait of color within a population can evolve over time. Throughout the exercise, the instructor interrupts the activity to ask multiple-choice questions using clickers to judge students' understanding of the concept. For example, students are asked whether natural selection is happening after only one round of replication. For this activity to work, a flat surface that all team members can see is required. The small tables in the ALC work perfectly for this exercise.

During the activity, the instructor monitors the room, examines findings, and asks and answers questions. At the end of the activity, she leads a class discussion in which she asks teams to share their results and uses the differences among groups' findings to illustrate principles of natural selection. For instance, if a group did not start with any M&M's of the same color as their folder, they may never get a proliferation of any one color. This analysis helps illustrate the concept that natural selection can only act upon the genes present in a population gene pool.

The instructor remarks that the activity would be tricky to run in an auditorium-style lecture hall. This assignment might conceivably work in a conventional classroom, but its parameters could prove to be too daunting to make an instructor want to assign it, particularly in a large class of fixed rows and small desktops attached to each seat.

Related activities

The activity is supported by an out-of-class reading assignment on evolution and natural selection to be completed before class. After class, students take a graded online quiz on the subject to test their understanding.

Laboratory Experiments

Laboratory experiments serve as the foundation for many science courses. Typically, separate laboratory space is set aside for students; however, many experiments can be done in the ALC. Examples come from an introductory physics class (Beichner et al., 2007). In the ALC, students work in teams of three to four, seated at round tables that hold three teams. Teams work on two laboratory problem types: tangible activities (short, hands-on) and laboratory activities (longer, hands-on). Each of these takes place during a single class session and ranges from 10 to 50 minutes.

An example of a tangible activity asks students to find the coefficient of kinetic friction between their textbook and the table. Students slide their books across the table and estimate initial velocity and measure stopping distance. Laboratory activities are longer than tangible activities and focus on real-world problems. One lab activity asks students to determine the speed that a ball travels off the bat of a hometown baseball player who has a hit. Students watch videos of each batter and are provided with the distance markers in the local stadium as well as with the video output of the radar gun measuring the speed of each pitch (in miles per hour). This activity can be completed entirely at the ALC tables. For other labs, larger pieces of experimental equipment may need to be rolled into the classroom on carts, but all experiments for this physics course can be done within the existing space of the ALC.

During laboratory activities, students take on the assigned roles of manager, recorder, and skeptic. At the end of a laboratory activity, the instructor leads a class discussion to provide global feedback, answer student questions, and clear up common misconceptions (Beichner et al., 2007). An added advantage of using the ALC for labs is that it does away with the need for a separate laboratory space.

Related activities

To prepare for these activities, students read from a textbook prior to class. They also test their understanding of the reading with an online quiz or short assignment that must be completed before class. After class, students complete follow-up homework that asks more challenging questions than those they encountered in class (Beichner et al., 2007). This cycle of learning is repeated with each laboratory activity.

Ordered Steps in a Process

Some scientific processes or problem-solving approaches that students learn involve a series of steps that occur in a specific order. While memorizing the steps can be useful, in the activity example, which comes from a human biology course,[9] students go beyond memorization to predict how an outside force might impact a multi-step process. Each team of three or four students is given a collection of index cards; each card provides a single step in a multi-step cycle (e.g., the pathway that air takes from your nostrils to the alveoli of the lung, or the steps of the Krebs cycle). The cards are provided out of order to student teams. The first step in the task is for the teams to place the cards in the correct order on their tables.

After they have completed that task, the instructor provides each table with an intervention that perturbs a step in the cycle (e.g., a genetic mutation that results in a lost protein, a drug that blocks a certain enzyme in the steps, or a condition of low oxygen). Each team receives a different intervention, though in large classes, multiple teams can get the same intervention. Students then predict what will happen to the cycle and the disruption's subsequent effect, if any, on the human body. Teams are given time to discuss and generate an answer. At the end of the activity, the instructor leads a class discussion in which teams describe each intervention as well as the effect they predict it would have upon the system. Multiple teams working on the same question are challenged to address one another and agree or disagree with others' conclusions. This activity could be conducted in a classroom with conference-style tables; however, the added benefit of being able to share diagrams and notes on a whiteboard space provides students with further incentive to work together on the problem. This activity is preceded by a reading assignment to be completed prior to class.

Skill Development

In addition to understanding and applying theory and abstract information, some course learning outcomes involve the development of specific skills. The following three examples address the skills of generating a hypothesis, supporting a claim with evidence, and leading a discussion.

Teams Generate and Modify a Hypothesis

Hypothesis generation is a skill that transcends different scientific disciplines. Providing students with data to use in constructing a hypothesis lets students practice. An extension of this activity is to provide students with new data after they generate a hypothesis and ask them to determine whether the data support or refute that hypothesis.

Each team of four or five students in an introductory biology class for non-majors receives a question, such as, "Why does the giraffe have a long neck?," and must develop an evolutionarily based hypothesis to answer it.[10] The instructor lists the hypotheses student teams generate and asks students to use clickers to vote (individually, not by consensus as a team) for the most likely hypothesis. The responses appear on the main projection screen and on the individual table screens. The instructor reports that the majority of students typically chooses a naïve answer.

Next, the instructor provides the student teams with data related to their question. Data may take the form of a graph or chart or may be raw data that student teams have to graph themselves on their whiteboards. The teams are instructed to discuss what the data mean in the context of their chosen hypotheses. During this lively activity, the instructor circulates throughout the room, listening, observing, and responding to questions. After several minutes the instructor once again asks students to use clickers to choose the likely hypothesis. She reports that usually the vast majority of the students change their answer in this second round of testing to select a more appropriate hypothesis. The instructor then ends the class with a discussion synthesizing the skills students used in hypothesis generation. She points out differences in the class's responses before and after seeing the data and likens their actions to those used by researchers employing the scientific method.

Team members can write in a shared Google doc, on scratch paper, or on the whiteboard so that the whole team can contribute to the output. The logistics of this activity would be difficult in a traditional classroom with fixed seats and/or only one whiteboard.

Related activities

Students are prepared for this activity by having completed an assigned reading before class. After class, their understanding of the subject is tested by a brief graded online quiz. The quiz provides immediate feedback to the students about the accuracy of their answers.

Teams Answer Subjective Questions Using Evidence

Many academic disciplines require students to make arguments and support them with evidence. The instructor of a history class develops this skill in students by having them work on questions in teams.[11] In this activity, teams of two or three students receive a history problem. Teams must use primary historical documents to inform and justify their responses to questions that address the problem. The questions and problems assigned are similar to those a practicing historian might work on, such as, "What are the challenges of Jim Crow and the dynamics found within it?" Teams seated at round tables begin working on a list of questions, such as, "As an interpretive historian using the primary source reading that you are provided, how do you define *Jim Crow*? In responding, be sure to cite the sources that you use."

Teams discuss their answers, using the whiteboards to sketch notes and an outline. Sometimes they might use the table projection screens to pull up the reading and highlight particular passages that the entire team can see. During the discussion, the instructor walks around the room to listen to students' conversations and respond to questions. Students sit where they want and choose their own team members. After some time, the instructor tells all the students to move and join a different team. The instructor wants students to incorporate multiple perspectives when answering these questions, just as a practicing historian would seek out different perspectives when working on historical issues. The new teams receive another question, such as, "According to the sources, what aspects of life were affected by Jim Crow?" Again, students must support their examples with evidence from the primary literature.

The instructor remarks that the atmosphere of these discussions is energetic and, at times, loud. (In fact, he encourages boisterous discussion, telling his students that he "wants a noise complaint" from the classes next door!) At the end of class, the instructor leads a discussion to synthesize what students have done during the exercise. He is intentional about drawing comparisons between how the students approached these problems and how professional historians approach these problems. The instructor has used this activity in a traditional classroom, though he says it is much more difficult to do. He must limit the opportunities students have to record their responses to questions, and there is not as much opportunity for him to move around and interact with each of the teams.

Related activities
Students are prepared for these activities by completing assigned readings of selected primary sources before coming to class. Early in the semester the instructor also models how to approach answering these questions by going through one of the questions in front of the class. Students eventually apply the answers they generated in teams during class to a related written assignment.

Small-Group Discussion Leading

The ability to lead a discussion is an important skill for teachers to master. An activity in a graduate-level education course held in an ALC was designed to provide students with more practice in leading discussions and giving constructive feedback to their peers.

Teams of four to six students are equally distributed according to teaching ability so that novices are matched with advanced instructors. Over the course of two or three class sessions, individual members of a team lead a 10-minute discussion on the assigned reading for the day. In the ALC all team discussions occur simultaneously with one team per table, so several discussions happen at once and make efficient use of in-class time. Discussion leaders are encouraged to use the whiteboard or projected images as part of their discussion. Each team also has an instructor serving as an expert facilitator who models giving constructive feedback to the discussion leader following the discussion. Following the lead of this expert facilitator, team members provide structured feedback to the student discussion leader.

Since implementing this activity, the instructor has found that both the quality of discussion facilitation and the quality of constructive criticism among peers has increased. Student feedback also indicates that most students found this exercise useful for their development as future college instructors. The layout of the ALC with spacious separate tables and boards and screens at each table makes the logistics of this activity much easier to manage than it would be in a traditional classroom. Before using the ALC for this activity, the instructor had to reserve multiple classrooms to run the team discussions concurrently and to give each discussion leader access to a board and a projection screen. This example illustrates how one ALC can support the activities of multiple classrooms in a single physical environment.

Topic Introduction

In the epigraph to this chapter, an instructor reflected on the need to prepare "everything but the lectures." In ALCs, discussion and occasional mini-lectures take the place of lectures that tend to predominate day-to-day curriculum in traditionally designed, particularly auditorium-style, classrooms. This change in curricular approach means the category of "everything but the lectures" confronts instructors with significant choices: How will they teach content in ALCs in the absence of regular, lengthy lectures? What, exactly, constitutes *everything else*? The activities described in this chapter up to this point provide part of an answer to that question. Developed and implemented by faculty who teach in ALCs, these activities give instructors tools for teaching content while fostering student achievement of various learning outcomes. Those outcomes include synthesizing disciplinary ideas, using evidence to support arguments, collaborating to produce and present a single document, applying foundational or new knowledge in academic and real-life contexts, and developing skills in leading a discussion.

Another part of the response to what constitutes *everything else* in an ALC concerns non-disciplinary elements, such as a general course introduction at the start of the semester. Instructors should give thought to how they want to introduce their course on the first day of the term, whether they are teaching in an auditorium, an ALC, a small seminar room, or outside on the quad. In considering the broad category of *everything else* that emerges with the diminishment of classroom reliance on lectures, we propose that faculty teaching in an ALC eschew lectures at these moments as well. In this section, we present two activities instructors can use to introduce their courses on day one. These activities can be used in most classes, regardless of discipline, program level, or student ability.

Four Corners Topic/Background Questions

Using an activity to introduce your topic on the first day of class accomplishes two goals. First, it provides an opportunity to motivate students about the importance of the topic, and, second, the topic introduction sets expectations for active learning from day one. One approach that can be used to introduce many topics is the four corners topic/background questions activity. The instructor writes four questions on the whiteboards in each corner of the ALC. Questions can concern the course topic and may even be used to probe students' background knowledge. Example questions for different courses include:

- What is one way that you use chemistry in real life?
- How do you approach a major writing project?

- What word comes to mind when you think of ethics?
- What three words come to mind when you think of how the popular media portrays mental illness?

Divide the class into four groups and send each group to a corner. Direct each student in a group to write an answer to the question on the whiteboard and to discuss their responses with each other. After a few minutes, ask the groups to rotate and move to the next whiteboard question. Have them read the responses already there and add any new ones they can think of. Continue this round-robin until students are back at their original whiteboards, and then convene a full-class discussion to address some of their answers to the questions you posed. You might address misconceptions, allay fears, teach a bit of content, or explain to students how your course will help them achieve certain learning outcomes. After class you might want to record the responses with your cell phone camera and show them to students at the end of the semester to demonstrate how far they have come and how much they have learned during the semester.

The whiteboard and the open space of the ALC make this activity easier to accomplish than in a traditional classroom. In a traditional room, large sheets of flip chart paper could be posted on the walls of the classroom, but the whiteboards allow for more space for student responses. Likewise, the ALC's open arrangement allows for students to cluster more easily around the question and to write (and edit cleanly, with the whiteboard's eraser) their responses.

Syllabus Scavenger Hunt

The syllabus scavenger hunt is an activity to use on the first day of class.[12] It is designed to address multiple goals for the day: Introduce the syllabus, introduce the course management site, act as an icebreaker, provide students with practice speaking in front of the group, and create a sense of community. The instructor begins by describing and enumerating the goals of the activity. Students are divided into teams of four. Each team is assigned an aspect of the syllabus that they are responsible for learning more about and summarizing to the rest of the class. Categories include assignments, course objectives, attendance policy, and grading. Student teams have 15 minutes to learn more about their topic, which includes searching the course website and the course management site and preparing a brief presentation. Each team has five minutes to present their syllabus category summary to the rest of the class and respond to student questions. The instructor wraps up with a whole class discussion and fields any remaining questions. He states that since he started using this activity, the number of questions about the syllabus he gets in the second week has decreased. An instructor could scale this exercise for a larger class by having multiple small groups study the same category and then call on one of those groups randomly to present; thus, all groups need to be prepared to present. The non-presenting groups can be asked if they have anything to add to the presentation just given.

Conclusion

The activities described in this chapter range from short in-class undertakings with little support from outside assignments to semester-long projects supported by multiple out-of-class graded and non-graded activities that provide students with feedback on their performance. Many of these examples take advantage of cycles of learning in which students are exposed to the topic outside of class by way of a textbook or primary paper reading or video lecture followed by active engagement with the course material in the ALC. This engagement ranges from collaborating to answer problem-set questions, leading small-group discussions, and presenting posters, writing assignments, collecting data from simulations and websites, to generating data through experimentation. In almost every example, students work in small teams, typically assigned by the instructor, and they can remain together for part of or the entire class session or semester. Team members may be assigned roles and can be held accountable for their contributions, or they can work in collaboration without assigned roles.

Among instructors who have compared the experiences of teaching in both a lecture hall and an ALC, a common theme emerges. Instructors describe that when they conduct activities in a traditional classroom, they compromise on the quality of student–student and instructor–group interactions. In traditional classrooms, the quality of student–student interactions lessens in the face of logistical difficulties that compel students to try to face each other and share resources. Likewise, instructors experience a reduced ability, perhaps even an inability, to interact with every group in the room due to logistical constraints presented by tight rows of student seating, making it difficult to monitor activities and provide feedback. Instructors teaching in ALCs report stronger interactions with student groups in these contexts as a result of a room design that allows for an instructor to approach every student. As you mull over how to prepare *everything else* you need to engage and teach students in your ALC, we encourage you to use and modify the activities presented in this chapter to help your students achieve the learning outcomes in your course.

Notes

1. Thanks to Sue Wick, Mark Decker, David Matthes, Robin Wright, Anna Mosser, Brian Gibbens, Anna Strain, and Michael Burns, University of Minnesota.
2. Thanks to Lee-Ann Breuch, University of Minnesota.
3. Thanks to Michelle Driessen, University of Minnesota.
4. Thanks to Murray Jensen, University of Minnesota.
5. Thanks to Scott Simkins, Auburn University.
6. Thanks to Guy Rohrbaugh, Auburn University.
7. Thanks to Jigna Desai, University of Minnesota.
8. Thanks to Sehoya Cotner, University of Minnesota.
9. Thanks to Cheryl Neudaur, Minneapolis Community and Technical College.
10. Thanks to Sehoya Cotner, University of Minnesota.
11. Thanks to Robert Poch, University of Minnesota.
12. Thanks to Bill Rozaitis, University of Minnesota.

Appendix 5.1: Complete Calendar of Activities for Genetic Engineering Project Within the Context of the Course

Bold: Assignments *Italic:* Quizzes, Exams, Projects		LRQ: learning readiness quiz PEA: post exam analysis		Readings are from Freeman and colleagues' textbook, unless otherwise indicated		
		Monday	**Wednesday**	**Friday**	**Sat/Sun**	
Week 1	Preparation reading/assignment:	Sept 1	Sept 3	Sept 5	Sept 6–7	
Nature of Science	– Study Guide 1 – Reading: • Online references listed in Study Guide 1 • pp. 16–17, The Big Picture	Labor Day: no class	*LRQ1* Guided Inquiry 1	***Mastering Biology* to be done before beginning of class.**	**Metacognition due in Moodle dropbox by 11:55 p.m. Sunday.**	
Week 2	Preparation reading/assignment:	Sept 8	Sept 10	Sept 12	Sept 13–14	
Principles of Evolution	– Study Guide 2 – Reading: • Chapter 25 • Section 2.4 in Chapter 2 • **Skim** Section 28.2 in Chapter 28 (Don't memorize time periods or their events!) • Sections 28.3 and 28.4 in Chapter 28 • pp. 560–561 in Chapter 30	***Mastering Biology* due at beginning of class** *LRQ2* Guided Inquiry 2	Guided Inquiry 2, continued Project Team Work: project introduction	Project Team Work: What constitutes a good project?	**Metacognition due in Moodle dropbox by 11:55 p.m. Sunday.**	

(Continues)

Appendix 5.1 (*Continued*)

Bold: Assignments *Italic:* Quizzes, Exams, Projects	LRQ: learning readiness quiz PEA: post exam analysis		Readings are from Freeman and colleagues' textbook, unless otherwise indicated	
	Monday	**Wednesday**	**Friday**	**Sat/Sun**
Week 3	Sept 15	Sept 17	Sept 19	Sept 20–21
Biomolecules — Preparation reading/assignment: – Study Guide 3 – Reading: • Sections 2.4 & 2.5 in Chapter 2 • Chapters 3, 4, & 5 • pp. 84–88 in Chapter 6	**Mastering Biology due at beginning of class** *LRQ3* Guided Inquiry 3	Guided Inquiry 3, continued Project Team Work: evaluation of previous proposals and posters	Project Team Work: prioritized project ideas	**Metacognition due in Moodle dropbox by 11:55 p.m. Sunday.**
Week 4	Sept 22	Sept 23	Sept 26	Sept 27–28
DNA Replication, Mutation, Cancer — Preparation reading/assignment: – Study Guide 4 – Reading: • Chapter 15 • Section 16.4 in Chapter 16 • Fig. 12.3 & The Cell Cycle, pp. 222–223 • Section 12.4 in Chapter 12 (but don't memorize details of the G1 checkpoint) • pp. 366–367, The Big Picture	**Mastering Biology due at beginning of class.** *LRQ4* Guided Inquiry 4	Guided Inquiry 4, continued Project Team Work *Download and read Take-home exam 1 (posted on Moodle site by Wed. noon)*	*Exam 1, 100 points: 25 points take-home, 75 points in-class*	*Submit completed Take-home exam 1 to Moodle dropbox by 11:30 p.m. Sunday.* **Metacognition due in Moodle dropbox by 11:55 p.m. Sunday.**

Week 5	Preparation reading/assignment:	Sept 29	Oct 1	Oct 3	Oct 4–5
Gene Structure and Expression	– Study Guide 5 – Reading: • pp. 304–312 in Chapter 16 • Chapter 17 • pp. 366–367, The Big Picture	**Mastering Biology due at beginning of class.** LRQ5 Guided Inquiry 5	Guided Inquiry 5, continued *Project Team Work: individual critique of team's top 3 project ideas due before class*	*Project Team Work: team submits prioritized project ideas by 10:00 p.m.*	**Metacognition due in Moodle dropbox by 11:55 p.m. Sunday.**

Week 6	Preparation reading/assignment:	Oct 6	Oct 8	Oct 10	Oct 11–12
Mitosis, Meiosis, Mendel	– Study Guide 6 – Reading: • Sections 12.1–12.2 in Chapter 12 • Through Section 13.3 in Chapter 13 • pp. 366–367, The Big Picture	**Mastering Biology due at beginning of class.** LRQ6 Guided Inquiry 6	Guided Inquiry 6, continued Project Team Work: annotated bibliography	Project Team Work: annotated bibliography	**Submit PEA 1 to Moodle by 10 p.m. Sunday** **Metacognition due in Moodle dropbox by 11:55 p.m. Sunday.**

Week 7	Preparation reading/assignment:	Oct 13	Oct 15	Oct 17	Oct 18–19
Gene Regulation	– Study Guide 7 – Reading: • Chapter 18 • Chapter 19 • pp. 366–367, The Big Picture	**Mastering Biology due at beginning of class.** LRQ7 Guided Inquiry 7	Guided Inquiry 7, continued *Project Team Work: submit annotated bibliography and outline of topic by 10:00 p.m.*	Project Team Work: project background	**Metacognition due in Moodle dropbox by 11:55 p.m. Sunday.**

(Continues)

Appendix 5.1 (*Continued*)

Bold: Assignments *Italic*: Quizzes, Exams, Projects	LRQ: learning readiness quiz PEA: post exam analysis		Readings are from Freeman and colleagues' textbook, unless otherwise indicated	
	Monday	**Wednesday**	**Friday**	**Sat/Sun**
Week 8	Oct 20	Oct 22	Oct 24	Oct 25–26
Evolutionary Mechanisms Preparation reading/assignment: – Study Guide 8, including Exploratory Questions – Reading: • Chapter 26	**Exploratory Questions, *Mastering Biology* due at beginning of class.** *LRQ8* Guided Inquiry 8	Guided Inquiry 8, continued Project Team Work: project background	Project Team Work: *project background due 10:00 p.m.*	**Metacognition due in Moodle dropbox by 11:55 p.m. Sunday.**
Week 9	Oct 27	Oct 29	Oct 31	Nov 1–2
Genetic Technology I Preparation reading/assignment: – Study Guide 9 – Reading: • Sections 20.1–20.3 in Chapter 20	**EQ9 due at beginning of class.** *LRQ9* Guided Inquiry 9	Guided Inquiry 9, continued Project Team Work: research plan *Download and read Take-home exam 2 (posted on Moodle site by Wed. noon)*	*Exam 2, 120 points: 30 points take-home, 90 points in-class (mostly on weeks 5–9; some questions from weeks 1–4)*	*Submit completed Take-home exam 2 to Moodle dropbox by 11:30 p.m. Sunday* **Metacognition due in Moodle dropbox by 11:55 p.m. Sunday.**

Week 10	Preparation reading/assignment:	Nov 3	Nov 5	Nov 7	Nov 8–9

Speciation	– Study Guide 10
	– Reading:
	  • Chapter 27
	  • Review pp. 516–517
	  • pp. 414 (Chemical Signals . . .)–416
		Mastering Biology due at beginning of class.
		LRQ10
		Guided Inquiry 10
			Guided Inquiry 10, continued
			Project Team Work: research plan
				Project Team Work: research plan and discussion/summary
				Deadline to submit any re-grade requests for in-class exam.
					Metacognition due in Moodle dropbox by 11:55 p.m. Sunday.

Week 11	Preparation reading/assignment:	Nov 10	Nov 12	Nov 14	Nov 15–16
Genetic Technology II	– Study Guide 11 – Reading: • Sections 20.4–20.6 in Chapter 20 **Deadline to submit any re-grade requests for take-home exam.**	**Mastering Biology due at beginning of class.** LRQ11 Guided Inquiry 11	Guided Inquiry 11, continued *Project Team Work: research plan due by 10:00 p.m.*	Project Team Work: discussion/summary and poster	**Metacognition due in Moodle dropbox by 11:55 p.m. Sunday.**

(Continues)

Appendix 5.1 (*Continued*)

Bold: Assignments *Italic:* Quizzes, Exams, Projects	LRQ: learning readiness quiz PEA: post exam analysis		Readings are from Freeman and colleagues' textbook, unless otherwise indicated	
	Monday	**Wednesday**	**Friday**	**Sat/Sun**
Week 12	Nov 17	Nov 19	Nov 21	Nov 22–23

Phylogenetics	Preparation reading/assignment:
	– Study Guide 12
	– Reading:
	  • Section 1.4 in Chapter 1
	  • Through Section 28.1 in Chapter 28
		Mastering Biology due at beginning of class.
		LRQ12
		Guided Inquiry 12
		
		Deadline to submit paper copies of PEA and whichever parts of Exam 2 you are analyzing on the PEA. Take-home exam materials must include points received for each question.
			Guided Inquiry 12, continued
			Project Team Work: draft discussion/summary due by 10:00 p.m.
				Project Team Work: poster	**Metacognition due in Moodle dropbox by 11:55 p.m. Sunday.**

Week 13		Nov 24	Nov 26	Nov 28	Nov 29–30

Cells	Preparation reading/assignment:
	– Study Guide 13
	– Reading:
	  • pp. 94–96 in Chapter 6
	  • pp. 106–119 & Section 7.6 in Chapter 7
	  • pp. 560–561 in Chapter 30
		Mastering Biology due at beginning of class.
		LRQ13
		Guided Inquiry 13
			Guided Inquiry 13, Project Team Work: finalize poster
			When your poster is ready, submit file to Imaging Center; deadline is 9:00 a.m. Monday, December 1.
				Thanksgiving break
				(No class meeting!)
					Metacognition due in Moodle dropbox by 11:55 p.m. Sunday.

Week 14	Preparation reading/assignment:	Dec 1	Dec 3	Dec 5	Dec 6–7
Project Wrap-Up	Review for Ultimate Quiz	*Must have poster file submitted to Imaging Center by 9:00 a.m. Monday* *Practice presenting poster with team*	*Project Poster Presentations* Poster critiques and nominations for best posters	*Ultimate Quiz*	**Metacognition due in Moodle dropbox by 11:55 p.m. Sunday.**

Week 15	Preparation reading/assignment:	Dec 8	Dec 10	Dec 12	Dec 13–14
Nature of Science II	– Study Guide 14 – Reading; see links in Study Guide to • *Kitzmiller vs. Dover Area School District decision*, pp 64–89 • **Skim** The Flagellum Unspun	Discussion of Dover and Intelligent Design Project 2 Team Work: *Submit IP Notebook*	**Last day of class** Discussion of evolution of the bacterial flagellum Best posters announced; course recap and instructor evaluations		*Team: submit final poster file to Moodle by 10 p.m. on Sat* *Individuals: submit Peer Evaluations* **Course survey due 11:55 p.m. Sunday; 5 extra credit points.**

Exam week	**Final exam is Wed., Dec. 17, 1:30–3:30 p.m. It will include weeks 10–15 (i.e., includes Dover and evolution of the bacterial flagellum), and cumulative material from earlier in semester.**	**Final exam will most likely be in our regular classroom. If this changes we will notify you.**

Appendix 5.2: Genetic Engineering Proposal Project Structure and Descriptions

Week	Project subtask	Subtask description
3–5	Teams choose their project topic	Your aim is to choose something to work on that is: a. Reasonably likely to succeed—based on established methods and reagents. It is not reasonable to first propose to discover a gene from some trait that you are interested in and *then* make changes in an organism with that to-be-identified gene. Neither is it reasonable to first propose to develop a new method of gene delivery and *then* use that method to get your gene construct into the recipient organism. A large part of your background and significance section addresses the earlier work by others that provides the foundation for your work. b. Novel—not a direct lift of a project published or described elsewhere. This is very important. You should build on the foundation of current scientific knowledge but there needs to be something different (and better?) about what you are setting out to do. Part of your background and significance section addresses the issue of originality/novelty of what you propose to do. c. Of sufficient benefit to be worth the risk to human health, animal welfare or the environment. While the issue of risk is mostly addressed in later sections of the proposal, the issue of benefit is central to the background and significance section.
6–7	Teams create an *Annotated Bibliography*	You need to identify sources that are relevant to each of the sections of your proposal: background on your process of interest, the gene you plan to modify, the organism you plan to transform/transfect, the method of DNA transfer, your methods for assessing success. You need to be able to explain to others in your group *why* a particular source you found is worth including (and citing) in your paper. Each paper you cite has a small or large evidential role. Nothing extraneous is included.

8	Teams write the project *Background*	You need to address the following questions in **1,000 words**. a. Why is the work being proposed new and interesting or important? What is the unmet need, unanswered question, or commercial opportunity that your work would address? b. What is the published work that provides the intellectual and technical foundation for each of the aspects of the project? As in all scientific writing, it is important to organize your thoughts, write precise sentences that follow each other in logical progression, and cite appropriate sources. Clarity, organization, and use of active voice wherever possible contributes to strong, effective writing. Inclusion of graphics, especially ones that would be suitable for inclusion on the poster version of the project, can enhance clarity and persuasiveness.
9–10	Teams write up the *Research Plan*	This begins with a brief statement of your specific aims (enumerated 1., 2., 3.), an outline of the methods/technical procedures you plan to use [not full protocols!], your experimental plan (where you describe the process of accomplishing each specific aim), and a description of the kinds of results (positive and negative) you might expect. This is where you sketch what you plan to do so your reader understands in detail how you intend to achieve your specific aims. It is inherently a detailed section, a place for you to present maps of the gene construct you plan to introduce into a recipient organism, for example. **This section must be no more than 1,200 words.** Figures (e.g., a flow chart of procedures) or tables can be added without their legends being included in the word count.
10–11	Teams write up the *Discussion* and *Summary*	In this section you will explore the alternative plans that you would take up if the main approach doesn't work, future studies (follow-up questions that the work proposed would enable you to answer in the future), and a statement of the safety and environmental issues that the project presents. The section should end with a summary of the main elements of the proposal as a whole, echoing the background and significance section. This is your last chance to argue the importance and interest of the work you propose. This section has a **800-word** limit. Again, figures can be included without their legend being included in the word count.

eÃ

Appendix 5.2: (*Continued*)

Week	Project subtask	Subtask description
12	Teams submit the poster draft for feedback from peers	Here you assemble the elements you've written after getting feedback on the various parts from the instructors. It involves collaborative editing, and incorporating comments from people within your team. Putting together this draft for peer review is also a chance to check your draft against the grading rubrics that will be provided to you.
13	Teams submit final poster draft	At last! This is where you incorporate the best of the feedback/comments of your peer reviewers. The challenge is to evaluate their suggestions, deciding whether to incorporate a suggested change or not, and to choose between potentially conflicting recommendations. It is particularly important that you ensure your proposal *flows* well and has a consistent voice at this stage as it has had many authors and suggestions have come in from many of your peers. This is your chance to make your proposal "bullet proof," ready for a critical reading by a demanding "study section" or "panel" that will decide whether and how enthusiastically to recommend your proposal for funding. In this case your instructors will be your final readers. The final proposal has a **3,000-word** limit.
14	Team presentations and peer review	You need to be able to communicate the essence of your proposal in 10 to 15 minutes using your poster as the visual aid. It is the place to direct your listener's visual attention while you talk, and the place to which you return your visitor's attention when there are questions. It is important to be clear, accurate, and moderately enthusiastic about what you are presenting, and in sufficient command of the material that you feel comfortable fielding questions.

Note. Thanks to David Matthews, University of Minnesota.

Appendix 5.3: Genetic Engineering Proposal Rubric for Annotated Bibliography

TEAM____

Rubric for Citation of Sources

	Exemplary 9–10	Exceeds Standard 6–8	Meets Standard Some of the Time 3–5	Below Standard 0–2	Team Score
Organization of citations, citation within text	All references are organized (e.g., in Zotero or RefWorks) according to Harvard style formatting for citing scientific sources, and all references are complete (include all information needed for someone else to find the reference). Text provides informative citations of sources of information (e.g., [Smith, 1997]) where appropriate.	Most references follow Harvard style formatting for citing scientific works and/or most references are complete (include all information needed for someone else to find the reference). Sources of statements made in the text are often cited appropriately within the text of the proposal.	Some references follow Harvard style formatting for citing scientific works, while others are in a different format or are incomplete. Some key statements in the proposal are not attributed to the source of the information, or references cited do not accurately match the text.	Several references fail to follow Harvard style formatting for citing scientific works or contain seriously incomplete information. Numerous key statements are not attributed to sources or the sources listed do not pertain to the text.	

(Continues)

Appendix 5.3: (*Continued*)

	Exemplary 9–10	Exceeds Standard 6–8	Meets Standard Some of the Time 3–5	Below Standard 0–2	Team Score
Content	All key references are from credible scientific sources; a few sources from the popular press or from non–peer reviewed. Websites are permissible, but are not the base of the reference list.	Most key references are from credible scientific sources; a few sources from the popular press or from non–peer reviewed websites are permissible, but are not the base of the reference list.	Several key references are from credible scientific sources or several sources are from the popular press or from non–peer reviewed websites and form the base of the reference list.	Most key references are from the popular press or from non–peer reviewed websites.	
Breadth	References cover the breadth of information needed to present the project background and a proposed treatment strategy.	References cover much of the breadth of information needed to present the project background and a proposed treatment strategy.	References cover only part of the breadth of information needed to present the project background and a proposed treatment strategy.	References cover only a small part of the necessary information needed for project completion.	

Appendix 5.4: Team Accountability Documentation Sheet

Today's date_____ Team _____

Team Accountability Documentation

This form is due in your team folder every Friday immediately after the end of class. It becomes part of your team's Intellectual Property notebook, which is part of the total 300 project points. Each team member needs to state explicitly what he/she contributed to the work of the team during the week (e.g., who found relevant references, drafted a section of the project proposal, gave feedback on a draft, interviewed an expert on the project topic, or researched a project element and explained it to the rest of the team). Once all team members have filled in their contributions you need to pass the sheet around your team so all can verify the claims made by others.

Name	What I contributed to the team work this week

Appendix 5.5: Rubric for GMO Poster Presentation

Poster critiques are done as a **pod**; use this sheet as a guideline and then record your scores, questions, and comments for the two posters assigned to you on **Survey Monkey**. Please take this seriously and make substantive, constructive comments, just as you hope to receive substantive, constructive comments. The quality of the review is worth 15 points (for each of two posters) to the team doing the review. Poster content 25 points

Team/pod whose poster you are evaluating: 20-___   Team/pod doing review: 20-___ pod___

Criteria	Excellent	Very good	Marginal	Lacking	Pts.
Overall logic behind making this new gene 5 pts. Is the reason for creating the new gene clearly explained? How will this modification affect the organism in which it is expressed?	Uses diagrams, labels, captions, bullet points effectively to explain logic for new gene and how it will solve a problem. Explains effectively how the modification will affect the organism and why. 4–5 pts.	Needs more information or detail to fully explain logic for new gene. Explains how organisms will be affected, but is not totally clear. 2–3 pts.	Diagrams effective but lacking adequate explanation, or diagrams not useful. Does not explain adequately how the change will affect the organism. 1 pt.	Diagrams or explanation ineffective in explaining point of project. No explanation of how the change affects the target organism. 0 pts.	
Molecular strategies 5 pts. Are parts of the new gene explained? What is the origin of the genes and promoters? How will they work?	Lists or provides a diagram with clear explanation of the genetic parts needed and overall strategy for creating the new gene. 4–5 pts.	List or diagram is present but it does not completely describe genetic parts and overall strategy for new gene. 2–3 pts.	List or diagram only marginally explains parts of new gene and strategy for making it. 1 pt.	Information provided is unclear; readers will not understand features of gene or how made. 0 pt.	

Diagram of novel gene 5 pts.	Are the parts of the new gene logically and accurately labeled?	Diagram of plasmid or DNA molecule is clear and well-labeled; diagram clearly relates to logic for making gene. 4–5 pts.	Diagram is mostly clear and well-labeled. 2–3 pts.	Diagram is missing key elements or is labeled in confusing way. 1 pt.	Diagram is missing or unclear or unhelpful in understanding gene. 0 pts.
Phylogenetic relationships 5 pts.	How is the gene of interest related to its paralogs and/or to its orthologs?	Phylogenetic relationship of your gene to other genes is diagrammed or shown as an MSA or lack of homology to other genes is explained. 4–5 pts.	Phylogenetic relationship (or lack thereof) is mostly clear and explained well. 2–3 pts.	Relevant information on phylogenetic relationships could be significantly improved. 1 pt.	Discussion of phylogenetic relationships is missing, obviously inaccurate, or unclear. 0 pts.
Flow of the story 5 pts.	Does the story flow logically? Is it clear how the new gene will solve a problem or affect the organism?	Poster does excellent job tying together the parts of the story so it flows logically to explain how new gene will change a situation. 4–5 pts.	Individual parts of poster are solid, but the story does not flow as smoothly or logically as it could. 2–3 pts.	Poster needs more work to make the story flow or to explain how the new gene changes anything. 1 pt.	Story presented on poster is disjointed or illogical. 0 pts.

(Continues)

Appendix 5.5: (*Continued*)

Poster aesthetics 5 pts.

	Criteria	Yes/No	One	Points
Title 1 pt.	Is the title concise, clear, interesting? Is it legible from 6 feet away? Are names of all authors and team included?	Yes. Title draws people in; all criteria are met. 1 pt.	One or more criteria not met. 0 pts.	
Organization and layout 2 pts.	Is the poster well-organized and easy to read? Does poster layout contribute to its effectiveness? Is the text sufficient to explain graphics? Are the main points clear?	Poster is easy to navigate so reader can follow story easily. Reader can find the message through the combination of graphics and text. 2 pts.	Poster is poorly organized; reader would be confused about order of parts and where to focus, or meaning of some graphics is insufficiently explained. 0–1 pt.	
Figures, images, diagrams 1 pt.	Are graphics interesting, relevant, easy to interpret? Do they illustrate key points? Is technical detail suitable for poster audience?	Each is attractive, easy to understand, well-labeled. Graphics and labels are large enough to see details. Use of graphics draws in viewers. No use of "shock" graphics. 1 pt.	One or more of the graphics are not relevant to the poster, not large enough or well-labeled, or are intended only to shock viewers. 0 pts.	
Visual appeal and quality 1 pt.	Does the use of color and choice of fonts enhance the poster's impact? Has text been carefully edited to eliminate errors?	Pleasing to look at; good use of color and graphics. No spelling or grammatical errors. 1 pt.	Color scheme or fonts may distract from effectiveness of poster; contains spelling or grammatical errors. 0 pts.	

Oral presentation of poster 20 pts.

Criteria		Yes	Somewhat	No	Pts.
Explanation of poster and answering of questions 10 pts.	Did the pod presenting the poster guide you through the poster confidently and effectively?	Presenters highlighted main points, explained the approach taken, and could answer questions about proposed work. 7–10 pts.	Presenters did a fair job explaining the project and could answer at least some questions about the proposed work. 3–6 pts.	Presenters struggled to explain the material, appeared to not understand parts of the project, or were unable to answer questions. 0–2 pts.	
Participation by all members 10 pts.	Did *all* members of the subgroup participate in presenting the poster?	All two or three members were actively involved in explaining the project and answering questions. 7–10 pts.	Not all members were equally involved. One or more didn't seem comfortable answering questions without help. 3–6 pts. **Name(s) of presenter who could not explain poster or answer questions:**	One or two members dominated the presentation while other members contributed very little. 0–2 pts. **Name of presenter who dominated:**	

Comments on content and oral presentation of the poster: To earn 15 pts. per poster critiqued, you must include substantive comments along with the rubric numerical scores in the Survey Monkey form. Be sure you have carefully recorded your scores AS A POD on this sheet before you transfer them to the Survey Monkey. Once you begin the survey you must finish your critiques of both posters in one session.

Appendix 5.6: Gas Law Worksheet

Kinetic-Molecular Theory and Gases

Model 1A: Kinetic-Molecular Theory and Pressure

Pressure is a measure of force per area: $P = \dfrac{\text{force}}{\text{area}}$

Temperature (absolute, in kelvin) is proportional to kinetic energy (energy of motion)

KE = $1/2$ m(speed)^2

Ideal gas particles (Assumed by Kinetic-Molecular Theory):

- Are in constant, random, straight-line motion until they run into something
- Do not have attractive forces between one another
- Have elastic collisions with one another (don't lose energy, KE total is constant)
- Occupy very little space compared with the volume of the container

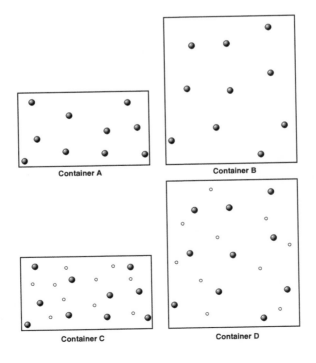

Container A   Container B

Container C   Container D

1. How many gas particles are in container A? Container B?
2. If the temperature of both A and B are the same, which container do you THINK will have the higher pressure? Why? Use the definitions in the model to explain.
3. If the temperature of all four gas samples is the same, can you place them in order of increasing pressure? If so, give your reasoning. If not, what other information would you need?

STOP HERE FOR CLASS DISCUSSION

Model 1B: Kinetic-Molecular Theory Simulations

Instructions:

One student should open the "simulations" tab of our class Moodle site and open the simulation under "week 4." This may take a moment to load.

"Play" with the simulation as a group for a minute or two to gain an understanding of how it works.

Reset the simulation and add some of the "heavy" gas to the container. View the energy histogram (under "measurement tools") and record the pressure and temperature.

Reset the simulation and add the same amount of the "light" gas to the container. View the energy histogram and record the pressure and temperature.

4. What do you notice about the energy histograms, pressure, and temperature between these two (heavy and light) gas samples?

Reset the simulation. Add the same amount used in the last two steps of "heavy" and "light" gas to the container at the same time.

5. What do you notice about the pressure, temperature, and energy histograms of this mixture? Are they related at all to the separate heavy and light gas samples from earlier? How?

Model 2: Where does the Ideal Gas Law come from?

6. Brainstorm in your group. Make a list of as many factors that you think can affect the pressure of a gas.

Instructions:

One student should still have the simulation open. Another group member should open Google Docs and start a new spreadsheet (create/spreadsheet) for taking data points and graphing.

Design an "experiment," using the simulation, to explore how the factors you listed in Q6 affect the behavior of a gas sample. Your group should focus on changing one factor only to begin with. Collect data in the form of numerical values from the simulation.

Graph* the data and identify any trends present. Have your labeled graph (day of week, table, and group number) ready to share with the class on the monitor. Also "share" the document with me.

Continue experimenting and collecting data, looking for trends between the other factors/variables you listed in Q6. These will be shared with the entire class.

*Graphing tips:

Place each variable in a column—do not put units on each value.

Select the "graphing icon (chart editor)," then select the "charts" tab, then "scatter," then the top graphic.

Give your graph a title and make sure the axes are labeled, including units.

STOP HERE FOR CLASS DISCUSSION

Applications: Gases

A. Determine the mass of C_3H_8 that would be required to react with 32.3 L of oxygen gas at 422°K and 1.25 atm. $C_3H_8(l) + 5O_2(g) \rightarrow 3CO_2(g) + 4H_2O(l)$

B. Determine the partial pressure of methane (CH_4) present in a gas mixture that contains only methane, 20.0% N_2, and 35.0% Ar, and has a total pressure of 3.89 atm.

C. How many times faster will UF_6 containing U-235 effuse than UF_6 containing only U-238?

D. What is more dense at STP, SF_6 or Ar?

E. An atmospheric chemist places SO_2 and O_2 gas in a 2.00L container at 800°K and 1.90 atm. When the reaction occurs, the pressure falls to 1.65 atm. Find the moles of SO_3 (the only product) formed in the reaction.

STOP HERE FOR CLASS DISCUSSION

Note. This activity is the intellectual property of Professor Michelle Driessen at the University of Minnesota and may not be shared on the open web or uploaded into any study site.

Appendix 5.7: Epithelial Tissue Histology

Model 1: Structure of Epithelial Tissue

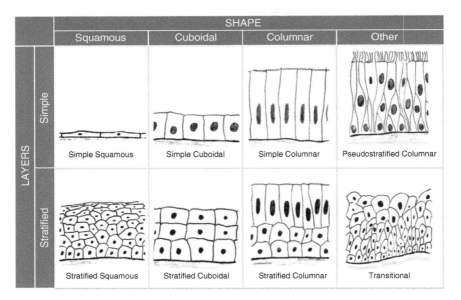

QUESTIONS:

1. Describe the morphology (shape) of the following epithelial tissue cells.

    a) Cuboidal:

    b) Columnar:

    c) Squamous:

2. Write a grammatically correct sentence to describe the difference between simple and stratified epithelial tissue.

3. Reviewing your answers to questions 1 and 2, what two characteristics do you think are used to classify epithelial tissue?

4. Based on your examination of Model 1, which epithelial tissues <u>do not</u> conform to the naming classification rules you described in question 3? (*The manager* should have two different team members state a tissue and describe its structure).

5. Compare pseudostratified columnar epithelium and simple columnar epithelium and answer the following questions:

   a) How are these two tissues the same?

   b) What differentiates pseudostratified columnar epithelium from simple columnar?

6. The bottom (basal) layer of stratified epithelial tissue may have different cell shapes from the top (apical) layer. Which layer determines the shape classification of the tissue? Provide evidence to support your answer.

7. Name the specific type of epithelium described by the following: <u>a tissue that consists of multiple layers of cells, in which the top layer is composed of columnar cells.</u>

8. Before answering as a group, each person should individually complete this question by themselves. Once everyone is done, complete question 9 as a group.

    a. Label the apical surface on each epithelial tissue photomicrograph.
    b. Label the basal surface on each epithelial tissue photomicrograph.
    c. Draw a bracket to indicate the location of the epithelial tissue.
    d. Name the specific epithelial type under both tissue photomicrographs.

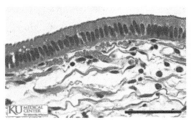 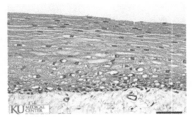

Images courtesy of The University of Kansas

Tissue = _____   Tissue = _____

9. Discuss and compare your individual answers to the previous question with your group. (The manager should ensure that all group members share their answers). Develop a group consensus and write the best answer.

10. The majority of dust is composed of human skin cells. What does this indicate about the rate of mitosis for epithelial tissue?

11. Epithelial cancers are the most common types of cancer. Answer the following questions together as a group:

    a) Briefly explain what cancer is.

    b) What do you think makes skin so susceptible to uncontrolled cellular growth?

6

MANAGING STUDENT GROUPS

The people around me on my team acted as support and helped hold me accountable. If I failed they failed, and I'd feel guilty if I dragged them down, so I worked harder.

—An ALC student

Much of designing strong learning experiences in Active Learning Classrooms (ALCs) boils down to understanding how student groups work. This quickly becomes apparent in student responses on surveys about the room. Many students spontaneously mention the health or dysfunction of their group, and how the group dynamics shaped what they learned in the classroom. Helping students understand the essential importance of collaboration in ALCs and attending to the vitality of student groups is a critical task that instructors must address in their course planning as well as throughout the term.

Ample research has demonstrated that groups help students learn (e.g., Johnson, Johnson, & Smith, 1998; Slavin, 1990, 1996; Springer, Stanne, & Donovan, 1999; Strobel & Van Barneveld, 2009; Tomcho & Foels, 2012). Researchers have concluded that working collectively provides the following benefits to students:

- Exposure to multiple perspectives (e.g., Johnson et al., 1998, 2013; Tinto, 1997) and increased openness to diversity (Cabrera, Colbeck, & Terenzini, 2001);
- Improved occupational awareness (Cabrera et al., 2001); and

- Lifelong learning, increased problem-solving abilities, and greater satisfaction with learning (e.g., Johnson et al., 1998, 2013); positive attitudes toward course materials (e.g., Johnson et al., 1998; Springer et al., 1999); persistence (Braxton, Milem, & Sullivan, 2000); and, if introduced in the first year, increased likelihood that a student will persist to the second year of college (Braxton, Jones, Hirschy, & Hartley, 2008; Loes, An, Saichaie, & Pascarella, in press; Tinto, 1997).

Additionally, working in groups is one of the more promising means of promoting higher-order thinking skills at the post-secondary level (Freeman et al., 2014; Johnson & Johnson, 2009; Loes et al., in press; Tinto, 1997). ALCs are intentionally designed to allow students to work together, which can provide opportunities for their growth in any of the aforementioned dimensions.

With these multiple benefits of group work, however, are several potential drawbacks. Many instructors worry about various aspects of introducing group work into their classes, such as the following: To what degree will students resist this method? How do I create groups to maximize the potential for learning? How do I create the conditions for constructive group dynamics? The goal of this chapter is to address challenges that instructors encounter when managing groups for learning and teaching in ALCs. Table 6.1 outlines the topics we address in the chapter, such as group formation, size, promoting accountability, group dynamics, dealing with dysfunction, and social loafing. These issues may emerge in traditional classrooms as well, but given that the design of ALCs foregrounds group work for most activities, it is crucial that ALC instructors address them effectively.

The literature on the specifics of group learning is vast. Arendale (2004) found over 8,000 entries in the ERIC database that contained the terms *collaborative, cooperative,* and *learning communities.* McKeachie and Svinicki (2014) documented that terms for collaborative and cooperative learning are used interchangeably and frequently conflated. We provide our rationale in the section as we discuss the ways instructors address issues with student group work and the principal role those issues play in learning and teaching in ALCs.

Defining Groups and What They Do

The umbrella term of *small groups* in higher education is associated with assembling students into groups (usually fewer than eight) as a means of fostering active learning (Davis, 2009; Michaelsen, Knight, & Fink, 2004).

TABLE 6.1
Chapter 6 Topics

Areas	Topics
Defining Groups and What They Do	Common characteristics of small groups Developing group outcomes and objectives
Assembling Individual Students Into Groups	When to form groups Ways to form groups Group size Group roles Group duration
Promoting Group Success	Group accountability Group dynamics Group dysfunctions
Groups Outside of the Classroom	Group work in blended, hybrid, or online settings
Assessing Group Learning and Productivity	Weighting grades to promote group work Avoiding grade curving Peer assessment
Closing Group Activities	Group accomplishments and peer reflections Thank-a-group-member

Small-group learning has evolved over the last five decades and now encompasses many nuanced strategies, such as

- Cooperative learning (e.g., Johnson et al., 2006; Slavin, 1990, 1996);
- Collaborative learning (e.g., Barkley, Cross, & Major, 2014; Bruffee, 1993);
- Peer instruction (e.g., Crouch & Mazur, 2001; Mazur, 1997);
- PBL (e.g., Major & Cross, 2004);
- POGIL (Moog, 2014); and
- TBL (e.g., Michaelsen et al., 2004).

Complicating matters, all of the approaches listed may vary by discipline as well (Davidson & Major, 2014; Pascarella & Terenzini, 2005).

Despite the nomenclature associated with these various group methodologies and strategies, we use the term *groups* for this reason: It is the broadest definition, while presenting the fewest constraints, that describes students working together to achieve a joint goal. Accordingly, in what follows we will not distinguish among the strategies listed but instead discuss them together, using the term *groups* to refer to them collectively. Defining a specific strategy for group work in the context of different assignments, however, may help instructors apply the type of pedagogy more effectively.

Common Characteristics of Small Groups

Broadly speaking, Davis (2009) suggested the framing of group work should focus on the learner or student (i.e., student-centered learning) and the application and practice, or "hands-on" nature, of the work. Researchers of group learning have asserted that groups promote the development of skills across the spectrum of higher-order thinking (e.g., Davidson & Major, 2014; Davidson & Worsham, 1992; Prince, 2004; Terenzini, Cabrera, Colbeck, Parente, & Bjorkland, 2001; Weimer, 2013) and student engagement (e.g., Padgett et al., 2010; Tinto, Goodsell, & Russo, 1993). Moreover, instructors often remark that working together toward a common goal improves student learning (from retention to mastery) of a concept, task, or topic. Researchers also have suggested that students develop the capacity to reach mastery through a complex and challenging objective that no single student could reach alone (e.g., Johnson et al., 1998; Michaelsen et al., 2004). They observed that the level of group formality and structure may shape student achievement and group dynamics (Davidson & Major, 2014).

Many strategies to promote student learning with groups contain common elements, which we have distilled into the following categories, based on research from several decades on the topic:[1]

- *Accountability*: All group members are individually accountable and responsible to ensure work is done in a timely and complete manner (Crutchfield & Klamon, 2014; Michaelsen et al., 2004).
- *Group processing*: Groups set goals and conduct frequent assessment of performance (Anson & Goodman, 2014) to increase functionality and eliminate inefficiencies. A key component of this process is self- and peer reflection.
- *Interaction*: The work must be done together, often synchronously, though some individual work (done asynchronously) might be required to complete the collective goal. Goodsell, Maher, Tinto, and Associates (1992) suggested that "learning is inherently social" (p. 12) and often happens when students interact through discussion and tasks in group settings.
- *Interdependence*: Group members rely on each other to achieve the goal, objective, and/or task. The group's success or failure is dependent

on all members' performances. Some methods of group work (e.g., cooperative) rely on interdependence in more formal ways than others (Johnson et al., 1998); higher levels of participant interdependence enhance outcomes for students (Tomcho & Foels, 2012).

- *Skill development*: Ample opportunities for students to build on prior knowledge and skills (hard and social) are integrated into the process. Felder and Brent (2007) stated that this category also includes collaborative skill development, such as decision making, conflict management, and trust building.

Instructors unsure of the precise detail of a specific method should know that, in general, small groups of students working as a collective have shared goals and interdependent tasks, and how they reach this state can be determined by selecting among a set of pedagogical approaches. We will highlight these features throughout the chapter and point to ways the instructors integrate these elements into their teaching in ALCs.

Developing Group Outcomes and Objectives

Learning outcomes and objectives are primary drivers of what students will be able to know, do, and value as a result of completing a course (e.g., Beichner et al., 2007; Crutchfield & Klamon, 2014). Suskie (2009) stated that much confusion surrounds outcomes and objectives because they are often interchanged. She described outcomes as "the end rather than the means" and the "why" (p. 116). The objective is the "means to the end," the tasks related to reaching the goal (p. 117). In turn, course learning outcomes and objectives should guide how groups will function during the course term. Consider the following questions when determining learning outcomes for your ALC course: What ideas or concepts should endure for students one month, one year, and one decade after they complete a course? What competencies or levels of mastery should a student be able to demonstrate after finishing the course?

For example, Jon Berndt Olsen at the University of Massachusetts has the following statement related to course outcomes in the syllabus for History 101; Western Thought Since 1600:

This course aims to develop your ability to *think critically*—to read and think about complex historical issues beyond the simple facts of the case. Certainly the facts are important, and the exams and papers will make sure that you are learning them. But beyond that, you will learn to think like an historian, trying to understand not only the "what" of history, but also the "why."

Olsen then links the course outcomes to an objective specifically meant for the groups, which is listed on the syllabus. In doing so, he is able to point to the alignment between course outcomes and objectives:

> Teams should analyze the three documents and seek out differences and commonalities. Are the three ideologies presented here—National Socialism, Fascism, and Stalinism—three variations of the same thing or very different in their core values? Using the whiteboard, create a visual representation of these three worldviews.

To check the students' understanding, Olsen gives an individual quiz as well as a group quiz on the material. He stated that the students quickly learn who has and has not read the material during the group quiz portion of the exercise. Students in groups are good about holding members accountable during the process, he contended, because of the multiple steps involved. After the quiz, the group members must work carefully to identify the similarities and dissimilarities of the article based on their reading of the text. Finally, the students have to determine the best way to communicate their interpretation of the articles as a group, how they will represent this interpretation on the whiteboard during class, and who will present the information.

Beichner and colleagues (2007) encouraged instructors who teach in ALCs to think beyond content coverage (i.e., using the course texts' tables of contents) to determine course outcomes and objectives. Many of the ALC instructors we worked with said that learning to be an effective member of a team is a stated outcome of their classes. To be clear, this outcome does not mean instructors implement group work for the sake of group work, but rather that they connect group work to content- or process-related goals. Content-related goals need to concern subject matter and often include the development of skills. Process-related goals can be associated with activities and habits. For example, a process goal for a course might be for students to learn to work collaboratively. Of course, each instructor, program, college, and institution may have its own goals, but the literature on group learning suggests that alignment between objectives and tasks ensures adherence to some of the good practices for small-group work.

Assembling Individual Students Into Groups

For groups to accomplish their objectives, ALC instructors need to consider when to form groups, the ways they have groups come together, how many students should be in a group, whether group members should be assigned formal roles, and how long groups will stay together. The literature is replete with strategies to construct, coordinate, and condition groups in ways optimal for ALCs, and we will conyextualize these approaches in experiences from ALC instructors in the following sections. Appendix 6.1 contains an overview of these topics and can be used as an "at a glance" reference that cites relevant literature.

When to Form Groups

While some instructors, especially those new to ALCs, may make use of informal groups that have less structured arrangements and goals, many ALC instructors assemble formal groups[2] early in the term (on the first day or during the first week). Forming groups early in the term requires intentional and consistent effort before the class begins, and even before the course is taught in an ALC. Forming formal groups early in the term may serve to emphasize the instructor's intentions for group work (Hillyard, Gillespie, & Littig, 2010; Johnson et al., 1998). Early formation allows group members to begin to get to know each other so they can start bonding and work to become a cohesive unit (Johnson et al., 2013; Levi, 2013; Michaelsen et al., 2004).

A common practice is to spend part of the first day or two explaining expectations to students and laying the groundwork for group formation. Ambrose and colleagues (2010) stated that establishing ground rules linked to course objectives is another important consideration for instructors. A communication professor gives students a reading about the research on team cohesiveness during the first class session. She is intentional and direct in explaining to students that the course grade is heavily based on group work. Some students dislike this style of teaching and elect to drop the class. She is then able to determine groups after the first class period. One professor of Spanish and Portuguese does not form teams until the second week of class. She allows the students who are sitting at a table to get to know each other over the first four or five class sessions so the students have some time to interact in informal ways before formal groups are determined.

There are some drawbacks to early formation as well, namely the distribution of student abilities and skills and the fluctuation in student enrollment. The main challenge is that class rosters are often not finalized until a few weeks into the term. To manage both of these issues, a resource economics professor has new students join groups from which other students have dropped. Early formation may hinder the balance of "member resources," which entail the different attitudes, abilities, skills, and socioeconomic background characteristics a student brings to class (Michaelsen et al., 2004). Proponents of group work suggest that instructors strive to distribute these resources, such as academic ability and diversity (e.g., gender, race/ethnicity), as evenly as possible in groups. Another strategy is to combine members who have joined after the first day (Oakley, Felder, Brent, & Elhajj,

2004), typically before the add/drop period for classes has closed and course rosters are finalized. He lets his students know there will be fluctuation during the first few weeks but that most of the teams will be set from day one. Thus, while early group formation has great benefits, you should anticipate some fluctuation in the initial groups as a natural consequence and simply plan for it.

Whether students are assembled into groups on the first day of class or during the early weeks of the course, ALC instructors widely agreed that students should be working together from the earliest class period possible. Early group work also applies to instructors who have students rotate and/or switch groups during the term. Regardless of first day or early formation or whether students will rotate or switch groups, it is important for instructors to consider how the groups will be formed.

Ways to Form Groups

Forming teams can be a complicated process. Opinions about how to form groups are many and varied (e.g., Barkley et al., 2014; Barr, Dixon, & Gassenheimer, 2005; Davis, 2009; Johnson et al., 1998). There is very little empirical research, however, on which method best promotes student learning or enhances the learning experience.[3] This section features four approaches ALC instructors can use for group formation: random, instructor-generated, self-selected, and mixed. We will also present advantages and drawbacks to each approach.

Random

Research from a number of fields supports the random formation of groups as the simplest and most efficient approach (Nilson, 2010). Some instructors use software, such as spreadsheets and web-based random number generators (e.g., www.random.org), and learning management systems (e.g., Moodle, Blackboard) to help with this process. Others implement low-tech and traditional methods. For example, a music therapy instructor gives students a number when they walk in the room, and the number corresponds with a table number in the room. Another approach used by ALC instructors is to have students count off by the number of desired students per group until every student has been assigned to a group. Random assignment is an equitable way to form groups (Barkley et al., 2014) and works well in large classes with broad and diverse member resources that therefore are more likely to be randomly distributed.

There is no consensus, however, about the effectiveness of forming groups through random assignment. Disadvantages to this approach include risks to group cohesion and unequal distribution of students from underrepresented backgrounds as well as the unequal distribution of member resources. Oakley and colleagues (2004) suggested that instructors should endeavor to keep students from underrepresented populations together, especially early in a curricular sequence. This may help some students who might otherwise feel isolated to have a greater affinity with the group. Proponents of instructor-generated groups, Michaelsen and colleagues (2004) posited that random formation simply leaves too much to chance. McKeachie and Svinicki (2014) stated that instructor-determined groups are more likely to result in a balance of member resources across groups.

Instructor-generated

Instructors must first determine the criteria that they will use to form groups, and recognize that there are advantages and drawbacks to their choices. An essential part of this process is knowing something about the students who are enrolled in the course. One popular method entails using a pre-class questionnaire (via e-mail or learning management system) or in-class exercise at the onset of the term.[4] Instructors can solicit information about the backgrounds of the students (e.g., grade point average, major, level of math preparation). By knowing the students' background characteristics, the instructor can balance the distribution of member resources (Michaelsen et al., 2004). An English professor who teaches a course on dystopia, video games, and comic books has her students fill out a survey so the instructor can look for common characteristics and interests. The questions ask students to identify the type of gamer they consider themselves (e.g., casual versus hard-core), types of gaming platforms they own and have access to (e.g., next-generation, PC-based), and the types of games that they would like to explore (e.g., role playing, strategy). Knowing some of these background characteristics, instructors who generate groups can work to ensure better skill development for group members and diversity of member resources per group.

Another spin on this method is to assemble students into groups based on common interests. A drawback of forming groups based on common interests is that the resulting groups might be more homogeneous than those established by other methods (Barkley et al., 2014). This uniformity can affect skill development as well as group interaction. The English professor mentioned previously admitted that the "hard-core" gamer group can be very intense. In different iterations of the course, she has split up those who identify as "hard-core," given the deeper knowledge they can share with less experienced gamers. This peer-to-peer knowledge sharing is an important takeaway for instructors teaching in ALCs. The literature revealed that in group settings the more academically gifted students can help the academically challenged students (Nilson, 2010). Brooks and Solheim (2014) found that all students, regardless of academic ability, tended to benefit from working in groups in ALCs, with the greatest gains coming from students who were in the lower quartiles of the class. Instructors who generate their own groups can seek to distribute student characteristics and member resources and know that both academically challenged and gifted students will thrive.

Just as software is available to help in the formation of random groups, instructors can use another program to assign students to groups more deliberately. One tool instructors might consider using in this regard is the Comprehensive Assessment of Team Member Effectiveness (CATME; www .catme.org). This free tool allows instructors to input the desired criteria on which to base groups (Loughry, Ohland, & Woehr, 2014). Instructors also have the option of selecting from a bank of questions provided by CATME developers. Tools within a campus learning management system may also have features that allow instructors to assemble students into groups based on instructor-generated criteria.

Self-selected

Some instructors prefer to let students self-select into groups. For proponents of self-selected groups, Brookfield and Preskill (1999) suggested that students feel more comfortable and more motivated when they are able to self-select group members. For logistical purposes, it might simply be faster to assemble students based on where they are sitting in a classroom. Barkley and colleagues (2014) stated that students might also find this process to be more "fair" than other strategies. Bacon, Stewart, and Silver (1999) indicated that self-selected groups might be more efficient for short-term projects because students may already know each other and thus need to spend less time in the early "formative" stages of group development.

Davis (2009) posited self-selection might work well in smaller classes or for classes designed for majors or upper-division students. A biochemistry and molecular biology professor lets the teams form naturally in an upper-division course, assuming advanced students have different preferences and capabilities than lower-division students:

> I never intended for that to happen, because I wanted to balance diversity and all, but these are upper-level students and they know each other. They probably already have study groups. Why should I fight that? Sit with the people they can work with. If teams found that they needed more expertise in an area, like a mathematician or a chemist, then we could do some trading. Students didn't trade very much, so I just sort of let it go. Those (self-formed) teams worked better than they had before [in previous iterations of the course].

Arguments against self-selection include the lack of balance in group members' academic ability and resources. The lack of balance in under-represented students, especially during the "first two years of a curriculum" (Oakley et al., 2004, p. 11), might further isolate them (e.g., Felder & Brent, 2001). Davis (2009) proposed that shy or underrepresented students might have a difficult time joining a group. Davis also stated that "groupthink" (p. 195) may affect self-selected groups because the need for group solidarity may trump the generation of alternative ideas. McKeachie and Svnicki (2014) posited that some students dislike self-selected groups because of the social pressure they face to join with friends. Michaelsen and colleagues (2004) suggested that instructor-formed groups are likely to move students beyond where they initially sit early in the course. Finally, levels of accountability may vary widely due to the students' familiarity, or lack thereof, with each other. Students who are highly familiar with each other may spend time off-task discussing cocurricular or extracurricular issues. From our research on social context, we know that social distraction in the ALCs can lead to poorer learning outcomes. Students who are not familiar with each other, however, may further resist working together. By anticipating these varied student responses, ALC instructors can plan to address problems with students' membership in self-selected groups as issues arise.

Mixed

The literature on group formation is growing but lacks empirical conclusiveness (Moreno, Ovalle, & Vicari, 2012). As one instructor put it, "I've tried everything. There really is no silver bullet." Several ALC instructors employ a "mixed methodology" to the formation of groups, drawing on some aspects of the instructor-generated methods and of other approaches. One simple extension of the random count-off method mentioned previously is the "line up and count off" approach based on selected characteristics.

First, have students line up around the room according to certain attributes that you have pre-selected, and then have them count off to form their teams. For instance, you could begin by asking how many students have a certain amount of experience with the topic (e.g., laboratory experience, writing experience, or math background). Have these students form a line. Next, ask the remaining seated students to answer another resource question (e.g., Have you taken a biochemistry class? A composition class? Have you had two or more classes in this major?). Have these students line up behind the first group. Continue asking questions in this way until all students are in line with each line positioned behind the one before it. If any students remain seated, ask them to line up as well. Finally, starting at the head of the front line, have students count off by the number of teams you will have in your class (e.g., 1–19; instruct all ones go to Table 1, all twos to go to Table 2, etc.). One student from each line should count off in turn. In this manner, you will randomly distribute students in groups, but you will not run the risk of one group having more than its fair share of student resources.

Anson and Goodman (2014) suggested that groups could be formed according to when the class members have availability (see Oakley et al., 2004, for a template). For example, if four members of a class are able to meet at 1 p.m. on Tuesday and Thursday, the instructor could put these students into a group. This assignment ensures students have common times outside of class to meet. Common work time is an important feature of blended, hybrid, and flipped approaches to teaching that can be successfully paired with ALCs (e.g., Baepler, Walker, & Driessen, 2014).

Determining the most productive way to assemble groups for different assignments will come with experience. All of the instructors to whom we have talked have modified their group formation methods to a greater or a lesser extent based on their experiences teaching in ALCs.

Group Size

Depending on the type of space you have available and the class size, the number of students per group may vary. Tomcho and Foels (2012) found that learning outcomes do not vary systematically with group size, so the decision about how large to make student groups can be determined on the bases of administrative considerations and the student experience. For example, Michaelsen and colleagues (2004) suggested that groups of more than eight can be difficult to manage. A biochemistry and molecular biology professor stated that finding the right number for a team can be a challenge: "You want the teams not to be too big to avoid social loafing, but not too small so personal dynamics come into play. . . . I've found five, six, or seven work best for me." Many of the ALC instructors we spoke with use teams with three to six members. Groups in this range promote interdependence such that it allows an instructor to design activities too substantial or complex to be completed by a single student. A math instructor said, "Four to six per team works, but I've found five works best for me. The tasks can be big enough, and challenging enough, so that all members need to be involved to solve the problem." Groups of this size can use the various skill sets possessed by group members (Davis, 2009). While groups of four permit the use of pairs of two, groups with odd numbers ensure no "ties" occur when deciding on a course of action or other group processes.[5]

Other factors that influence this decision can include the type of furniture in an ALC or the pedagogical strategy the instructor employs. For example, in many ALCs, large tables seat up to nine students. In this case, instructors can consider forming sub-teams. Beichner and colleagues (2007) promoted the use of the "rule of three," by which there are three teams of three at a particular table. An astronomy instructor, for example, has a "three-team" and a "table team (of nine)." The team of nine is based on the number of seats at the physical table itself, while the "three-team" often works on elements of an assignment and confers with the table team to deliver the final product. A resource economics instructor prefers groups of nine because the multiple perspectives from a large group can add creativity and bring different strengths to the group projects. He said that the smaller sub-teams are useful too, particularly for difficult topics, because they can afford a greater level of intimacy for a conversation or topic.

Group Roles

The literature endorsing the assignment of group roles is mixed. Much of the literature that supports group roles indicates that groups function best when given structured tasks with clearly outlined expectations (e.g., Bacon et al., 1999; Oakley et al., 2004). Providing students the chance to operate in roles is one way to help groups organize and engage different skills. Roles are also useful to help promote interdependence (Barkley and colleagues 2014), which in turn is a predictor of student learning in classes that use group activities (Tomcho & Foels, 2012). For example, Van Horne and colleagues (2014) found that when an instructor assigned students in a group basic roles (e.g., recorder, manager, skeptic), the act of performing in those roles changed the level of student engagement. To ensure greater levels of participation, the instructor also rotated roles so that each student experienced every role in a group.

David Matthes of the University of Minnesota has a few unique ways to prepare students for group roles and work. Matthes presents students with guidelines entitled "General Instructions for Pods and Teams" (see Appendix 6.2). Available as part of the students' course materials, this reference is a primer on how the groups will function as pods (smaller groups of 3–4 students) and whole table teams (9–10 students). This document contains a useful illustration to represent Matthes's expectations of independent or group work per assignment. He uses the illustration throughout the course to indicate visually on assignments and activities whether a student is expected to work alone, in a small team (pod), as part of a larger group (table), or as part of the entire class.

Matthes's handout also includes descriptions for roles group members will play at each group and level. To ensure no one person is overextended or plays a singular role, Matthes created a "Team Pod Role Assignment Grid" (see Appendix 6.3), which helps the students rotate through the roles.

Each team is given a grid and asked to fill it out. Students then follow the role assignments on the grid for their pod and their team based on each week of the semester. For example, Albert Chang, Marie Green, and Estella Torres[6] are all in a class that is using the assignment grid. They sit at the same table. Albert fills the first slot on the grid (first name, last name), which puts him in Pod 1. In this role, Albert serves as the coordinator of the table team for the first week of class. Marie fills out the second slot, which places her in Pod 2. Marie serves as the coordinator of Pod 2 for the first week of class. Estella fills out the third slot on the grid, placing her in Pod 3. Estella serves as the coordinator of Pod 3 for the first week of class. The other members of the team (not listed here) would fill out the rest of the grid and assume the roles according to the sequence laid out by Matthes in this example.

Opponents of assigned group roles (e.g., Britton, 1990; Michaelsen et al., 2004) recommended that roles emerge naturally as teams interact and work on skill development. Critics of roles also suggested that if students are assigned to roles, they might not get a chance to develop other skills or might have an imbalanced workload, which can negatively affect group dynamics (Bruffee, 1995). Michaelsen and colleagues (2004) argued that assigning and determining roles is needlessly time-consuming and that students are often able to sort themselves out while working on an assignment or project. By assuming or assigning themselves roles, groups are better able to function because they have had autonomy over the process.

Group Duration

Instructors frequently ask, "How long should the groups remain intact?" Michaelsen and colleagues (2004) asserted that groups need to stay together for the duration of the course. Remaining together allows them to build trust as well as the cohesion necessary to perform tasks effectively and efficiently. However, Tomcho and Foels (2012) found that groups of brief duration (one to three class sessions) promote student learning better than groups of longer duration (half to the whole term). Nevertheless, many instructors said it is easier to manage groups that remain intact for longer periods, especially in larger courses. An astronomy instructor pointed out that keeping groups together for the course can also foster relationships for student success:

> I think establishing the fact that these are permanent groups helps students to get to know group members. It would be smart to know how to contact them should you miss class, or you want to study, or you want to share materials, to tell them that students who go to class and work with their groups do better.

It is important to determine whether the size of the groups align with the learning objectives for the session, unit, or term. For example, a music therapy professor prefers to switch groups after every major project to give her students the opportunity to interact with a variety of participants. She stated that working with different classmates helps students learn to manage different personalities, skill sets, and perspectives. There are drawbacks related to short-term group duration, however. For example, it might be difficult for a group to reach a cohesive state over a shorter period of time. In addition, if a group is together for just a handful of class sessions, the opportunity to generate peer feedback is limited.

Promoting Group Success

Instructors should not assume that simply putting students in groups will be met with favor, nor will students inherently be able to perform as a fully functioning unit right away (Michael, 2006). In fact, much of the literature cited thus far in this chapter includes advice on how to help groups evolve and achieve their goals. For groups to be successful, ALC instructors need to promote group success. Central topics to consider in promoting group success are group accountability, dynamics, and dysfunction.

Group Accountability

For groups to function with accountability, the instructor must make that expectation clear to students early in the course. One way to articulate this expectation is to describe in the syllabus how groups will be held accountable. Clear presentation of expectations (e.g., using rubrics) throughout the term leads to better student experiences with group work (Bacon et al., 1999).[7] A communications professor who uses a TBL approach has the following statement on the class syllabus:

> This is a Team Based Learning [(TBL)] course. TBL is a collaborative learning model that uses problem-solving and constant assessment as a basis for teaching problem-solving and decision-making skills. TBL groups are formed at the beginning of the semester and stay constant throughout. TBL uses both individual and group-based assessment in the form of assignments, activities and in-class tests.

By noting that the course will include group assessments in the syllabus, the instructor is clearly demonstrating the intention to use groups to promote student learning and accountability. Davis (2009) suggested that instructors take time to make clear why they are presenting a team approach in their syllabus and then spend the initial part of the first in-class team meeting elaborating on the subject. ALC instructors could consider giving a quiz about the syllabus to get students working together from the start of class and to ensure students have covered the part of the syllabus that addresses group work.

Oakley and colleagues (2004) suggested giving further guidance to shape the preliminary interactions of groups and to discourage a "divide-and-conquer policy" (p. 11). An instructor might say, "Students, do not divide and conquer. It might seem more efficient, but when the assignment is a truly collaborative effort, both academically gifted students and academically challenged students benefit." However, Davis (2009) stated that instructors can promote interdependence by suggesting students divide the workload. How a group manages its tasks and goals is likely determined by how self-organized and directed a group becomes. Nilson (2010) proposed that instructors tell students they will be in the roles of both leaders and followers while working in groups. In this way, students come to the realization that they need to assume a collective responsibility for each other and their work.

Another way to promote interdependence involves having individual teams generate criteria for group conduct and behavior—in essence, a team contract. ALC instructors have used a few variants of this contract. For example, David Gross, a biochemistry and molecular biology instructor at the University of Massachusetts, Amherst, said:

> I have students on the first or second day—depending on when the teams form—talk about group behavior and what kind of group behavior they know that they show, constructive and destructive. I have them design what they think would be an effective team member. I tell them we're going to do peer reviews and those peer reviews are going to be based on what the team came up with as a collective. They work for 10 to 15 minutes on that to figure out what is good behavior, and in the beginning they get it in their heads as to what their own expectations are. I think it helps them build teamwork and buy into the idea [of teamwork].

ALC instructors, like this one, can let individual groups formulate how they will hold each other accountable. Instructors might want to provide a few guiding topics for self-governing groups to address, like how to manage time and what skills are needed for certain assignments or projects. Once the group has reached a consensus or majority, the members can formalize the document as a contract for the group, and each member signs it.

Another approach to designing team contracts is for individual teams to determine some of the key criteria on which they will be evaluated. Then, in a discussion with the whole class, the teams offer one or two suggestions they would like in a contract. Instructors can help guide the conversation to address the common characteristics of groups (e.g., the criterion of being on time concerns accountability; actively listening to others concerns group processing). Once each team has a chance to provide suggestions, the instructor can use the themes that emerge and distill the items into a contract. An environmental sciences professor used this approach and said it was easier for him to codify the terms for the contract after group discussion. The contract can be distributed in class and or posted on the learning management system so students have ready access to it and can reference it when questions about accountability arise. Moreover, the groups and the instructor can refer to the contract as a source for discussion if dysfunction arises in the group. Alternatively, a variation of this process is for the instructor to present a set of criteria for group behavior policy that students can review and alter.

In addition to requiring group contracts, an instructor might choose to show groups how to devise a plan to manage tasks and projects successfully (Davis, 2009). Groups can draft a plan of action and submit it to the instructor (or teaching assistants) for feedback. Instructors could structure assignments so students have to submit elements of a project in stages. Structuring activities is an important way for instructors to plan for the different stages of group work. If a team is conducting a research project, for instance, they might submit a literature review, research questions, and sections about data collection and analysis separately for feedback from instructors. Group members can identify parts of the project to which they contributed. The final product might also indicate in which sections group members made contributions. Let's say five students—Lin, Manfred, Jose, Kate, and Ryan—worked together as a group to produce a final paper. They could divide their contributions to the final paper as follows:

- Statement of purpose (Lin, Manfred)
- Literature review (Jose, Lin, Ryan)
- Research questions (All)
- Data collection (Kate, Ryan)
- Data analysis (Ryan, Kate, Manfred)
- Findings (Manfred, Jose, Lin)
- Implications (Jose, Kate)
- Final draft (All)

The activities can be structured in ways that also allow team members to provide frequent, formative peer evaluations on the performance of assigned tasks as well as on attitudes toward the group itself (Oakley et al.,

2004) so members have the opportunity to build on strengths and address limitations.

Group Dynamics

Positive group dynamics are crucial to successful collaborative, cooperative, problem-based, or team-based learning approaches.[8] Students do not always have the skills or motivation, however, to make groups work in ALCs. Petersen and Gorman (2014) suggested ALC instructors build in time for groups to interact. The following are three approaches used by ALC instructors to promote constructive group dynamics:

1. A biology professor allows students to name their teams. Students can have fun with this low-barrier activity. It gives each team an identity and promotes interaction, as all members of the team must agree on the team name.
2. Early in a course, an environmental sciences faculty member uses stages of group development (Tuckman, 1965; Tuckman & Jensen, 1977) with students to help them discuss how groups perform and identify stages of their groups' development progression. Tuckman and Jensen (1977) asserted that groups move through five stages: forming, storming, norming, performing, and adjourning. The instructor asks students about the characteristics of each stage and some potential issues that may occur during the stages. This process raises awareness of group dynamics early in the term. Instructors who use this process can also refer back to it during the term and ask groups to determine their current stage as a means of facilitating an ongoing discussion about dynamics.
3. A math instructor has her students work on an application activity early in the course. The scenario is based on the location of three retail distribution centers; the instructor asks how students would make recommendations for a fourth center, given the addresses of the existing three. The problem has several answers but requires students to think about components beyond multivariate calculus, such as cost of fuel and traffic patterns. By working together early in the course, students are able to see how solving such a problem requires different skills, as well as the talents of several members, to complete the task on time.

More generally, Oakley and colleagues (2004) suggested that groups do not always function efficiently and that it is important for instructors to provide groups with opportunities to perform effectively and efficiently. In doing so, students will interact more, often building social bonds as well as

Image 6.1 First-year engineering students in Jean VanderGheynst's Introduction to Engineering Design at the University of California, Davis completing a team-building activity called "Surviving on the Moon."

Note. Photo by Tiffany Johnson.

interdependence as they strive to achieve a shared goal. Oakley and colleagues stated that instructors who set expectations and provide preliminary instruction on effective team practices will help foster sound group dynamics. Another way to support the building of social bonds in a group is to have students engage in an ice breaking activity at the start of a new topic. While there are many ice breaking activities, try to choose one that challenges the team to quickly use their collective expertise to solve a problem (see Image 6.1).

Group Dysfunctions

Couch potatoes (Oakley et al., 2004), *free-riders* (Hall & Buzwell, 2012), *hitchhikers* (Oakley et al., 2004), *lone wolves* (Barr et al., 2005), and *social loafers* (Latane, Williams, & Harkins, 1979) are terms for problematic group members who do not make equal contributions to group success. No matter the classification, each behavior has the potential to derail groups in ALCs. Instructors should work to decrease students' negative attitudes about group work at the onset of and during class (Hall & Buzzwell, 2012). The following are some ways ALC instructors have responded to and managed students' negative attitudes about group work:

- A chemistry instructor allows groups to fire a member of the team if the dysfunction is problematic; however, she uses a specific technique to ensure such groups follow a regulated process. Students can fire a member, but they have to give the group member under scrutiny warning and enumerate what she or he needs to do to prevent being fired. The group then presents their case to the instructor for a decision. She says in all her years of teaching, no one has ever been fired, probably due to the forced communication students would need to undergo to instigate a firing.

- A political science instructor employs a progressive process to help with dysfunctional groups. The first step is the students address the issue themselves; if that does not work, the second step is a mediated session with the instructor. If that course of action fails, then the third step is the instructor resolves the problem for the students by making an executive decision. In his experience, his classes never moved past the first step because the teams have been able to work out their differences.

These examples reflect the research on this topic. The literature on dysfunctional groups suggests that the instructor should allow the group to try to solve the matter internally and should resist reassigning team members (e.g., Davis, 2009; Johnson et al., 1998; Nilson, 2010). A physics instructor agreed: "I tell them to work it out. The reason they are in groups is to learn to deal with diverse people and situations. I step in when needed, but almost all of the groups are able to sort things out."

Other strategies include asking groups to review the group contract as a means to facilitate a discussion about how to address the issue. Frequent (three to five times per term) peer feedback (addressed later in the chapter) is another good way to structure conversations about contributions and responsibilities (Davis, 2009). Some ALC instructors allow members to leave a group, but only if another group will accept them. It is uncommon that other teams will accept a member who leaves her or his original group.

An activity called "Coping With Hitchhikers and Couch Potatoes on Teams" is also useful (see Oakley, 2002; Oakley et al., 2004). In this exercise students consider scenarios in which a group is experiencing dysfunction, with some members hitchhiking (relying on the goodwill of other group members to carry them along) and others exhibiting characteristics of a couch potato (not pulling their weight). As groups work through the exercise, they may become aware of some of these characteristics or learn to curb habits that lead to behaviors associated with dysfunctional group members.

Groups Outside of the Classroom

Active learning instruction often requires students to be exposed to content before and after class, which allows instructors to use class time for activities promoting application of ideas, creating interaction between students and instructors, and providing immediate feedback to students. How instructors structure activities will determine how class time is spent, which is often achieved by setting expectations from day one of the course. For example, a communication instructor stated the following to her class on the first day:

> Much of the group work will be done in class; however, you will need to work outside of class to prepare for in-class assignments and for your final project. The amount of group time you will need outside of class will be largely determined by how efficiently you use your in-class group time.

Group Work in Blended, Hybrid, or Online Settings

Thinking about what students will do in and out of ALCs is also an important consideration for instructors who plan to use blended, hybrid, or online modalities and flipped methodologies (Barkley et al., 2014). Both the literature and instructors with whom we worked suggest giving students an individual assessment beyond the reading and activities they conduct out of class and then giving the same assessment as a group when they convene in a face-to-face setting (e.g., Michaelsen et al., 2004). A physics instructor who uses the flipped approach has students watch videos before class and take a quiz on the material when they arrive in class. He then spends time in the ALC helping them problem solve, which he describes as his most valuable time in the classroom. Cloud (e.g., Google Docs) and collaborative tools (e.g., wiki) also allow groups to manage projects in class and are points at which the instructor can promote and monitor group interactions (Boettcher & Conrad, 2010).

Assessing Group Learning and Productivity

Assessing groups can seem daunting; however, there are several strategies to help ALC instructors measure learning and group performance. These strategies include grade weighting, avoiding grade curving, and peer evaluation. We explore assessment in Chapter 7 but will touch on a few strategies here.

Weighting Grades to Promote Group Work

One way to promote buy-in is to weight the grading structure in such a way as to promote group accomplishments. Ludmila Tyler, biochemistry and molecular biology instructor at University of Massachusetts–Amherst, allows groups to determine how percentages of grades will be awarded: "The weight of each major component will be set, with input from the students, no later than the second week of class. The percent weights for major components will be within the ranges listed below." Weighting within each category (e.g., for individual versus team quizzes) will remain at the values indicated in Table 6.2. Students vote on the range of percentages during class. Tyler said

TABLE 6.2
Syllabus Excerpt: Weighted Grading Percentages

	Percent of total grade
Individual iClicker responses	5–25%
Individual assignments	5%
Quizzes	10–25%
Individual quizzes, 70% of the quiz grade	
Team quizzes, 30% of the quiz grade	
Team activities and assignments, usually in-class	5%
Team projects	30–55%
DNA informational flyer, 15% of the project grade	
Sequencing proposal, 35% of the project grade	
Final project (BMB in Other Fields),	
50% of the project grade	
Individual personal statement	10–15%
Individual presentation reviews plus guidelines	10–15%

that she sets a few ground rules: (a) The individual grade weights must be within the specified ranges; (b) the total must equal 100%; and (c) the entire class must, within a specified time (e.g., by the end of the class period), agree on a single grade-weighting scheme. Tyler said, "This last requirement provides incentive for being thoughtful about grading priorities (particularly individual versus team work), but has the huge practical advantage of stream-lining grading, which is especially important for my large classes."

An English professor employs a similar technique but has an even broader range of grade percentages for her students, and she plays the role of mediator in the large-group discussion about grades. First, she presents a range of grade percentages to her students (e.g., 65% for individual and 35% for team), and the teams discuss and agree on a range they favor. Then, the students partici-pate in a large-group discussion about how their team arrived at their percent-ages for the grade balance. As the mediator, the professor explains to students that distribution of work is more manageable and students learn better when performing in groups. She says sometimes these explanations help tip the stu-dents' decisions in favor of group work receiving a higher point percentage. In addition, she says it helps highlight the fact that group dynamics matter.

Avoiding Grade Curving

Beichner and colleagues (2007) suggested that faculty teaching in ALCs avoid curving the grade, at least for individual students. A curved or norm-referenced grading scheme does not promote collaboration because it pits students against each other in competition for a scarce resource: a high grade (Nilson, 2010). Beichner and colleagues (2007) suggested that faculty who have concerns about using a grade-curving approach should redistribute the percentage weight of assessments to encourage participation and buy-in—for example, by shifting the distribution of points toward lower-stakes assessments (e.g., homework) and away from higher-stakes assessments, like midterms and exams. However, norm-referenced grading might be beyond the control of an individual instructor.

Peer Assessment

A central component of assessing groups in ALCs is using peer and self-assessment. For example, several instructors at University of Massachusetts–Amherst use iPeer (http://ipeer.ctlt.ubc.ca) to allow students to reflect on their individual and team contributions and performance. Students are asked to score their contributions based on a set of points that they can assign to themselves and teammates.

Peer evaluations also play a big role in Tyler's biochemistry course, as mentioned earlier in this chapter. Tyler uses the following language in her syllabus:

> All team scores will be modified based on peer evaluation. <u>Unless everyone on your team contributes absolutely equally throughout the semester, you will not all receive the same scores on team quizzes, activities, and projects.</u> Each student will be required to evaluate the contributions of his or her team members approximately four to six times during the semester. At the end of the semester, the evaluations will be averaged to generate a multiplier for the final team scores.
>
> *Example 1:* Student Lazy's team scored 100% for the team activities during the semester. Lazy's team members reported that he contributed, on average, 50% of his fair share of the team's work. Lazy's final score for the team activities would therefore be 50% (calculated as 100% × 50% = 50%). Similarly, Lazy would receive only half credit for the team quizzes and projects.
>
> *Example 2:* Student Hard-working's team scored 75% for the team activities during the semester. Hard-working's team members reported that he did more than his fair share and contributed, on average, 120% of the team's work. Hard-working's final score for the team activities would therefore be 90% (calculated as 75% × 120% = 90%). Similarly, Hard-working would receive 20% more credit for the team quizzes and projects.

By providing the disclaimer and setting the expectations in the syllabus, Tyler is able to foster student buy-in. Moreover, by providing the calculations for two fictional students, her students are able to quickly grasp how the assessment will work and the value of the group approach to promote success.

One might also consider the number of times students and groups are allowed to give feedback. For example, a Spanish and Portuguese instructor has her students conduct three self-evaluations and three peer evaluations during the term. She says that allowing her students to receive and give formative feedback throughout the term will help them become aware and address individual and group performance before it is too late to change.

We should acknowledge that some students may try to set the peer evaluation terms in their favor. For example, an environmental science professor said in an early iteration of his ALC course, the students tried to "game the system" and assign everyone high evaluations when not all members were making equal contributions. To ensure students are accurately representing contributions, Michaelsen and colleagues (2004) suggested allowing students a pool of points and not allowing them to assign any one student the same number of points. Barkley and colleagues (2014), Davis (2009), Michaelsen and colleagues (2004), and Oakley and colleagues (2004) all have helpful templates that can provide guidelines for self- and peer evaluation forms.

One strategy ALC instructors may consider including is a team feedback exercise, which Anson and Goodman (2014) linked to a structured team improvement process and self-reflection. ALC instructors comment that they frequently incorporate self-reflection as the first step in the peer reflection process. Another approach is to give the students a chance to provide feedback to themselves in the peer reflection process. ALC instructors have stated that many of the students are quite honest and will speak up when they are carrying an imbalanced portion (too little or too much) of the workload.

Peer evaluation helps students reflect on all of the dimensions of high-functioning groups (accountability, interaction, interdependence, skill development, and group processing). By including peer evaluation, ALC instructors can prompt students to hold constructive conversations about how the group is performing and address issues where they arise. Instructors can use this feedback to help students become aware of and improve their behaviors. Anson and Goodman (2014) wrote, "Without feedback, students will not be able to learn to improve their behaviors—this time, or the next time around" (p. 33). The process might be time-consuming, but the literature and practical input from ALC instructors suggest it is a worthwhile endeavor as students learn more from positive team experiences than negative ones (Bacon et al., 1999).

Closing Group Activities

The *adjourning* or *ending* of the group is worth noting. Tuckman and Jensen (1977) defined this stage as one where the group's tasks end and disengage (i.e., the course ends). Before you disband a group after completing a project, you might want to assign activities that bring closure to the group. In this section we'll review some of these activities, including group accomplishments and peer reflections as well as ways group members can express gratitude to each other.

Group Accomplishments and Peer Reflections

Many instructors feel it is important at the group's end to revisit the group's accomplishments. Eggleston and Smith (2002) stated that instructors can tell the class as a whole that completing the course is an accomplishment in and of itself. This is also an excellent opportunity to connect how learning course topics will serve students in future academic, professional, or personal endeavors. This is an important consideration for instructors who have been working as a collective in their learning objectives. Instructors who gave a pre-course survey or pretest might have students retake the pre-exam again. Following the test, the instructor can show the results to the group to show the changes and how their understanding of the subject matter has evolved.

ALC instructors might have the groups review the group's contract individually, at first, and then talk about how well members met the terms of the contract. Groups might talk about certain aspects in depth (e.g., being on time, respecting everyone's opinions) or what they found the most or least valuable about the group experience in the ALC. One way to codify this experience for students is to ask them to identify one aspect of the group learning experience that they can bring to their next group situation.

Instructors might also encourage students to include elements from the course as artifacts or mementos. An education professor has students put a collaborative project in an e-portfolio for the course. More informal ideas include a group photo and set of group practices or principles they can apply in future group interactions (Petersen & Gorman, 2014).

Thank-A-Group-Member

Petersen and Gorman (2014) suggested that instructors provide students with an opportunity to thank a group member for the support they gave to each other during a final course meeting. This demonstration of gratitude might be done informally in a small-group discussion, through written thank-you notes, or by standing up and making a few short comments about the group members who positively affected the class experience for one another. Many ALC instructors find that this happens naturally, but allowing time for it during a class meeting may help the students see how a group process reaches closure.

Conclusion

Weimer and Lenze (1997) recognized that instructional methods are "eminently learnable," and working with groups requires very little, if any, formal training. Managing groups is not always intuitive or easy; however, there is a wealth of literature (empirical and practical) to support the pedagogical strategies and methods instructors may employ in ALCs. Working with groups takes vigilance and consistent guidance from instructors. As instructors think about how to leverage groups to promote student learning, it is equally important to think what students will do when they are assembled into groups.

Notes

1. Substantial research on collaboration, cooperation, groups, and teams exists, and includes Arendale, 2004; Bacon and colleagues, 1999; Barrows, 1986; Brubacher, Payne, & Rickett, 1990; Cohen, 1994; Cuseo, 1992, 2002; Davidson & Major, 2014; Felder & Brent, 2001; Goodsell and colleagues, 1992; Johnson and colleagues 1998; Kagan, 1992; Michaelsen and colleagues, 2004; Millis & Cottell, 1998; Prince, 2004; Tomcho & Foels, 2012.

2. Johnson and colleagues (1998) stated that formal learning groups work together for a sustained amount of time (one period, but often several weeks, if not longer), have a shared set of learning goals, and require interdependent work by all members to complete objectives. With formal groups, another goal is to build a collective sense of cohesion and member support (Barkley et al., 2014; Michaelsen et al., 2004).

3. Moreno and colleagues (2012) found some learning advantages for instructor-generated groups based on pre-class subject matter knowledge, communication ability, and leadership ability.

4. Oakley and colleagues (2004) have a useful template for instructors to use or modify for this activity. The template includes categories for academic (e.g., major, year of study) and demographic (e.g., race/ethnicity, gender) details, personal interests (e.g., hobbies, favorite movie), and availability.

5. Nilson (2010) suggested that teams of three to five are large enough to ensure members have the chance to interact equally both in discussion and during work on collective projects and tasks. Smaller groups tend to allow for members to rely upon each other to achieve a complex task but should be large enough to prevent social loafing or freeloading (Hall & Buzzwell, 2012).

6. These names are fictional and used for educational and explanatory purposes. Any likeness to actual individuals is coincidental and unintended.

7. Instructor clarity has been shown to enhance a host of other college outcomes as well, such as academic motivation, critical thinking, persistence to the second year of college, and likelihood of matriculating (e.g., Loes & Pascarella, 2015; Loes et al., in press; Pascarella & Terenzini, 2005).

8. The literature in psychology and the social sciences is extensive. A recent publication by Levi (2013) contains an overview of much of this research.

Appendix 6.1: Overview of Advantages and Drawbacks of Group Characteristics

Topic	Type	Advantages	Drawbacks
When to Form Groups	First Day of Class	Formal group formation allows teams to bond and connect from the first day of class, which can benefit cohesion and ease interaction (Johnson et al., 2013; Levi, 2013; Michaelsen et al., 2004).	Students may decide to drop a course, which can create an imbalance of member resources and/or members per team.
	First Few Weeks of Class	Allows instructor to have a finalized course roster to set groups without risk of students dropping the course.	Groups miss out on a few sessions to bond and build cohesion early in the term, a crucial time in the course.
How to Form Groups	Random	• Supported by research in numerous fields (e.g., Nilson, 2010). • Random formation may ease the administrative work (e.g., no pre-course survey, configuration time). • Not time-consuming (Davis, 2009). • Perceived as fair by students (e.g., Barkley et al., 2014). • Distribution of member resources equal by chance (Davis, 2009).	• Not fully supported by literature as the most effective method (e.g., McKeachie & Svinicki, 2014; Michaelsen et al., 2004; Moreno et al., 2012). • Group cohesion may be slower due to lack of familiarity with group members (Nilson, 2010). • Underrepresented students could be separated, a concern during early stages in a curricular path (Oakley et al., 2004). • Distribution of member resources can be unequal by chance (Michaelsen et al., 2004).

(Continues)

Appendix 6.1: (*Continued*)

Topic	Type	Advantages	Drawbacks
	Instructor-Generated	• Supported in the literature (e.g., Michaelsen et al., 2004; Oakley et al., 2004; Svinicki & McKeachie, 2014). • Instructors can achieve the desired balance of member resources (Michaelsen et al., 2004; Oakley, 2004).	• Member resources could be unbalanced (Michaelsen et al., 2004). • May isolate students in certain student populations in the classroom (Oakley et al., 2004).
How to Form Groups	Self-Selected	• Many students favor this approach (Brookfield & Preskill, 1999; Davis, 2009). • Students often sit with friends and/or are reluctant to move after first few days of class (Bacon et al., 1999; Michaelsen et al., 2004). • May work better in smaller courses, upper-division courses, cohort-based courses, and graduate courses (Davis, 2009; Oakley et al., 2004). • Cohesion may occur sooner, thus allowing groups to move into performance stages quicker (Bacon et al., 1999). • Accountability may be strong due to familiarity of peers (i.e., "We won't let our team down, they are our friends").	• Member resources could be unbalanced, overly homogeneous (Michaelsen et al., 2004). • May isolate students who do not have friends or acquaintances in the classroom (Oakley et al., 2004). • Underrepresented populations may find it difficult to select into teams (Goodsell et al., 1992; Oakley et al., 2004). • Groupthink may overrule creative ideas for the sake of solidarity. May have a higher probability of academic misconduct (e.g., cheating; Oakley et al., 2004). • Accountability may be weak due to lack of familiarity with peers (i.e., "I don't know these people nor do I owe them anything"; loafing) or increased familiarity—which might hinder time on task (i.e., socializing).

		Advantages	Disadvantages
Group Size	Small Teams (3–4 members)	• Allows members to fully utilize skills. • Minimizes opportunity for social loafing; accountability greater with smaller numbers. • Cohesion may occur sooner, thus allowing groups to move into performance stages more quickly.	• Groups may lack diverse opinions/members. • Groups may not be able to accomplish complex tasks.
	Large Teams (4–8 members)	• More members results in greater diversity of membership and perspectives (Tinto, 1997). • Groups are more likely to be able to accomplish complex tasks.	• Higher potential for social loafing. • Lack of interdependence due to size. • May not allow members to fully develop/utilize skills and/or experience different roles.
Group Duration	Short term	• Student can assume multiple roles during the term. • Students are exposed to a greater diversity of their peers' member resources. • Easier to manage dysfunctional teams.	• Groups may not become cohesive during short lengths of time. • Groups may not be able to give frequent peer feedback.
	Long term	• Increased ability for members to become a cohesive unit due to long-term collaboration (Bacon et al., 1999). • Groups might be able to handle more complex tasks due to time for project development. • Students may be able to play multiple roles during course.	• Students may not get a chance to interact with other classmates; loss of large class community. • Greater chance for social loafing due to project/course length.

Appendix 6.2: General Instructions for Pods and Teams

This semester you will work through several class activities in pods of 3 to 4 (everyone sitting at one arc of the table) and as an entire team of 9 to 10 (everyone sitting at the entire table).

Each person has a role in the pod and in the team; these roles will rotate each week so that each person has a chance to perform each role during the semester, and learn from that experience. See the role assignment grid in your team folder.

Work in a pod   Work in a team   Work as a class

Team Roles (1 per team)	Pod Roles (1 per pod)
Team Manager: Gathers materials the team and the pods need; makes sure everyone knows their roles for the activity; keeps team on task and on time; ensures that team completes the tasks by the deadline and that all reports are filed on time.	*Pod Coordinator*: Ensures that pod completes its tasks on time and that all pod members are participating and on track; ensures that pod's assignments are posted or turned in as appropriate; keeps a log of the concepts the pod discusses and makes sure the team reporter is informed of the pod's work.
Team Reporter: Keeps a record of team's work and completes team reports; gathers material from each of the team's pods prior to class discussion; asks questions on behalf of the team and shares team's answers with class. While the team reporter should generally be the one who answers on behalf of the team after a particular pod- or team-level activity or discussion, it is also okay for others in the team to contribute to class discussions or ask questions when they have something new to add to the class discussion.	*Pod Technician*: Performs all technical operations, including using the computer, manipulating models, writing on the whiteboard or other media.
Team Analyst: Examines how team is working and ensures that all members are actively listening and participating; makes observations to the team about group dynamics and suggests changes or improvements; this might include observations about what worked well for the team on a given day, or what seemed to be a less effective strategy or tendency.	*Pod Talent*: Contributes ideas, insight, skills, effort, and talent to the pod's work; identifies areas of need and fills them; supports coordinator's and technician's efforts; reflects on pod's creative/productive process, boosts morale when needed, and plays "devil's advocate" role when pod seems to be thinking narrowly.

Appendix 6.3: Example of Role Assignment chart for Table Team (9 students) and Pods (3 students)

Team Pod Role Assignment Grid   Team:20-____

Week	1	2	3	4	5	6	7	8	9	10	11	12	13	14	15
Date	1/21	1/28	2/4	2/11	2/18	2/25	3/4	3/11	3/25	4/1	4/8	4/15	4/22	4/29	5/6
1 first name	1	2	3	1	3	2	1	1	1	1	3	2	1	3	3
last name	Crd	Tec	Exp	Crd	Exp	Crd	Crd	Tec	Exp	Tec	Exp	Exp	Crd	Tec	Tec
2	2	3	1	1	1	2	2	2	2	3	1	3	2	1	3
	Crd	Tec	Exp	Tec	Crd	Tec	Crd	Tec	Exp	Exp	Crd	Exp	Crd	Tec	Exp
3	3	1	2	1	2	3	3	3	3	1	1	1	2	3	1
	Crd	Tec	Exp	Exp	Crd	Tec	Crd	Tec	Exp	Exp	Tec	Crd	Tec	Exp	Crd
4	1	1	1	2	3	1	1	1	1	2	1	2	3	1	1
	Tec	Exp	Crd	Crd	Crd	Tec	Tec	Exp	Crd	Exp	Exp	Crd	Tec	Exp	Tec
5	2	2	2	2	1	1	2	2	2	1	2	3	1	2	1
	Tec	Exp	Crd	Tec	Tec	Exp	Tec	Exp	Crd	Crd	Crd	Crd	Tec	Exp	Exp
6	3	3	3	2	2	2	3	3	3	2	2	1	1	1	2
	Tec	Exp	Crd	???	Exp	Exp	Tec	Exp	Crd	Crd	Tec	Tec	Exp	Crd	Crd
7	1	3	2	3	3	3	1	1	1	3	2	2	2	2	2
	Exp	Crd	Tec	Crd	Tec	Exp	Exp	Crd	Tec	Crd	Exp	Tec	Exp	Crd	Tec
8	2	1	3	3	1	3	2	2	2	2	3	3	3	3	2
	Exp	Crd	Tec	Tec	Exp	Crd	Exp	Crd	Tec	Tec	Crd	Tec	Exp	Crd	Exp
9	3	2	1	3	2	1	3	3	3	3	3	1	3	2	3
	Exp	Crd	Tec	Exp	Exp	Crd	Exp	Crd	Tec	Tec	Tec	Exp	Crd	Tec	Crd
10	#1	#2	#3	#4	#5	#6	#7	#8	#9	#1	#2	#3	#4	#5	#6
	Exp	Exp	Exp	Exp	Exp	Exp	Exp	Exp	Exp	Exp	Exp	Exp	Exp	Exp	Exp

1, 2 or 3 = Your pod number for the week. ?# = Your pod number unless another pod is missing one

Team roles for the week:	Crd = Manager	Tec = Reporter	Exp = Analyst
Pod roles for the week:	Crd = Coordinator	Tec = Technologist	Exp = Expediter

If there is a tenth person on a team, that person switches roles with another teammate (#1-#9) each week, as shown. The person switched with becomes an expediter for the week.

Note. Thanks to David Matthes from the University of Minnesota.

7

ASSESSMENT AND
FEEDBACK

I think the hardest thing about team-based learning/ALCs is assessment.

—An ALC instructor

nstructors new to teaching in an Active Learning Classroom (ALC) sometimes have difficulty designing assessments for learning that happen in
such a unique space. For instance, in some cases, collaborative activities
might best be measured with collaborative assessments. Faculty, though, may
be hesitant to use collaborative assessment approaches, either because their
department or college requires the use of traditional exams or because they are
unsure of exactly what to use and how to use it. The ALCs also pose an assessment challenge for instructors who use traditional exams. Because the small
tables compel students to face one another—the very feature we otherwise
laud—students may be more tempted to engage in academic misconduct.
In this chapter, we will address both of these concerns by providing multiple examples of collaborative assessment and feedback strategies successfully implemented by ALC instructors. We will also address strategies for
traditional, non-collaborative assessments for instructors who choose to use
these approaches. To make it easier to envision how the approach might be
adapted for your teaching we do not limit most of the examples to the context of a specific course or topic.

We describe strategies for both informal and formal assessment that take
advantage of the affordances of the space and we exclude approaches that
are significantly limited by the space. For instance, role-playing, performance
exercises, or any assessment that requires the entire class to observe an individual (or small number of students) do not tend to work well in the ALC
environment, with their lack of a single focal point. Accordingly, we will not
report on them here, though, of course, a flexibly designed space may make
some of those strategies more manageable.

Advantages afforded by the space for collaborative feedback and assessment include the small tables that allow students to interact easily. Whiteboards and projection screens showing student work allow instructors to quickly scan the room to assess student progress and provide feedback during activities. The open configuration of the room's furniture provides instructors with easy access to any student to give one-to-one feedback. However, as mentioned previously, the configuration of the space may prove challenging for administering traditional exams. In this chapter we will describe different types of assessments and methods for providing instructor and peer feedback used successfully by ALC instructors.

Assessments

Exams

As in traditional classrooms, instructors in ALCs administer exams as one way of assessing students' learning. In this section, we will present strategies for using collaborative, open-book, and traditional exams in ALC spaces.

Collaborative exams

Testing students collaboratively may be desirable in situations in which students are learning collaboratively. By completing collaborative exams, students can benefit from the strengths of each person in the group when the team is asked to demonstrate knowledge and understanding of a subject. Typically, questions on collaborative exams are complex with no single correct answer, and they require the input of students with different perspectives. Collaborative testing has been shown to enhance learning, including the performance of both high- and low-performing students and students with test anxiety (Giuliodori, Lujan, & DiCarlo, 2008; Pandey & Kapitanoff, 2011; Rao, Collins, & DiCarlo, 2002). Increases in test performance are attributed to students' having good discussions, remembering information better, and having an increased ability to think about the information (Kapitanoff, 2009).

In a higher education teaching course, an instructor at the University of Minnesota typically uses a collaborative exam as the final because much of the work assigned during the term is completed collaboratively. Throughout the semester, students individually create a syllabus for a course they have chosen to design and work in teams to design and deliver course content, to peer review documents, and to engage in classroom activities. The instructor creates a final exam that asks each team to work collaboratively to design a first-year seminar course.[1] Students have time before the final exam date to choose the topic and submit a brief written description for feedback from the instructor. On the day of the exam, student teams have two hours to create three learning aims for the course; create an assessment for each aim; and describe the types of learning activities, technology, and course materials they will use. They are allowed to use any resource in the planning of their course. During the activity, they sketch out their courses on the whiteboard or use the projection screen to work on a collaborative document. When finished, each team presents its proposal to a mock panel of deans composed of two or three faculty members from different departments. The "deans" and the instructor provide oral feedback to the students after each presentation. This type of final examination demonstrates the usefulness of working with a team for course planning and models how students can organize their time when planning an actual course in their future careers in higher education. The fact that students can put together a fairly complete course proposal in a little over two hours also increases their confidence in their ability to design educational curriculum.

Two-stage collaborative exams also work well in the ALC. In the first stage, students answer exam questions individually as they would on any typical exam. Once completed, individual exams are turned in to the instructor, and students immediately receive the second stage of the exam to work on with their team. The student's final score is some combination of the individual and the group exam scores, often with the group score accounting for a lower percentage of the overall exam grade. The second-stage exam questions may be a subset of the questions, frequently the most challenging items, from the first-stage exam. They may be identical to the first-stage exam questions or slightly modified to make them easier to complete in less time. Students discuss the questions at their tables, evaluating approaches for solving and answering the questions. Because students have just attempted these questions on their own, and some portion of exam credit is tied to their group responses, these discussions tend to be focused. Students who have taken two-stage exams have reported that the exams benefit their learning (Rieger & Heiner, 2014). For example, a student in an upper-division statistics class remarked that it was a great way to take an exam. Under the individual exam conditions, he struggled with the questions and was eager to immediately confirm his methods with his classmates during the second stage. He said that it was a true learning experience because he had just grappled with the material and knew exactly what he needed to find out from his classmates. "There's nothing like the lonely intensity of an exam," he said, "to drive you back to your group for confirmation." One instructor who uses collaborative exams described how students prepared: "People from the same table got together and studied ahead of time; even though they assigned each other areas of specialization, they tried to get together to discuss—I mean, oh my God, I should pay for that kind of activity."

Open-book exams
Some instructors use open-book collaborative exams in class. Typically, students are allowed to access resources and discuss answers with each other. This approach has the added advantage of reducing the possibility of cheating at the ALC's round tables. Open-book exams are usually scheduled so that students do not have enough time to begin a de novo search for an answer but do have time to refer to their notes if they come into the exam with an understanding of the material being tested and a list of appropriate resources to refer to quickly. This approach is a good way to emphasize exam preparation, including how to approach solving a complex disciplinary problem that requires the use of resources. Furthermore, this approach more closely resembles how professionals in many disciplinary fields solve real-life problems (i.e., accessing available resources and discussing solutions with colleagues).

Traditional exams
The same tables that allow students to face one another present some challenges for instructors who give traditional exams. Sitting in close proximity makes it very easy for students to see one another's exams, even unintentionally. Furthermore, even if an instructor patrols the room during an examination, it simply is not possible to monitor all tables at once. Overcoming this challenge is a major concern for many instructors new to teaching in an ALC. Students also find it uncomfortable because they do not want to be inadvertently perceived as cheating if their eyes innocently wander. Collaborative exams, of course, conveniently eliminate this issue. (Another way around the problem is to substitute projects for exams, which will be described later in this chapter.) These methods have worked well for many instructors; however, there may be some subjects and courses where these types of assessment approaches may not be appropriate or would not conform to a department's conventions. Next we describe several methods for responding to this problem.

Some instructors use a narrative exam format such as a written essay or procedural explanation. This format makes it more difficult for students to copy from one another with a quick glance, or if students do copy from a neighbor, the similarity of the responses will be more apparent than with responses to multiple-choice or short-answer exam formats. Some instructors eliminate the problem by moving the exam to a more traditional classroom space, such as a large auditorium or an institution's testing center, if available.

Image 7.1 Students arrange folders to maintain privacy during an exam.

Alternatively, if the ALC has enough empty seats, it may be possible for students to seat themselves so that there is an empty chair between each of them. Another approach is to have half of the students move into a different room for the exam, creating enough space in both rooms for students to have space between themselves and a neighbor. Of course, a test proctor would be required for both rooms. Many of these approaches require some logistical shuffling.

An easier method may be to provide some privacy during a traditional exam by having students put up blank manila folders on each side of their work area to create a line-of-sight barrier between themselves and other members at the table (see Image 7.1). Folders can be provided by the instructor and distributed to each table on exam day or the instructor can require students to bring their own barriers. Incidentally, the folders are a convenient conveyance to submit and return materials such as exams, worksheets, homework, and so forth.

Another approach is to administer different versions of the same exam. A professor of biochemistry and molecular biology distributes different colored answer sheets (red, blue, yellow) to use with exams that correspond with three versions of the test. Students with the same colored answer sheets do not sit next to one another. The same instructor teaching a different course in an ALC brings in laptops (via a laptop cart) for all students to take individual exams. The students log in to the online homework system at the institution to complete the exam electronically. He has done direct comparisons between paper exams and online exams and found no difference in grades and averages. An informal poll of the students revealed that almost all students gave the online exam a positive review.

Quizzes

Collaborative quizzes

Collaborative quizzes differ from collaborative exams in that quizzes are usually focused on a smaller subset of material, are shorter, and are often in an easy-to-grade format (e.g., multiple choice, true–false, short answer). Collaborative quizzes provide students with the benefit of tapping into the knowledge and skills of their teammates to answer questions about course content. These assessments have been used for different purposes in courses. Michaelsen, Knight, and Fink (2004) advocated using collaborative quizzing as a way to prepare students for in-class activities designed to apply and extend what they learned from the course reading. Termed *readiness assessment tests* (RATs), these quizzes are given at the beginning of each new major unit of instruction to test student understanding of the assigned reading. Students take the quizzes individually, turn them in, and then immediately take the same quiz again in teams together, discussing and advocating for the answers they selected. The process of taking the quiz individually measures student learning, while the process of taking the quiz together further deepens learning and promotes confidence as students advocate for their answers and consider other students' explanations. As with cooperative exams, quiz scores are based on percentages of both the team and the individual scores (Michaelsen et al., 2004). The quizzes are graded in class to provide rapid feedback to the team on student performance (IF-ATs, described later, are one way to accomplish this quick feedback). Doing well on the quiz instantly tells students that they have the background knowledge needed to engage in upcoming activities related to the course content. Michaelsen and colleagues (2004) suggested that students be provided with an opportunity to appeal any questions they may have missed on the group quiz. As students construct their argument for their answer from their course readings and other resources, they are further learning the material (Michaelsen et al., 2004).

Collaborative quizzes can also be used to introduce a new course topic or check for misconceptions. A biology instructor uses the Immediate Feedback Assessment Technique (IF-AT) for this purpose. The IF-AT includes scratch-off answer sheets for multiple-choice questions.[2] A correct answer is confirmed when an asterisk is revealed in a scratched box. The instructor first has students take a multiple-choice quiz on their own. Then she asks them to take the quiz as a group, discussing answers and coming to consensus. To encourage persistence in the face of an incorrect answer, partial credit is given if groups get the correct answer on the second or third try. She reports that teams almost always outperform any individual in the group, which also helps to demonstrate the value of working collaboratively. Quiz scores can be recorded as a combination of the individual and the team quiz scores (Cotner, Baepler, & Kellerman, 2008). Another instructor modified the collaborative quiz process so that student teams discuss the answers to each question during class but answer the quiz on their own sheets rather than on a single team form.

Collaborative quizzes can also be used as a team-building exercise when groups are first formed. K. A. Smith (2004) recommended that students in groups be given a task to work on together as a way to foster team cohesion prior to receiving class assignments. The quiz can be about course material, or it could be on unrelated material. One instructor uses a current-events quiz from Slate's website (www.slate.com) as a team-building activity. Like the activities just described, team members first take the quiz individually and then take the quiz as a team. The teams usually perform better than any individual member, which demonstrates the advantages of working together. Alternatively, the quiz could cover a reading about a specific pedagogical approach that will be used in class (e.g., TBL or POGIL). This activity provides students with information about the benefit of the teaching approach used by the instructor.

After the quizzes are scored, the exercise can be used as the basis for a large-group conversation about the process of working together. This may be surprising to students who expect that the material covered in class will only be about disciplinary content, and it sets the stage for the instructor to discuss the importance of teamwork skills. This conversation provides an entry point for the instructor to ask questions such as: How did your team make decisions? Was the vote unanimous or by majority? Did one person dominate? Did all team members contribute equally? If not, why not? Students can be asked to draw on this experience to draft a statement establishing how the team will work together during the term.

Clicker quizzes and questions

Personal response systems, or clickers, that allow tracking of student responses and identity can also be used for graded quizzes. Some instructors who use this system pose a few questions each class session as a quiz that counts toward the final grade. Clickers can enhance participation and engagement in the material and can incidentally increase attendance (Bruff, 2009).

Typically, clicker-question responses are individual; however, some instructors allow students to confer with their teammates before answering the questions. A slight variation on this approach is to ask students first to answer the question on their own and then to confer with their neighbors and try again (Mazur, 1997; M. K. Smith et al., 2009). The final score could be based on a combination of the first and second answers or just the final answer. Both of these approaches encourage student collaboration and allow team members to benefit from each other's strengths. Clickers can also be used for informal assessment to provide feedback to the instructor and to students about their mastery of a topic. In this case, they would be used as described here, although points would not be awarded, and it would not be necessary to track student identity. We will talk more about feedback methods later in this chapter.

Traditional quizzes

We have described multiple methods for collaborative quizzing; however, an instructor may prefer to use traditional quizzes—that is, quizzes students take individually during class. As was described for exams, the arrangement of the ALC poses some challenges for this approach. Quizzes are usually designed to be easy to grade and to take a minimal amount of class time; however, some of the suggestions described for traditional exams may not be appropriate approaches for quizzes (e.g., written essays or procedural explanations may take too long for students to complete and for instructors to grade). More practical methods, as described in the traditional testing section, may be to have students put up physical barriers or to have the instructor administer different versions of the same quiz.

Projects and Presentations

Presentations of posters and other visual output of projects

The configuration of an ALC is ideal for poster presentations by student teams. Posters or other visual output can be mounted on the whiteboards around the perimeter of the room. Alternatively, electronic versions of posters can be displayed on individual table projection screens. There are some advantages to using the projection screens rather than the whiteboards for this purpose. For one, animations or videos can be displayed. Instructors can also call up an individual presentation to display on all of the monitors to use the poster as an example for commenting and providing public feedback. Also, the electronic files displayed on the projection screens can be saved on a course management site for later viewing and referral, perhaps with annotations or audio narration. This approach can be particularly helpful for students who have a visual or learning disability and need an accommodation to view the material in a different format or at another time.

A disadvantage of this method over mounting posters on the whiteboards is that projection monitors are sometimes placed higher on the wall, making it more difficult to point to specific information as the presenter is speaking, though a laser pointer can help. Moreover, some projection screens are significantly smaller than a poster might be.[3] Other visual objects, such as drawings, photographs, and certain artwork, can be displayed for student viewing and discussion.

Student media presentations

Projection screens allow students to display materials easily for the entire class to view. Students can connect their electronic devices to project to the entire room, showing videos, PowerPoint slides, websites, or other Internet resources. The instructor can control which source is displayed on the main projection screen and the student monitors. In this way, multiple students' findings and projects can be presented in a short amount of time to allow for public feedback from the instructor and students from other teams.

The existence of multiple projection screens in a collaborative space also permits instructors to assign media-production projects. An English professor has student teams work on their individual projection screens to design and build a video project together over multiple class sessions. At the end of the term, they hold a "showcase day" during which all student teams reveal their team videos, which are graded by the instructor.

Grading Approaches

Most of the assessment approaches we have described in this chapter are collaborative. To encourage students to work collaboratively, it is worth revisiting your grading system. Instructors typically use one of two general schemes for assigning course grades: normative-referenced grading and criterion-referenced grading. Normative-referenced grading refers to assigning scores and grades based on some predetermined distribution formula. This distribution formula could take the shape of a bell curve, ensuring that the majority of the grades fall in the C range with fewer grades in the B and D ranges, and fewer still in the A and F ranges. Criterion-referenced grading refers to assigning scores and grades to pre-determined values or cut scores.

Normative-referenced grading

Some propose that the use of normative-referenced grading increases fairness for student grades across multiple sections with different instructors. This approach would mitigate the differences in grading standards or teaching effectiveness between sections. Without it, a student's grade could depend on whether they have a hard or easy grader or a more or less effective instructor rather than on their mastery of the material. Another argument in favor of norm-referenced grading is that it helps to prevent grade inflation, the phenomenon of successive cohorts of students earning higher and higher grades each year. A department or college may encourage this grading approach to identify the top students in a class and to preserve the exceptional nature of an A grade.

A disadvantage of norm-referenced grading is that grades are necessarily assigned based on the performance of other students. Accordingly, some students can receive inappropriately low grades if there are many high performers in the class. Likewise, this approach can result in inappropriately high grades if there are many poor performers in the class. Furthermore, the grade may not reflect the level of mastery of the material; if most students do poorly on an exam, a low score could earn an A, even if the student who earned that A grade does not understand the material. Another drawback to this approach is that students are indirectly discouraged from working collaboratively. With a zero-sum grading approach, students end up competing against one another for the top grades. If one student scores high, another student necessarily must receive a lower grade. This requisite balance can deter students from working together and helping one another's learning (Piontek, 2008).

Criterion-referenced grading

Criterion-referenced grading refers to assigning student grades based on some predetermined criteria. The breakdown of grade assignments may be based on a percentage of correct answers (e.g., 90% = A, 80% = B, etc.). Ideally, each assessment should be graded according to a rubric that all students can access. With criterion-referenced grading, the number of students who receive each grade is not affected by the scores of other students. Another advantage to criterion-referenced grading is that students are not penalized for helping other students perform better, hence eliminating a potential disincentive to collaborative learning. If all students master the material above a defined level, all students could conceivably earn As. Likewise, if no students master the material, no students would pass the course. A disadvantage of this system is that it takes time to articulate specific grading standards, which preferably would be done before the start of a course (Piontek, 2008).

Generally, if you want to encourage your students to work collaboratively, criterion-referenced grading is recommended (Svinicki & McKeachie, 2011). Some departments and colleges, however, have grading policies in place that require all instructors to use a particular form of grading that may preclude criterion-referenced grading. Beichner and colleagues (2007) have suggested that instructors in this situation distribute course points among homework, tests, quizzes, and other assignments rather than on two or three high-stakes exams. More weight on homework encourages students to do it; less weight on exams makes it possible for students to do well in the course despite one bad performance, though their grades would still be influenced by the performance of other students.

Feedback

Whether you are teaching in an ALC or a traditional classroom, offering feedback to your students helps them learn content more deeply and demonstrates your interest in their learning as much as they can during your course. This section describes ways that instructors can provide feedback and can guide all students in the ALC to share productive feedback with their classmates.

Methods for Providing Instructor Feedback

When you teach in an ALC, you can offer your students feedback in ways that might be more familiar than you think. In this section, we describe ways that you can provide focused, relevant feedback to individual students and to student teams.

Whole-class discussions

At first glance, the ALC can look like a chaotic, uncontrollable environment for a whole-class discussion. However, instructors are able to call on an individual team, an entire table, or a particular student quickly and easily. Often, instructors in ALCs use the whole-class discussion as a way to wrap up and synthesize team activities. Involving the entire class in the discussion gives the instructor the opportunity to provide feedback to one student's response in a manner that will benefit the entire class. These discussions can also reveal to the instructor the areas in which students are having difficulties, inform students of different answers and approaches used by their classmates, and permit the instructor to provide additional information or perspectives.

An instructor can determine in multiple ways which individual students or groups to call on. She can ask for volunteers; call on a specific table, team, or student; or randomly call on students, teams, or tables. Asking questions and calling on students randomly allows the instructor to quickly assess the understanding of a representative student in the class (Dallimore, Hertenstein, & Platt, 2012). When instructors respond to one student's answer (e.g., "Correct" or "Something is missing; can anyone else help?"), they provide feedback to the entire class. One example of a random approach used by several instructors is to project a virtual "magic eight ball" that randomly selects numbers to identify a specific group (e.g., Group 27; see Figure 7.1).[4] The instructor can choose to allow the group to confer and select a spokesperson to answer the question, or the instructor can call on a specific member of Group 27 for an answer. Another instructor summarized the possibilities for choosing students for feedback in the ALC: "So I have three different

Figure 7.1 Magic Eight Ball Random Number Generator.

ways I can call on someone: either by the whole table, by a pod of three within a table, or I can [point to] a name card and say, 'Hey, Joe, what did your pod decide?'"

Displaying student notes

The whiteboards around the room can be used to display student work on in-class problems or activities to make information easily accessible to the team and for instructor feedback. By asking students to do their work on the whiteboard, the instructor can walk around the room and quickly scan what students are doing to identify teams that are on track and teams that need intervention. In this way, the instructor can also determine how well the class as a whole is mastering the material. If many groups' work reveals problems, the instructor can stop the activity for a quick, whole-class mini-lecture or question-and-answer period and then allow teams to resume working. If most student teams seem to be working well on an activity, the instructor can check in only with those groups that are having difficulty. One chemistry instructor, for example, uses students' work on the whiteboards to determine whether they have tackled all steps in a multi-step assignment. She stated that some teams think they are finished before realizing that the activity requires more work. She can spot those teams quickly as she circulates around the room and prompt them to continue by asking just a question or two about their work.

Another advantage of displaying teams' work on the whiteboards is its visibility to other teams. It lets classmates see the work of their peers, allowing students to compare their work to that of other groups that may have arrived at a different answer, presented a different conclusion, or followed a different process. This approach permits students to see the diverse possibilities for solving problems. Additionally, students can provide feedback to one another as they observe the work of the other teams. Some instructors encourage students to move about the ALC and look at the responses of other teams to foster this practice. This method is sometimes referred to as a "gallery walk," and it is a good way to expose students quickly to the thinking and approaches of their classmates on a common problem.

Preparation for exams

When you help them prepare for exams, you can help your students synthesize what they have learned during the term and show that you care about their performance (Svinicki & McKeachie, 2011). This practice allows students to receive feedback in time to change what and how they study for the exam.

Circuit-training exam preparation

For this study activity, the instructor creates several activities and questions that will help students review for an exam and then designates tables as stations through which student teams will rotate. For example, the instructor could stock the first station with copies of a cooperative quiz of previous course material and the second station with a prompt for students to design an experiment. The third station might ask students to analyze and critique a piece of writing selected by the instructor. The fourth station can ask teams to derive a model to explain a given set of data. To check comprehension and reduce frustration, answer keys should be placed at each station, and students should be instructed not to look at them until they have finished the task.

Teams should be allowed a set time at each station—say, 10 minutes—to answer the question together and compare their answer to the answer key. Projecting a countdown clock with an alarm can help students stay on track and signal when it is time to move to another table with a new activity. The instructor resets the clock and repeats the countdown until all students have experienced each activity. It is best to reserve some time at the end of the hour to wrap up with a whole-class discussion during which students can ask questions that arose at different stations. This fast-paced studying technique helps students stay on task and also indicates the level and the kind of answers the instructor will be looking for on the exam. If study questions and answers are posted on the course management system, students can later review areas that troubled them.

Methods for Providing Peer Feedback

Some instructors assign projects and ask students to peer review a classmate's assignment. The in-class peer review is designed to be part of the learning process. Peer review allows students to recognize strengths and weaknesses in a classmate's or another team's project that may provide insights that can lead to strengthening their own projects. The small tables in the classroom allow for easy conversations among students during the feedback session, and the open configuration of the space allows the instructor to circulate among tables, check progress, and answer questions as they arise.

Contribution to a collaborative document

One key advantage of individual projection screens is that they allow larger student groups to work on electronic documents collaboratively. A single laptop can be viewed simultaneously by two or three students; however, when the teams are larger, it is difficult for all members to see. In the ALC, student teams can use a single electronic device easily to contribute and respond to a team-designed collaborative document, like a Google doc projected on their table screen. Likewise, teams can use their laptops to contribute to a class-wide collaborative document or wiki that is projected to all the screens. For example, a music therapy professor assigns a student during each class period to take notes on a class wiki. The wiki is occasionally projected on the screens in the room and is also available electronically so students can check it at any time during class for details they missed. The notes are also available on the wiki in the course management system to everyone after class.

Pass-pass-pass peer feedback

A biology instructor takes advantage of the room's open configuration to randomize partners in a peer-feedback activity she calls "pass-pass-pass." Students complete a writing assignment and put their name on it. Then all students pass their paper to a person near them. Students continue exchanging papers for a minute or so until the instructor tells them to stop. Whichever paper the students have at the end of this exchange is the one that they will peer review. The biology instructor has remarked that students enjoy this activity "beyond what common sense would predict," and it is not unusual for students to talk loudly and to laugh throughout the exchange process. A variation of this peer-feedback activity is used by a different instructor who asks students to wad up their completed paper assignments into a ball and toss the balls around the room on cue. Again, assignments end up distributed randomly for peer review, and many students enjoy the unconventional activity.

It is important to prepare students for peer-review activities to achieve useful results. Providing detailed rubrics is one way to facilitate peer feedback. Instructor-designed rubrics that outline the important elements of an assignment and a description of requirements for different performance levels helps students focus their comments on useful and relevant aspects of the assignment. Using a rubric also frees students from having to make value judgments about peers' work (e.g., "This was good." or "You did a great job."). By using the language of the rubric for their feedback, students can refer instead to whether the standards for each element were met. Peer reviewers can then focus on the concrete aspects of the project (e.g., "Three of the four elements were present in your assignment." or "The rubric asks for a thesis statement, but I couldn't find one."). This focus helps students who receive peers' feedback to address and correct the most important aspects of the assignment in a subsequent draft. Though creating a detailed rubric takes time, the effort is offset by more effective peer evaluations; a finished product of higher quality; and, accordingly, less instructor grading time.

Student-designed study guide

Some instructors encourage students to codify what they have learned as part of their exam preparation and incentivize this synthesis by creating an assignment that compels them to design shareable study guides. A biology instructor, for instance, divides the course content into sections corresponding to textbook chapters and assigns each team a section. Teams must create a study guide in class for their assigned section, using a collaborative document displayed on their projected screen. Teams exchange study guides and perform peer review on another group's guide. The main goal for the peer reviewers is to spot and correct any errors; however, the close reading done by the teams also helps them more deeply learn some of the material for the exam. At the end of the exercise, all study guides are made available for all students to use to prepare for the exam.

Conclusion

The ALC helps facilitate collaborative forms of assessment that align well with the collaborative approach to learning often used in these spaces. The ALC's design also allows for easy and rapid visualization of student work, whether on the whiteboard, the projection screen, or paper, which helps facilitate instructor and peer feedback. Traditional written exams and quizzes that students take individually can be a challenge in the space; however, there are multiple techniques to help mitigate these problems, including the use of temporary physical barriers or alternate test formats. Because the design of the room facilitates collaborative work, it is worth considering whether the grading scheme in use facilitates or undermines student collaboration. A normative-referenced grading system, in which student scores are determined in relation to their peers' scores, may counteract the collaborative process instructors are trying to instill in their students. A criterion-referenced approach, in which scores are determined based on attainment of a priori determined standards, reduces the drive for competition among individual students and may encourage student collaboration.

Notes

1. Thanks for this example to instructor Ilene Alexander, University of Minnesota.
2. See www.epsteineducation.com/home/about/default.aspx to order IF-ATs.
3. See Chapter 5 for a description of a poster session project in an introductory biology class.
4. Thanks for Mark Decker who built the magic eight ball random number generator and helped popularize this technique. By allowing a random number generator to determine which team to call upon, an instructor distances himself from being the one who selects people who will be in the spotlight. The instructor can't be perceived as playing favorites or choosing someone who hasn't hidden herself well enough. Students quickly realize that everyone needs to be prepared to answer a question or report results: It's the will of the Magic Eight Ball.

8

SUPPORTING ALL STUDENTS

Throughout this book, we have described the many advantages of an Active Learning Classroom (ALC) for student learning, but your move to the ALC and the innovations you design may create unintended hurdles for some students. In this chapter, we describe learning challenges the space presents for some students. Particularly relevant to our discussion are students with physical disabilities, students whose native language is not English or who are from a different culture, and students with learning disabilities. Specifically, we will talk about the challenges that are a direct result of the physical space itself or due to the types of learning activities engendered by the space.

The number of students with disabilities attending college has been steadily rising, and some of these students may find the space challenging. According to the National Center for Education Statistics (2013), 11% of undergraduates reported having a disability in 2007–8. The Americans with Disabilities Act (1990) mandated that institutions of higher learning provide reasonable accommodations for all qualifying students to access academic programs, and so, in new classrooms, we need to be mindful of the barriers the spaces may present as well as how to help students compensate for these issues.

Another group of students who may face challenges in the space are students for whom English is not their first language. Enrollment of international students in U.S. colleges and universities increased from 110,000 students in 2001 to 524,000 students in 2012 (Ruiz, 2014). From 2012 to 2013 the number of foreign students at American colleges grew 8% (*The Chronicle of Higher Education*, 2015). Another way to have a sense of the number of international students in the United States is to look at the number of higher education institutions that host 1,000 or more international students. Those institutions increased from 139 universities in 1999–2000 to 231 universities in 2013–14 (Institute of International Education, 2014).

With such a large and growing number of international students in the United States, instructors should be cognizant that the heavy reliance on verbal communication in ALCs may prove challenging to students who are nonnative English speakers. Challenges may include difficulty understanding the fast-paced speech of instructors and classmates, formulating verbal responses quickly, and speaking understandably in front of one's team or the entire classroom (Andrade, 2006). In such a diverse classroom, cultural differences can also lead to misunderstandings due to students' being unfamiliar with U.S. idioms, humor, and popular culture references. These differences may also influence the value placed on verbal expression as a way of demonstrating subject mastery. Accordingly, when designing and delivering their courses, instructors in ALCs should consider the impact of the space on students with disabilities and on students whose educations are grounded in different languages and cultures.

Attending class in an ALC can pose challenges for some students with learning disabilities as well. Even a busy ALC in which students are very much on task can produce visual and auditory distractions that may interfere with student focus. As we've noted elsewhere, ALCs have many and competing sources of stimulation: monitors and whiteboards on the walls, students talking during activities, and open laptops that are easily visible. Any one of these distractions could draw students away from the learning activity at hand, and together they can create more distraction than could be found in a typical traditional college classroom. The potential for distraction is compounded by a lack of a central spatial focal point: Students cannot rely on having a single spot in the room—such as "the front of the room"—on which to focus and tune out competing visual and auditory information around them.

As we have seen, many creative activities in ALCs rely heavily on oral communication, and this expectation can create another challenge for a student who has been used to listening passively to and processing a lecture. What can seem like simple communication to some students—talking to the person seated next to them, responding quickly to a question posed by the instructor, asking a question or presenting information to the entire room—can be daunting for others. Similarly, we may design activities or classroom routines that take advantage of the open space in an ALC and that allow students to move around the room during class sessions, although we might find that physical movement during class may be difficult for some students with mobility impairments.

Different students may be negatively impacted by one or more of these challenges. In particular, the multiple distractions and lack of a central focal point may be especially challenging for some students with learning disabilities, attention deficit/hyperactivity disorder (ADHD), students on the autism spectrum, as well as students with certain anxiety disorders (VanBergeijk, Klin, & Volkmar, 2008; Wolf, 2001). Lack of a central focal point can be difficult to negotiate for students with visual or hearing impairments, especially for students who may use an interpreter. Noise distractions can be challenging for students with hearing impairments or for nonnative English speakers. Reliance on verbal communication may be especially challenging for some nonnative English speakers (Andrade, 2006) and students on the autism spectrum (VanBergeijk et al., 2008). Finally, activities that require movement throughout the room can challenge students with mobility or visual impairments. Some of the very features that we prize highly about these rooms or that are by-products of other positive elements can create formidable barriers for some students. We need to be aware of this possibility as we design activities for and conduct class in an ALC.

For each of these challenges we will suggest practical, proactive steps you can take to help reduce the barriers to learning for certain student populations. The strategies we suggest are modeled upon Universal Design for Learning (UDL) principles that ask instructors to consider the needs of all potential students when designing learning environments and proactively create "instruction that is responsive to diversity in learning" (Scott, McGuire, & Shaw, 2003, p. 372). These principles provide guidelines for creating inclusive classrooms for the benefit of all students (Scott et al., 2003). A common example of an application to address the UDL goal that instruction is accessible to people with diverse abilities in the classroom is the addition of closed captioning to videos. This action makes it possible for students who are deaf or hearing impaired to follow the content of a video. Relevant to teaching in the ALCs, closed captioning also benefits nonnative English-speaking students. In fact, many students without health or language barriers express appreciation for the addition of subtitles to videos. Implementing UDL principles can result in elimination of the vast majority of individual accommodations needed.

All of our suggestions in this chapter are designed to address the various challenges of the space while still maintaining academic rigor. Furthermore, all of our suggestions assume that no changes need to be made to course goals, objectives, and standards. The focus here will be to enact reasonable and flexible accommodations that will increase the potential for all students who attend a class in an ALC to succeed. See Table 8.1 for a list that summarizes the suggestions we offer in this chapter. Moreover, many institutions have disability resource offices and offices to support international and non-native English-speaking students. Our suggestions are intended to complement,

TABLE 8.1

Summary of Suggestions to Support All Students in an ALC

REDUCE UNNECESSARY VISUAL DISTRACTIONS
• Have students blank their projection screen when it is not needed. • Develop a personal electronic device usage policy, perhaps collaboratively. • Acknowledge that in the ALC students may have their backs to the instructor at some times. • Stand by the main projection screen when speaking for longer periods. • Verbally telegraph your next movements to students. • Provide students with physical barriers to set among themselves for more private test-taking, or schedule exams in a different space.
REDUCE UNNECESSARY AUDITORY DISTRACTIONS
• Provide closed captioning for videos. • Incorporate periods of quiet time to allow students to reflect, think, or write. • Have a cue or signal to indicate that students should stop talking and direct their attention to you. • Encourage students to use the table microphone when speaking. • Use the microphone when you speak. • Supplement oral information with screen-reader-accessible written details. • Encourage students to pair their team discussions with note-taking.
SUPPORT VERBAL COMMUNICATION IN CLASS
• Be clear with your students on the first day of class that your course will require verbal interaction. • Acknowledge that some students may feel uncomfortable speaking in front of the class. • Provide time for students to think before asking for a response. • Hold off calling on the first student with his or her hand raised. • After calling on a student, give him or her time to discuss the question with teammates. • Assign roles to teams and provide guidelines for the roles. • Move some discussion topics online. • Provide clear guidelines for what is expected when speaking in class.
MINIMIZE UNNECESSARY MOVEMENT
• Have students display posters and other presentations electronically on the individual table screens. • Use an application like VoiceThread for providing oral comments on posters or other presentations.

(Continues)

Table 8.1 *(Continued)*

SUPPORT STUDENTS IN INFORMATION ORGANIZATION
• Provide a copy of your slides and notes. • Provide an organizing framework. • Break larger projects into smaller tasks that receive feedback. • Ask students to identify areas of confusion.

not supplant the input of those staff. We recommend you contact them with any questions or concerns you have.

Articulating Expectations on the First Day of Class

It is important to tell students on the first day of class what they will need to do to succeed in your course. Include your expectations for verbal communication, working in teams, and movement in the room. Providing this information at the start of the term helps nonnative English speakers and students with disabilities plan how they will meet the course requirements, seek additional assistance, or request disability accommodations if needed. This is also a time students may decide to drop the course and add a different one.

During this first class session, ask your students to submit any disability accommodation requests. (Ideally, disability accommodations will be in place before the first day of class.) Some students may be reluctant to reveal a disability to you for fear that it might be held against them and negatively impact their grade (Alexandrin, Schreiber, & Henry, 2008). You can address this apprehension by stating in your syllabus and in person that you want all students to succeed in your course, and that you will make every reasonable effort to create a positive learning environment for everyone. Inform students that to do so, you need to be aware of anything that might prevent them from learning in your class. The following is an example of a statement concerning access to the course that one ALC instructor tells students on the first day of class:

> I want to say a few words about access. I think that it is very important for all students to have complete access to the course. Sometimes there are aspects of a course that make it difficult for some students to fully participate. For example, students with disabilities may need accommodations so that they will have the same level of access to the course as other students. I encourage you, if you have a disability that requires such an

accommodation, to approach me after class, visit office hours, or contact me immediately so that together we can make such arrangements. Also, if you have not visited Disability Services to receive a letter certifying and explaining your disability, you should do so as soon as possible. You will find them very helpful. If you have never been diagnosed with a learning disability, but have reason to believe that you have one, I encourage you to visit Disability Services to explore this option and receive the help you need and deserve to have full access to your college education. Every student has a right to full educational access and I want to do whatever is necessary to make certain that you gain such access in this course. Please read the syllabus statement for further information, including the campus address of Disability Services. (Pedalty, 2008, p. 80).

Some instructors collect contact information from students in a first-day-of-class survey sheet. You could include a question such as, "Is there anything I need to know about you to help you succeed in this course?" Assure students that their responses will be kept confidential.

Minimizing Unnecessary Classroom Distractions

The ALC has many potential distractions that compete for student attention. These include visual and auditory distractions that may interfere with some students' concentration or make it difficult to translate text and listen to and understand speech. In this section, we identify some of those distractions and suggest ways to minimize or mitigate them.

Visual Distractions

One obvious visual distraction is the presence of multiple projection screens throughout the room. Most ALCs have a main projection screen to which students are able to direct their attention; however, the individual table screens are still visible on the periphery to students or can even be within their direct line of sight. When individual table screens are projecting different content, the level of distraction is even greater. It's quite natural for students to survey the room to see what others are up to; though beneficial, this scan of the room can also draw students away from what they are assigned to be doing at the moment.

Off-task use of laptops during classes (e.g., checking e-mail or social media) presents yet more visual distraction. Evidence shows that laptop multitasking can hinder the performance of the laptop user and also affect the performance of students within view of the multitasker's computer screen (Junco, 2012; Sana, Weston, & Cepeda, 2013). This visual distraction is more common in the ALC due to the room's open configuration, which grants most students direct views of their neighbors' laptop screens.

Another common complaint from students in the ALC is that there is no single focal point or "front" of the classroom. One student stated, "I don't like having to turn around every two minutes to see who is speaking or see a screen. There needs to be a central point of focus." A central point of focus, however, is a challenge to establish in an ALC. Because of the room layout, at any given time during a class session students may have their backs to the projection screen, the whiteboard, their tablemates, or the instructor. The latter may cause additional concerns for some students who, for cultural or other reasons, feel it is rude not to face the instructor at all times. This lack of focal point can also contribute to increased levels of visual distraction that students experience as they search to find the speaker or locate a visual aid.

Visual distractions can be particularly challenging for students with learning disabilities, ADHD, or certain anxiety disorders, or who are on the autism spectrum (VanBergeijk et al., 2008; Wolf, 2001). Students with hearing impairments who need to read lips may be affected by a lack of direct line of sight to the instructor's face. Students with vision impairments may find it difficult to read a board or the main projection screen if they do not have a direct line of sight to it.

Minimizing visual distractions
One principle of UDL is that instructors deliver content so that necessary information is communicated effectively, regardless of the student's sensory abilities (Scott et al., 2003). This presentation of content includes ensuring text is readable and accessible and distractions are minimized whenever possible to aid student focus.

A strategy for supporting students distracted by the multiple projection screens is to make sure that those screens are blank when visual information is not needed. An instructor can elicit the help of the entire class by instituting a policy that requires student teams to turn off their table's projection screen when they are not using it. As with many new policies in ALCs, instructor reminders may have to be used early in the semester to help students grow accustomed to the rule.

To discourage off-task laptop use and the visual distraction this practice engenders, the instructor can facilitate a discussion with students early in the semester about the consequences of laptop use in the classroom. The instructor can mention that laptop multitasking impairs the learning not only of the multitasker but also of students with sight lines to their multitasking classmates' screens. In other words, students' decisions to mind their computers at the wrong time have consequences for those around them. The instructor can briefly summarize the research literature related to multitasking distraction (Junco, 2012; Sana et al., 2013) to help make the point. This research summary can lead to a full-class discussion in which students are tasked with designing a laptop (and electronic device) usage policy for the classroom (Sana et al., 2013). Although it may take more time early in the course, eliciting student input for the policy may lead to better student compliance.

General laptop policies instructors have invoked are (a) students are allowed to use their laptops throughout the class, but the content must be related to the current course activity, and (b) students are asked to close their laptops for brief or extended periods of time during a class session to reduce distractions, aid individual reflection activities, or direct attention to a new task. The following is an example of a specific laptop policy included in an instructor's syllabus:

> The ALC is designed for the use of electronic devices to support your learning, and I encourage you to bring your laptops, tablets, or smart phones with you to class as they may be useful resources for completing in-class assignments. Keep in mind, however, that using personal electronic devices in the classroom can also be a distraction, not only for you but also for other students who can see your screen. Because of the arrangement of the space, some students will have an unobstructed view of your computer screen, which may be difficult to ignore. Please respect your classmates and me by not using your devices for non-class related tasks such as checking your Facebook page or catching up on your e-mail, and minimize laptop use during periods of lecture and whole-class discussions. For class activities that I deem may need your undivided attention, I may ask you to close your laptops for brief periods of time.

As you develop your policy for students' use of electronic devices, be aware that some nonnative English speakers may use their smart devices to look up definitions or background information related to something being discussed. While this action is related to the course's content, it can also be temporarily distracting to the student and those around her. Instructors may want to address this use of smartphones in their discussion by encouraging students not to rely too heavily on their technology, as they may lose the big picture while searching for a detail. As a final note, the open arrangement of the ALC allows easy and respectful enforcement of a laptop policy. An instructor can simply move toward and stand near a multitasking student; this action is often enough to discourage the distracting practice.

One approach that we do not recommend is to ban laptop use in the classroom. This policy would negate an important advantage of ALCs, namely access to smart devices that allow students to quickly identify electronic and

Internet resources and work with them collaboratively. Furthermore, some students need laptops and specialized software for note-taking due to visual and physical impairments.

To support students who find the lack of a central focal point visually distracting, an instructor has several options. She can begin early in the semester by acknowledging that the physical nature of the classroom may result in students having their back to her at some points during the class session, and that, while seeming odd at first, this position is nonetheless perfectly acceptable. She can take a further step and enumerate the ways that she will help reduce the time any single student faces her back by speaking from different parts of the room at different times and by visiting each table to answer any student's questions. Students with hearing impairments can be seated facing the center of the room to more easily see the instructor and sign language interpreters, if they are present. Nevertheless, there may still be challenges from the instructor who moves about the room and the multiple screens and monitors viewable from all directions.

Students with visual impairments can be seated with unobstructed views of the main projection screen and the table screen. The instructor can write or draw using a document camera projected to the room screens rather than write on the whiteboard, so that students can reliably locate and read the instructor's writing. Additionally, the instructor can direct student attention throughout a class session. When delivering information to complement slides on the main projection screen for extended periods of time, for example, she can stand in front of the screen when speaking. In this way, students can simultaneously see the screen and instructor, reducing the need to continually shift their heads back and forth between the two. A remote slide advancer can facilitate this arrangement by untethering the instructor from a central podium.

While moving about in a particularly large ALC, the instructor can verbally telegraph her next movements to focus student attention. She can tell students, "I am moving to the main projection screen where I will talk about XYZ for a few minutes." Or, "For the next 15 minutes I will be walking around the room and checking in with individual tables. Raise your hand if you have specific questions."

Finally, visual distractions can also add more stress to an already stressful activity: test-taking. Taking tests in an ALC presents the visual distraction of all of the technology equipment as well as the added distraction of sitting across from other students at the tables. This arrangement may be difficult for students on the autism spectrum (VanBergeijk et al., 2008). Some approaches to mitigate this difficulty are to provide students with physical barriers for test-taking. Alternatively, exams could be scheduled in proctored testing rooms in which student desks face the front of the room, if available, and individual students may be accommodated by taking tests in a more private space away from their classmates. Often, disability resource offices have testing centers for such purposes. Providing extra time for taking the exam is another common accommodation for students who may have difficulty taking exams in the ALC.

As mentioned previously, providing deliberate support for students distracted in an ALC by following UDL principles can result in a decreased need for formal accommodations. One instructor commented:

> I expected the ALC environment to be the exact opposite of what students with distraction-free settings could handle, but it wasn't that way at all. Usually after a few classes into the semester, they report that they don't feel like they need as many accommodations. After five or six semesters [of teaching] there has never been a student who has [chosen to take] the test in a different setting.

We do not suggest, however, that instructors can anticipate and prepare for every scenario involving a student with a disability. The most accessible classrooms may still need to be modified for some students' learning needs.

Auditory Distractions

Group work typically increases student conversations, a common noise distraction in the ALC that intensifies ambient noise levels and that can interfere with students' ability to hear or translate audio media, as well as student and instructor speech. Of course, increased noise levels can occur in a traditional classroom; in an ALC, however, increased noise levels are layered on top of the multiple visual distractions not present in a traditional room. Auditory distractions may be particularly challenging for students with hearing impairments who have difficulty hearing the speaker's voice. Auditory distractions can also be challenging for students on the autism spectrum due to the difficulties some students may have in filtering out certain kinds of noises (VanBergeijk et al., 2008). Nonnative English speakers can also be negatively affected by auditory distractions when listening to and translating English because translation requires focused concentration on a single voice.

Minimizing auditory distractions

As we mentioned previously, to follow UDL principles instructors need to communicate information effectively, regardless of the ambient conditions of the student's sensory abilities (Scott et al., 2003). This clear communication relies, in part, on minimizing distractions whenever possible.

As mentioned in the introduction to this chapter, providing closed captioning for videos benefits students with hearing impairments, nonnative English speakers, and most likely everyone in the classroom. An ALC instructor who added closed captioning to her videos for a hearing-impaired student found the addition of the written script useful to help understand quiet, accented, or quickly spoken English in videos. As a consequence, she now provides closed captioning for videos shown in all of her classes. Many disability resource offices can assist with this support. Alternatively, uploading text to YouTube is easy, fast, and fairly accurate unless it involves technical jargon or foreign language. (Instructors or teaching assistants can correct typos and other inaccuracies generated in the automated transcriptions.)

To mitigate noise and other distractions, vary your instructional methods throughout the class period (Scott et al., 2003). For instance, many ALC instructors who rely heavily on small-group discussion as an approach to student learning are also mindful to include whole-class discussions in which all students are silent except the one who is speaking. To support students with mild hearing impairments during whole-class discussions, encourage speakers to use their table microphones. In fact, many instructors in large ALCs make microphone use a classroom policy. To avoid the "disembodied voice effect" (hearing a voice through the classroom speakers but not being able to locate the source of the voice), students can be instructed to either state their name and table number or wave their hand momentarily when beginning to speak. This display may seem awkward at the start, but it can be quite helpful to listeners in the room and can quickly become routine.

Including periods of silent reflection to provide relief from noise distractions is a beneficial pedagogical strategy. Some instructors call for periods of quiet time to allow all students to reflect, think, or write. This reflection could be as simple as providing a two-minute respite between activities to allow students to refocus and mentally consolidate what they have just learned. In fact, Fink (2013) encouraged instructors to use in-class reflection in combination with some form of communicating information and providing experiences or activities as a necessary component for active learning.

Getting students' attention during times of noisy group discussions and activities can be difficult. It's useful for the instructor to have a regular cue or signal to indicate that students should stop talking and direct their attention to him. The cue could simply be speaking into the microphone stating that it is time to wrap up discussions. Other cues include sounding a tone or chimes or asking students to raise their hands and stop talking when they see the instructor's hand raised.

The use of clickers (student response systems) is another approach to mitigating noise distractions. A clicker question with a choice of answers is posted on the projection screens for students to read, think about, and select an answer. Another approach some instructors use is to intersperse table group discussions with discussion pairs. The proximity of students' partners makes it easier to hear what they are saying or to ask for clarification for anything they don't understand.

You can also decrease noise distraction effects by supplementing speech with written delivery. Written information could be an outline of the salient points presented in PowerPoint slides projected to all student table screens, or written material might be distributed as a paper handout or as a shared Google doc or projected to individual table screens. Accessible written content allows students who use screen readers to have easy access to the information and may help hearing-impaired students follow the presentation. Some instructors of large classes have a teaching assistant take notes during the class and make them available to all students on the course management system.

Similarly, for small-group discussion when ambient noise can be a distraction, encourage students to pair their discussions with team note-taking of some kind, whether on the whiteboard or on a shared electronic document. The additional visual cue may make it easier for students to attend to the discussion in spite of background noise and also provides additional cues for nonnative English speakers. An added benefit to this approach is that the instructor can quickly view the progress individual teams are (or are not) making. If notes are written on the whiteboard, encourage students to take a picture and share it with the rest of their team after class. The use of a microphone is suggested for the instructor during these potentially noisy events, even if the instructor has a voice loud enough to project to the entire room. A microphone allows a single familiar voice to rise above the din.

Incorporating many of these approaches into a single class session ensures that student learning and understanding will not rely solely on team conversation with its inherent distractions. Furthermore, use of varied pedagogical activities is a sound teaching strategy in its own right (Fink, 2013).

Another distraction to consider can be the by-product of successful teaching: students become friends with their tablemates. Close interaction with the same classmates every day can naturally lead to student teams feeling increasingly comfortable together and developing friendships that may extend outside the classroom. Indeed, it is often touted that one of the benefits of having students work in teams in large classes is that they are more likely to form relationships with their classmates, which helps reduce the feeling of anonymity some students might feel early in the college experience. However, being surrounded by friends during class may tempt or distract students to engage in social conversations not related to the course material. One way to address this challenge is to build team accountability in every class session. To keep conversations focused on the course topic require teams to turn in finished pieces of work at the end of every class session.

Supporting Students Through Other ALC Challenges

In addition to visual and auditory distractions that can hinder student concentration, other classroom challenges can reduce the accessibility of course content for some students. Among them are reliance on verbal communication for activities in an ALC, requirements for movement in the classroom, and presentation of complex course content.

Reliance on Verbal Communication

As described previously, many ALC activities involve verbal communication, such as student discussion with a partner, student team discussion, and students asking questions or presenting to the entire class. Of course, all of these forms of communication could take place in a large traditional classroom, but it is more likely that student discussions will take place regularly in an ALC. Many students enjoy verbal interaction with their classmates and are not daunted by asking a question or presenting information to their instructor and all of their peers; other students, however, find it quite challenging. Students especially intimidated by activities that require verbal communication for learning include some nonnative English speakers (Andrade, 2006), students on the autism spectrum (VanBergeijk et al., 2008), students with ADHD, and students with particular anxiety issues (Wolf, 2001).

Students who are not fluent in English may have difficulty quickly processing what others have said or expressing their thoughts during a fast-paced verbal activity in an ALC (Andrade, 2006). A cultural component can make verbal communication in classroom situations more difficult as well. Kim (2002, 2008) has shown that not all cultures equally value verbalization as a form of demonstrating mastery of the subject. As such, activities that require sharing ideas through speaking (thinking aloud) may put students from some cultures at a disadvantage.

Some students on the autism spectrum experience challenges with verbal communication in different ways. Some of these students may have difficulty communicating appropriately or interacting in socially appropriate ways with team members. This situation may take the form of a student dominating a conversation or speaking too long on an esoteric topic not of interest to other students (VanBergeijk et al., 2008). These behaviors may also be distracting to other members of the team or the entire class.

UDL principles call for equitable and flexible use so that instruction is accessible to people with a wide range of individual abilities (Scott et al., 2003). As we mentioned previously, make it clear to students that participating fully in the course means they will need to speak. Provide them with a brief description of the verbal tasks you will expect from them and how these will contribute to their learning and their grade in the course. You may also want to provide guidelines or a rubric for speaking. These guidelines can encourage students to build on each other's comments and can communicate cultural and classroom norms to help alleviate the pressure that some students feel to speak perfectly. This forthright approach allows students to determine whether they can meet the requirements of the course before there is a penalty for dropping the class.

One way to provide guidelines for verbal communication is for instructors to define and assign team roles, such as facilitator or reporter for all teams. Defined team roles that outline expected behavior—such as, "The team recorder takes notes and reads those notes back to the team at the end of the discussion" or "The facilitator makes sure all students on the team are heard from and no one student dominates the conversation"—can render the boundaries of appropriate behavior explicit to students.

Acknowledge that some students may feel uncomfortable having to speak in class, but encourage them to keep trying to overcome that discomfort because you think it is important for them to master this skill. You can mention that many professions will require them to talk in public and that your class will provide a safe environment in which to practice these skills. This explanation also communicates to students with particular disabilities or nonnative English speakers that they are not alone in their challenges.

A simple suggestion for supporting those who find verbal communication in the ALC challenging is to give students a few moments to think about or write down an answer to a question you've posed prior to opening it up for discussion. This time lets students formulate their ideas and think about what they might say if called upon. This opportunity to reflect before talking can be particularly helpful for some non-native English speakers (Andrade, 2006). Additionally, if the responses are written, students can read from their notes when addressing the entire group, which may lessen their anxiety.

Some instructors hold off calling on a student with her hand raised until several students also raise their hands. Like the approach described previously, this pause in selecting a speaker allows students time to think before answering. Moreover, this tactic prevents the same quick-to-respond students from dominating discussions. Alternatively, an instructor can ask questions to be answered by clickers. This approach replaces the need for a few students to speak in front of everyone with an opportunity for all students to participate nonverbally and to gauge how well their classmates understand the day's content by reading responses to questions displayed on screen by the instructor. To include a lower-risk verbal component to this exercise, the instructor can add reflection time by asking students to formulate and share their response with their neighbor or their team before making it public to the entire class. These moments of exchange and discussion can give students a clearer understanding of the question and the day's content.

Some instructors use a random call technique to elicit student responses. In this approach, the instructor calls on students by using a random number generator or selecting note cards with student names. Often this technique can provoke anxiety in students who find extemporaneous speaking uncomfortable. One instructor supports his students by allowing the randomly selected student to confer with teammates at her table before giving a response. This technique is especially helpful for nonnative English speakers (Andrade, 2006). Randomly calling on students in a supportive environment may actually help students to feel more comfortable volunteering to participate (Dallimore, Hertenstein, & Platt, 2012).

Another possibility is to move some discussion topics online to an asynchronous discussion board on the course management system. This practice allows students to ruminate on and carefully compose their answer before posting or responding to a classmate's post and also benefits students who cannot speak or who speak with difficulty. Another advantage of this practice is that a record of the conversation is maintained for the instructor's and the students' future reference.

Depending on the assignment and learning outcomes for the course, a more extreme measure might be for a student with communication and social interaction challenges to work on a project alone. In fact, some specialists in disability service offices may suggest this strategy as an accommodation. The instructor would then need to decide if and how a team activity can be modified and supported to be completed by a single student.

Requirements for Movement

Some courses in ALCs require students to present their work to the entire class, which may require standing and moving around the room. This action can be challenging for students with mobility impairments. A UDL principle asks that instruction be designed to minimize nonessential physical effort to allow maximum attention to learning (Scott et al., 2003). Physical effort engendered in an ALC could include any activity that requires students to stand and move around the room, as might be required in, for example, a poster presentation session. In typical poster sessions, students stand by their wall-mounted posters to discuss their projects with audiences who move by to see, read, and ask questions about all presentations. To minimize movement challenges in this activity, instructors can ask students to display their posters electronically on the individual table screens and upload them to a course management system for all students to view during class while seated, or after class. Indeed, most posters will be designed in an electronic format before being printed, so to make them available on a screen as well should not impose much burden on the student. Students presenting electronic posters can prepare a written or audio narrative to accompany their presentation. Students with mobility impairments can view these online rather than having to navigate the physical space of the classroom. Written narratives have the added advantage of being accessible via a screen reader, thus benefiting students with visual impairments.

Another possibility for applying UDL principles to this activity is to use electronic commenting tools like VoiceThread so that students can comment on their classmates' posters outside of the classroom. This approach can be helpful for nonnative English speakers, as it provides the opportunity for students to prepare remarks before sharing them and to replay classmates' comments about their poster for review.

Presentation of Complex Course Content

Another UDL principle asks that instruction be designed in a straightforward and predictable manner and without unnecessary complexity (Scott et al., 2003). Disorganized and content-heavy instruction can be difficult for students to comprehend. In this section we describe four options that can help students navigate the complex material associated with a college course in an ALC: Provide students with a copy of your slides and written notes, give students an organizational framework, break larger projects into smaller tasks that receive feedback, and ask students to identify areas of confusion.

Provide a copy of your slides and written notes to students either before class as preparatory material, during class as note-taking material, or after class for review purposes. Providing your slides in a reader-accessible PDF format allows students with vision impairments to use screen readers to access the information. Having slides available before class can also allow sign language interpreters, if needed for a hearing-impaired student, to plan and prepare before class. Some instructors choose to provide only a portion of their slides during class to encourage students to fill in missing material, thus promoting active note-taking and a greater depth of processing the material during class (Kiewra, 1985). Complete copies of the slides can be provided after class. Making these notes available for all students is appreciated by many and helps reduce the stigma that a student with a disability may feel if singled out.

Providing an introductory outline for your class session is a simple way to help students organize their thoughts about that day's concepts and notes. You can refer to your outline as you move from one topic to the next during the class session. Moreover, providing verbal cues to your students ("The first point we will cover is . . ."; "The second point we will cover is . . .") when presenting new material may result in increased learning (Titsworth & Kiewra, 2004).

Helping students organize their time can also contribute to their understanding of complex course content. Some students on the autism spectrum or with ADHD may have difficulty organizing their time for large assignments and need explicit instructions as to when to begin research for a project or writing a draft (VanBergeijk et al., 2008; Wolf, 2001). A large assignment can be divided into smaller tasks with separate due dates; this arrangement will encourage students to work steadily on it. Receiving feedback from the instructor or peers will provide students with an indication of the quality of their work. See Tables 5.2 and 5.3 for examples of how larger projects are broken down into smaller elements.

Finally, to determine whether all students find the class material and activities clear, understandable, and accessible, you can finish each class session by asking students for the muddiest point: the concept from the class that they find most confusing. This polling can be done electronically using a shared Google doc that students can access through their laptops or simply by asking students to write on note cards that the instructor will collect. Some instructors include a list of the main outcomes of the class session to remind students of topics covered. Students can circle one or more outcomes that they found confusing. This activity could also be completed online after class or with clickers. Collect and analyze this information and revisit material students found confusing, either in the next class period or online before the next class.

Identify Reasonable Alternative Assignments

Sometimes a student will come to your ALC with a disability accommodation letter that outlines suggestions not described in this chapter. Occasionally, these accommodations preclude existing activities and assignments in a course. In many cases, it is possible to adapt an activity slightly to allow access for a student with a disability without affecting the underlying learning outcome and level of performance expectation. The following are a few questions to ask yourself if you encounter this situation: Is this activity necessary to fulfill the learning outcomes of my class? If so, can another activity substitute for this one (Sukhai, Mohler, & Smith, 2014)? For instance, students may be allowed to choose between giving an oral presentation or writing a report for a course assignment.

Having clearly defined learning outcomes for your course will help you identify alternative activities. There have also been other occasions in which the requested accommodation made the instructor reconsider his priorities. For instance, an instructor was asked to extend the time allowed for taking an exam for a student with a disability. He realized that it wasn't essential that students know material quickly; rather, they just needed to demonstrate mastery of the material. As a result, he extended the exam time for all students in subsequent terms.

Conclusion

With increased enrollment of students with disabilities and nonnative English speakers (Andrade, 2006; *The Chronicle of Higher Education*, 2015; Institute of International Education, 2014; National Center for Education Statistics, 2013; Ruiz, 2014), colleges and universities must respond by making learning accessible to a greater diversity of students. The move to an ALC may make some of your innovative course material and activities unexpectedly difficult for some students. Keeping UDL principles in mind when designing your class, you can use the suggestions in this chapter to benefit all students in your class, not just the students most negatively impacted by a challenge. The National Center on Universal Design for Learning (www .udlcenter.org) contains general UDL information, and WebAIM contains information related specifically to web accessibility (www.webaim.org).

To adapt these suggestions to your own courses and students, you should have a clear understanding of your course goals. Ultimately those goals will help determine how you can best support your students. We also want to reiterate the suggestion to use institutional support services for students with disabilities and for international and nonnative English speakers. We strongly recommend that you contact these professionals for support with your specific course and for your specific students, and alert your students to the services offered by these offices.

9

SUPPORTING FACULTY

If you don't prepare, and simply teach your class in the ALC as you would in a lecture hall, your teaching will eventually evolve, but through a painful process of discovery through trial and error rather than the more gratifying one of thoughtfully considered adoption of best practices.

—David Matthes, College of Biological Sciences, University of Minnesota

One of the greatest resources instructors have is each other, and bringing them together to exchange ideas, resolve problems, and inspire one another as they figure out how to teach in a new environment wisely takes advantage of fellow travelers with years of classroom experience. Discovering how to efficiently use the Active Learning Classroom (ALC) doesn't have to be a painful solo journey; indeed, ALCs can be a lever to gather instructors and to transform teaching, to make what happens in the classroom meaningful and memorable for students. This discovery can be made easier with the support of faculty developers and those with whom they work.[1] Faculty development professionals, too, have rich experiences, particularly in areas that could be helpful to instructors teaching in the ALCs. These colleagues can create both formal and informal events directly related to instructors' thoughtful adoption of best ALC teaching practices.

Researchers have explored the wide range and efficacy of faculty development initiatives to assess what has worked and to project the future direction that the field should take. Austin and Sorcinelli (2013) argued that supporting active learning is a core function for many of these initiatives and that "expanding such programs will continue to be a priority topic" (p. 89). Supporting active learning in ALCs is also a key recommendation that has emerged from research on the effects of the space on student achievement (e.g., Brooks & Solheim, 2014; Van Horne et al., 2014). For example, Van Horne and colleagues (2014) concluded that a research-based faculty development program is essential to producing strong student outcomes in

ALCs at the University of Iowa. Although some institutions may choose to take a less directed approach, our experience has been that many instructors welcome a professional venue outside of their classrooms to ask questions and test out ideas.

This chapter focuses on instructional and faculty development programming that can support instructors who will teach in ALCs. The intended audience for this chapter is faculty consultants and developers (henceforth consultants), although instructors might also find this chapter useful. We examine four traditional types of programs that vary in the intensity of resources upon which they draw and the depth of their engagement: workshops, training sessions, institutes, and learning communities. We also discuss additional ways to offer ongoing support through online resources and professional development funding. The strategies we present are meant as a starting point for what you might plan at your own institution and can be easily modified to fit an institution's unique character. Instructors and consultants likely will find Appendices 9.1 and 9.2, which catalog faculty development sessions related to teaching in ALCs, especially valuable. We mention each appendix in its relevant section in this chapter.

Workshops

Many professionals in teaching centers that support instructors teaching in ALCs already know how to design effective workshops, from informal experiences like brown-bag talks or reading circles to more tightly structured events focused on specific outcomes. Both informal and formal approaches have benefits and can be organized to complement each other to draw different audiences and appeal to the various ways in which instructors want to work.

Informal Events

The purpose of informal events (e.g., brown-bag gatherings) is to bring participants together to discuss subjects related to teaching or learning in ALCs. The facilitators of the sessions should feature a few overarching talking points as a means to structure the session and foster a conversational tone for the meeting. For example, consultants at the University of Massachusetts–Amherst hosted a series of "Lunch and Learn" workshops to promote conversations about active learning and ALCs for instructors. Providing lunch can boost attendance, and inviting a faculty member to co-lead a conversation can make the experience authentic for instructors, particularly if the gathering can be held in an ALC. Another loosely structured event is the "show and tell," in which instructors discuss their approach, process, and lessons learned from a particular aspect of their teaching, such as a classroom activity or an approach to student learning assessment. Consultants should consider inviting faculty from different disciplines so participants can hear how the ALC has affected how instructors approach teaching in their fields. How a political scientist uses the room, for example, may be quite different from how a geologist teaches in one.

These types of informal events can be low-risk ways for faculty to eventually explore more formal types of instructional development opportunities. Particularly if they are held in actual ALCs, the nature of the discussion and the room itself can help participants envision the ALC's possibilities and perhaps inspire them to attend more structured events.

Formal Workshops

Highly structured workshops focus on a particular issue or set of skills related to teaching in ALCs and have specific objectives for participants to achieve. In Appendix 9.1, we list a series of topics and descriptions for potential workshops, including key questions and activities for participants. As we mentioned in the introduction to this chapter, this list is meant as a starting point as you consider what you want to provide. Some of these workshops lend themselves to being offered as a series, while other topics can naturally be combined or expanded. For example, facilitators might want to combine a session on theoretical underpinnings and a session on research on ALCs into one event while expanding the sessions on course design or workshops related to forming, managing, and evaluating groups. Similarly, facilitators might choose to forgo microteaching sessions if participants haven't been formally prepared with a previous series of workshops. At both informal and formal events, the end of the session is a prime moment to gauge interest in developing some form of learning community. Asking the audience to prioritize a list of topics for future events will more likely generate enthusiasm and address their most pressing concerns.

Training Sessions

Training sessions typically address the use of the room's technology, such as how to use the instructor console, but they may also attend to other features of the space, such as managing the acoustics and lighting and instructor movement within the learning space. Although it may seem a simple thing, knowing how to use the basic technology in the room can increase an instructor's confidence and reduce stress.

Technology Training

As with many classrooms, ALCs offer ways to project different devices (e.g., laptop, tablet, Blu-ray, DVD, document camera), but one feature that separates ALCs from traditional spaces is a touch-screen control panel that allows instructors to orchestrate how information is displayed on the many screens in the room. The options available may overwhelm some instructors, but training sessions that increase instructors' proficiency with technology help them gain confidence and concentrate on teaching concepts or delivering student feedback (Van Horne et al., 2014). Technological prowess is a significant factor linked to student acceptance of the rooms, because survey data have indicated that many students perceive that their instructors are unskilled in implementing technology in ALCs (e.g., Dahlstrom & Bichsel, 2014; Walker, Brooks, & Baepler, 2011).

Technology Simulations

Florman (2014) noted that technology simulations specific to everyday situations that instructors are likely to encounter when teaching in an ALC might be useful in helping them practice using the rooms' technology. Simulations should focus on eventualities that instructors might simply have overlooked. The following are two sample scenarios to consider adapting for a simulation exercise:

- You plan to open the class with a YouTube video of a movie trailer. You then plan to play the first 10 minutes of the movie on the Blu-ray player. Following the 10-minute film clip, student groups will present the notes they took while watching the clip. The groups need to display their notes on the monitors around the room. Please conduct these tasks using the room's technology and instructor console. Be sure to attend to the audio, video, and lighting issues that may arise in this situation.
- You want to annotate a diagram to identify elements of a human cell. Then you want students to identify parts of an orangutan's cell on printed handouts distributed during class. You will select at random two members of the class to explain their answers. You plan to project these two students' handouts using the room's document camera. Please locate the annotation tool on the instructor's console and identify a way to project the annotation to all screens. Next, power on the document camera and determine how to project it to the monitors around the room.

We believe it is useful for instructors to experience the room from the student's perspective as well. Having instructors run through a series of activities they expect their students to do during class (e.g., project from a laptop, use table microphones) will inform instructors on the student experience—what access to controls they do and do not have, for instance—and how to troubleshoot some common issues students face while working in the ALC.

Technology Documentation

Consultants should provide documentation guides for the technologies that will be used in ALCs. The University of Iowa has a website that contains a "quick start" checklist and videos that show some key room features and technology in its ALCs (http://tile.uiowa.edu/technology). The availability of a documentation guide and a list of contacts if an issue arises in the space are essential to not only help prospective ALC instructors become familiar with the room's technology but also reference should technology malfunction.

Movement Training

ALCs are built to encourage instructor movement across the learning space, and many instructors are unaccustomed to the opportunities that ALCs provide in this realm. Several ALC instructors stated that moving in the space is an adjustment, but simply visiting the space and walking around the room before the first day of class can be useful in planning how to negotiate that space while teaching in it during the term.

One technique is simply to invite instructors to move about the space. After a few minutes, consultants should direct the participants to make a list, ideally on the whiteboards, about the details they notice in the space. Some will point to the tables, others the whiteboards. Some will notice the sound treatments and microphones. To move in the room and observe its features is a low-barrier way for instructors to experience the space and begin to learn how to best move in the ALC.

David McGraw, senior lecturer in Theatre and Performance Arts at the University of Iowa, conducts workshop sessions about movement and performance strategies in Iowa's ALCs. McGraw has instructors try a "counter cross" movement technique: After a student raises a hand to speak, the instructor should be positioned opposite the student while maintaining a moderate distance from the student. The moderate distance between the student and instructor encourages the student to speak louder so peers beyond those seated nearby can hear what is being said. The moderate distance of the instructor's position also gives other students in the room the chance to see the instructor's nonverbal reactions (e.g., facial expressions) to the question. The counter cross is effective in smaller spaces or when microphones are not in use. In larger spaces or when microphones are in use, such positioning will allow other students to direct their attention to the general area where the interaction occurs.

Another technique is to "move on the beat." McGraw suggests that instructors move when they change topics or concepts. He likens it to a "paragraph break": A new idea calls for the instructor to claim a new position in the space. Using this technique promotes movement around the learning space and helps to untether the instructor from the main console or station.

Acoustics and Lighting Training

Many ALCs feature acoustic and lighting features not common to more traditional spaces. Acoustic features should include sound treatments to help absorb the noise when activity and noise levels get high while students are working together. In some cases, ALCs are rooms that have been retrofitted and will have sound treatments that differ from those in rooms built from scratch. Pilot spaces at the University of Minnesota had load-bearing columns in the middle of the room, so speaking in these rooms required instructors to change their delivery and wear a microphone to ensure students could hear them during class. We suggest that instructors visit the space before teaching in it to see how the sound "moves" around the room when one is speaking. This testing is most easily done with at least one other person—perhaps a faculty development consultant or teaching assistant—for a more authentic experience of hearing a speaker from various points in the room. This visit is also an opportunity for consultants to invite instructors to select a consistent way to call the classroom back together from activities. You might try using a bell or chime to bring a large, loud group back together in a noisy learning space. A colorful prompt that suddenly appears on the monitors can also direct students to change their focus to you.

Lighting features may include various dimming settings. These settings can often be controlled from the instructor panel as well as the wall. It is useful for instructors to familiarize themselves with these controls. For example, lighting can be one low-impact way to regain the collective attention of the class during activities. McGraw begins class with lights at a lower setting and then increases the lights' brightness later in the class period, typically around the 25- to 30-minute mark. He says it is akin to "opening the blinds" in traditional spaces. The increased light, he believes, tends to bring up the energy level.

Open House Events

Other informal training offerings include an "open house" approach. This approach is very loosely structured and designed to allow instructors to become familiar with the ALC and its technology. Typically, such offerings are staffed by instructional support staff who keep an ALC open for a set period of time when prospective instructors can drop in to check out the room, have hands-on time with the technology, and ask any questions about the space or how to teach in it.

At Auburn University, consultants host Active Learning Happy Hours on the third Thursday of every month at The Hotel at Auburn University and Dixon Conference Center (which houses the restaurant closest to campus). Faculty who teach in the ALC spaces at Auburn prepare with a short reading or video (available on the Biggio Center for the Enhancement of Teaching and Learning website), and they gather to discuss the topic with consultants. According to Diane Boyd, who directs the Biggio Center at Auburn, typically these conversations quickly expand to a discussion of teaching successes and challenges in the rooms.

Institutes

Institutes are intensive immersions into an ALC that give instructors practical exposure to the rooms and the theories that support their use. Participants dedicate time to the development of their ALC courses and have opportunities to receive feedback from their peers who are also developing courses for ALCs. In designing and facilitating an institute, consultants should be thoughtful about the program's goals and what is expected of each participant. For example, should participants leave with a full course outline, completed lessons, detailed assessments, group learning strategies, or developing activities and assignments, or even all of these examples? Determining the goals of the institute will give the facilitator(s) a good idea of how to structure it and which topics to feature. An institute that requires drafts of completed lessons, for instance, might suggest a schedule that includes time for peer review; an institute that focuses on performative issues in the space might offer sessions for teaching practice.

Appendix 9.2 outlines a sample agenda for an ALC institute. Again, the topics, segment length, and participant outcomes will vary according to your goals, situational factors, and resources. If a building or an ALC space will be completed within a year, it seems reasonable to hold a series of institutes over that academic year to accelerate development efforts for faculty who will soon teach in that space. If ALCs are already established on campus, consultants should consider hosting annual institutes, perhaps during summer or over winter break, and invite experienced ALC instructors to participate in the programming. The sample agenda also includes time for microteaching sessions as the closing activity for the institute. Microteaching allows for real-world teaching and experience in the space and typically allows for valuable peer feedback.

As with all intensive instructional development interventions, it is important to consider the overwhelming amount of information that participants will receive in such programs. We recommend thinking carefully about the format, structure, and duration of ALC institutes to reduce the cognitive load and possible confusion. Formats for institutes include half day, daylong, and multiday arrangements. Regardless of format, institutes should have ample time for participants to begin working on their materials for teaching in ALCs. At Auburn, consultants build into the program a day between sessions to allow participants to reflect and recharge. Additionally, facilitators should consider organizing time for participants to exchange ideas with colleagues also participating in the institute. In essence, facilitators will have to guard against overwhelming the participants with information while permitting time to process and reflect on the information and to build skills and comfort with teaching in an ALC.

Learning Communities

Learning communities allow members to meet, discuss, and address a common topic more frequently than workshops or institutes. The literature on learning communities has suggested that having the support of peers through a community gives participants opportunities to bond around areas of common interest (Cox, 2004). More intensive than workshops and institutes, learning communities are designed for groups of instructors to address issues related to teaching and learning in an organized manner over a prolonged period of time, such as the academic year. Instructional support offices can open ALC learning communities to the entire campus or facilitate them for a specific department or discipline.

Consultants in faculty development offices should endeavor to create ALC learning communities as "safe spaces" for instructors to address failures, communicate successes, discuss challenges, express frustrations, and exchange ideas with peers in an open manner. Because many participants are often at the same stage in familiarity and experience with ALCs, they may encounter obstacles at similar junctures in the academic term. For example, instructors may discuss group formation experiences near the beginning of the term when groups are assembled and then follow up on the topic a few weeks later to see how groups are performing. If the community includes participants with varying levels of experience, however, then many ALC instructors find the first few weeks of the term is a good time to check in with their peers to discuss reoccurring issues (e.g., dysfunctional groups) and generate ideas for future development.

During conversations with a learning community at the University of Iowa, a professor of Spanish and Portuguese said that the learning community "helped me a lot to see what other people are doing. . . . We would say, 'Gee, I'm having this problem, what did you do?' It was about sharing experiences and seeing what other instructors did." Even seasoned ALC instructors benefit from a sense of community. An experienced biochemistry and molecular biology professor said,

> Get a core together and just meet on a fairly regular basis. Talk about successes and talk about problems because that is the way to learn about new stuff. The more you learn about it, the more you're going to find something good to do [in class].

In essence, learning communities provide instructors a format to exchange ideas and share lessons learned and strategies for success. Consultants might consider separate tracks for new instructors and for experienced instructors, although combining participants with varying ALC experience is certainly possible.[2] Boyd stated, "The energy of the novice helps the expert maintain vitality over time as well."

As many consultants know, the success of a learning community depends on multiple factors, such as structure, support, community, accountability, and observable products (Cox, 2004). We urge consultants to keep these matters in mind as they build communities around ways to teach in ALCs.

Ongoing Support

Supporting ALCs is an ongoing effort. Typically, many offices share the responsibility of consulting with instructors who teach in the space, maintaining the hardware/software, scheduling classrooms, and training instructors. Beyond programming, instructional support units can develop awareness campaigns, design websites and other online resources (e.g., guides, how-to references), provide professional development funds (awards/fellowships/grants) to promote the effective use of ALCs on campus, and work with other units to use the ALC as a platform for collaboration on campus.

Online Resources

Instructional support units should consider constructing a website that provides details related to the ALCs on campus. Consultants at the Center for Teaching and Faculty Development at University of Massachusetts–Amherst redesigned their website to include resources about active learning and programmatic offerings available for instructors' participation over the course of the year. Additionally, such units might provide contact information for support and classroom maintenance. Some institutions identify further reading, research, and instructional strategies that are related to ALCs. Bob Beichner, the founder of the SCALE-UP movement, created a resource that consultants and instructors could find quite helpful: a comprehensive list of institutions with ALCs (http://scaleup.ncsu.edu).

Another useful support resource is to present a frequently asked questions section to provide visitors with some introductory information on topics concerning ALCs. Providing this entry point could help instructors better articulate their needs for future ALC consultations or for participation in more structured programs like workshops and institutes.

Professional Development Funding

Awards, fellowships, and grants provide incentives to instructors considering teaching in ALCs. Modest awards from $500 to $2,500 can provide much-needed funding for faculty to purchase books and technology or attend conferences about ALCs or active learning in general. Larger amounts, upward of $10,000, could buy release time or fund the hiring of graduate teaching assistants for faculty members so they can dedicate more time to the development of an ALC course. Dahlstrom and Brooks (2014) found faculty are motivated to integrate more or better technology, such as ALCs, into their teaching practices or curriculum by the evidence that a particular innovation enhances student learning, but another important factor in motivating faculty to make such changes was having the time to (re)design a course and materials. Institutions could consider offering awards that permit release time to address faculty concerns about the time needed to develop materials for a course to be taught in an ALC.

Some institutions employ a fellowship model in which instructors apply to become an "ALC Fellow." Often competitive, a fellowship provides instructors release time to develop course materials for teaching in an

ALC. Institutions may also engage in a number of professional and instructional development programs to build capacity and community around the topic of ALCs. For example, the University of Massachusetts–Amherst took Michaelsen, Knight, and Fink's (2004) concept of TBL as the basis of a learning community and created two cohorts of TBL Fellows. The TBL Fellows used Michaelsen and colleagues's text as a template to structure their community meetings. For example, early in the term, the group focused on the basics of TBL (e.g., structure, methods) before exploring topics related to groups and group work.

If funding is not available, an institution could incentivize participation in faculty development events by allowing priority access to ALCs for faculty who participate in a series of workshops or institutes. This approach also allows consultants and staff in instructional support offices to know who is teaching in the rooms and to prioritize adequate support for instructors. For example, early in the ALC rollouts at the University of Iowa and the University of Massachusetts–Amherst, only instructors who were part of an intensive ALC development program (i.e., fellowships and institutes) were assigned to teach in the ALCs.[3] Staff in instructional support offices then knew that instructors had received a threshold level of training and were made aware of relevant active learning pedagogical strategies. Consultants can work to extend the relationship with instructors and provide further support through subject-driven workshops (e.g., developing assignments and activities, assessing student learning).

Collaborations

We also suggest that consultants work in partnership with other campus units as they devise a strategy to support instructors in ALCs. Some potential collaborators with expertise to be leveraged in this collaborative work are obvious, such as staff in educational technology units and university libraries, but others might not be as apparent, such as those in construction and design offices, institutional research, and the registrar's office. For example, consultants who work with the design teams can advocate for the instructors or identify faculty members to be a part of the process before an ALC is built. Members from institutional research offices are good partners for topics that range from research design to collecting institutional data on students who take classes in ALCs. Working with the registrar's office can ensure that instructors using active learning pedagogies will have access to teach in the space. Communicating and coordinating among multiple offices is challenging, but the efforts are certainly worthwhile to ensure coverage of the range of issues that relate to ALCs.

Conclusion

Supporting ALCs is both a challenging and rewarding endeavor. We urge institutions' administrators to support ALCs in terms of not only the physical space and the technology but also the instructors teaching in the rooms. Investing in an ALC is an expensive undertaking, and part of that investment should include providing faculty with the developmental opportunities to help them translate their course to take best advantage of the space (Brooks & Solheim, 2014). While it's always possible for instructors to make their own way in the ALC, and many may like that way best, others will appreciate the chance to work together, share their plans, and obviate what might otherwise be, as David Matthes pointed out in the epigraph to this chapter, "a painful process of discovery through trial and error."

Notes

1. We are aware that *faculty developer* encompasses an array of positions (e.g., educational developers, specialists, instructional consultants). We use *consultants* because it generally describes the role of those who provide pedagogical support (Sorcinelli, Austin, Eddy, & Beach, 2006) to instructors. We are mindful, however, that the conversation on what to call professionals who work in the field of *faculty development* remains fluid (Gillespie, Robertson, & Associates, 2010). We use *faculty* to encompass all instructors, from adjuncts to graduate teaching assistants. Much of this programming can be modified to address the needs of these audiences as well.
2. A community of practice (CoP) is another approach consultants may consider to support instructors teaching in an ALC. See Wenger (1999) for more on CoP.
3. These policies have since been modified to address the demand for instructors who want to teach in the ALCs on each campus, respectively.

Appendix 9.1: Sample Workshop Descriptions

Workshop	Description	Key Questions	Sample Activities for Participants	Notes for Facilitators
Theoretical underpinnings of active learning and ALCs	Raises awareness of theories that support active learning and teaching in ALCs	• What theories support active learning? • How do students learn? • How do students develop mastery (Ambrose, Bridges, DiPietro, Lovett, & Norman 2010)? • What are the multimodalities of learning (auditory, kinesthetic, visual, etc.) supported by ALCs?	Prior to the session, participants read whole/ excerpted articles about cognitive development. Participants discuss the pros/cons of active learning compared to traditional instructional methods.	Many who attend such a session will already have been "convinced" about the utility of the approach; however, it is important for participants to have a common context. The session could be combined with the research on ALCs workshop.
Research on active learning and/or ALCs	Covers existing research on the efficacy of active learning and the impact of ALCs	• What does the research say about active learning? • How do we know these classrooms are beneficial to students?	Participants read and discuss whole/excerpted articles about research on ALCs.	A brief history of ALCs might also be included for context (see Chapters 1 and 2).
Common teaching challenges in ALCs	Covers common challenges that arise in ALCs and provides an overview of responses to them	• How do I address student resistance and motivation? • How do I manage the physical layout of the ALC? • How do I ensure students with learning accommodations are able to succeed?	Participants describe teaching challenges they faced or anticipate facing in ALCs, and brainstorm with colleagues ways of addressing those challenges.	See Chapter 4 for more ideas on this topic. Petersen and Gorman (2014) also provided an overview of this topic. Chapter 8, on supporting students, addresses issues concerning students' accommodations.

(Continues)

Appendix 9.1: (Continued)

Workshop	Description	Key Questions	Sample Activities for Participants	Notes for Facilitators
Role of the instructor in ALCs	Covers new role of the instructor in ALCs	• How do I balance lecture and active learning? • What do I, as an instructor, hope to achieve in an ALC? • What are ways to set expectations for students and for myself?	Participants discuss ways to reduce lectures and increase opportunities for hands-on activities. Participants identify ways to communicate expectations to students in an ALC.	This session might also discuss consideration of ceding "control" of learning to students/groups. It is useful to emphasize that many ALC instructors find they are constantly shifting roles (e.g., teacher, guide, coach) in ALCs.
Course (re)design	Covers basics of course design, including aligning learning objectives with affordances of ALCs	• What do I want my students to be able to know or to do or to value as a result of taking the course? • Where do I start? • How do I develop a timeline for redesign?	Participants review an existing course or think about a new course and write or revise new learning objectives for a course. Participants begin by reviewing one week/topic/unit of their course to redesign.	These activities can be a lot to complete in one workshop. Facilitators may choose to have participants work on one week of a course to start the design process. This session is also an opportunity to consider working in groups or to have consultants partner with instructors.

Pedagogical methods and instructional strategies (blended, flipped, hybrid, TBL, PBL, POGIL)	Covers range of pedagogical and instructional approaches used in ALCs	• What instructional methods can I use in ALCs, and how do these approaches differ? • What is blended/flipped/hybrid learning, and does it work in an ALC?	Participants review and reflect on various instructional approaches that promote group work.	Facilitators should have participants review Davidson and Major (2014), who compare common approaches to collaborative, cooperative, and problem-based learning.
Working with groups	Covers ways to implement group work in ALCs	• How can I get my students to work together effectively? • How do I get student buy-in? • How do I form groups? • How many students do I assign per group? • What about couch potatoes, free-riders, and social loafing?	Participants review strategies to address and foster student motivation. Participants discuss group dynamics and dysfunctions.	Topics relevant to this session include helping students from diverse backgrounds succeed. See Chapter 6 in this book for more on groups. Oakley, Felder, Brent, and Elhajj (2004) is a good reading on this topic.

(Continues)

Appendix 9.1: (Continued)

Workshop	Description	Key Questions	Sample Activities for Participants	Notes for Facilitators
Activities and assignments	Covers assignments that work well in ALCs	• What will my students do in class? • What will my students do outside of class? • How do I build activities? • How can students practice mastering concepts?	Participants determine what activities students will perform during and outside of their ALC classes. Participants will scaffold learning activities.	See Chapter 5 in this book for an array of activities instructors use in and out of ALCs. Also see Suskie (2009, p. 158) and Barkley, Cross, and Major (2014) for collaborative activities.
Assessing student learning	Covers techniques to assess student learning in ALCs	• How do I know my students are learning? • What evidence of student learning do I need to collect? • How do I collect evidence of student learning? • How do I reduce the potential for cheating in ALCs?	Participants identify methods and tools to assess student learning. Participants adapt or design tools to assess student learning. Participants review and develop strategies to reduce academic misconduct and cheating.	See Chapters 6 and 7 in this book for an overview of ways to assess groups and student learning in ALCs. Facilitators should determine whether participants adapt or design assessments during the session or prior to the session.

Role of technology	Covers types and usage of technology in ALCs	• There is so much technology: Where do I start? • What technology works well in ALCs?	Participants consider ways to evaluate and integrate technology in ALCs. For example, what are five common technologies, and how are they used in an ALC?	This workshop could be combined with a training session on the basic functions of the room control panel. Facilitators should mention that some technologies are fairly low tech (e.g., whiteboards) but still need to be intentionally incorporated into lesson plans.
Wrapping up and looking ahead	Presents one activity and/or lesson in an ALC	• Am I ready? • What did I miss? • What is next?	Participants conduct a microteaching session and receive peer feedback. Facilitators may also provide feedback.	The session may span two meetings. It is important to allow time for instructors to reflect on the microteaching session. This session works best if included in a workshop series. Microteaching might work well in other programs as well, such as learning communities.

Appendix 9.2: Sample 3-Day Institute Agenda

Day 1: Time	Session Topic and Goals	Sample Activities for Participants	Notes for Facilitators
8:30–9:00	Breakfast	Optional, though a meal sets a good tone for informal interaction.	Some classroom maintenance offices do not permit food in classrooms, so breakfast might need to be in hallway or adjacent space.
9:00–9:10	Introductions and goals for institute: Introduce agenda, set expectations, and introduce participants.	Institute host outlines goals, introduces speaker(s) and overview of the institute. Participants introduce each other. Participants are introduced to the space.	Many instructors will not have been in an ALC before or have spent much time in one, so providing an overview will give participants an idea of what to expect.
9:10–10:00	Icebreakers: Help participants become familiar with each other, the space, and give the sensation of student experience (unsure, new ground) in an ALC.	Simple game/activity (see Beichner et al., 2007, for Ponderables and Tangibles) Discussion about what made this activity a success (table setup, space allows instructor to interact, students interact, objectives on screen, use of whiteboards).	This activity sets the tone for the institute and shows how introductory activities can be tailored to the space. Some might also resist participating, which the facilitator can address.

10:00–10:50	History, definitions, and overview of active learning pedagogy and ALCs: Expose participants to theory and conceptual foundations that support active learning. Secondary goals: To talk about ALCs, their history and emergence; to clarify misconceptions about what active learning is and is not.	Reflection exercise: Observe the space. What is new? What is familiar? What was your first reaction to the space and why? Reflect individually and then as a group. • Do you know of research that supports the emergence of ALCs? • What "rumors" (Beichner et al., 2007) or misconceptions have you heard about ALCs? • How will you approach teaching in ALCs? Allow time to debrief after activity.	Facilitators may choose to do a light treatment of theory, as many participants could already have a general idea of it. Another option is to provide some evidence on efficacy of ALCs. If the ALC is under construction, then play a video about another institution's ALC, and then have participants observe and reflect. Consider introducing common challenges that instructors face.
10:50–11:00	Break	Providing reflection questions during the break is a good way to bridge sessions. • What are two "rumors" you have heard about ALCs that you want clarified today?	Frequent but moderate breaks help maintain energy and give the sense of what can be accomplished in 50 minutes, a period that mirrors some typical class times.

(Continues)

Appendix 9.2: (Continued)

Day 1: Time	Session Topic and Goals	Sample Activities for Participants	Notes for Facilitators
11:00–11:50	Common challenges of teaching in ALCs: Present common challenges that arise for those new to ALCs and begin to provide insight into how to address them successfully	Building off preceding "rumors" or misconceptions activity, participants address these questions: • How do I plan to teach in the space? • How does my role as the instructor change in an ALC? • How do I address student expectations and resistance to ALCs? • How will I incorporate technology in an ALC? • How do I help students with accommodations?	A general overview of the common challenges is a good way to help participants realize the many components that go into successfully teaching in an ALC for the first time.
12:00–1:00	Seasoned ALC instructors: Voices of experience	During breaks, participants can generate a list of questions for seasoned instructors or socialize with other participants. We recommend providing key questions to discuss: • What new ideas have you heard that apply to your teaching? • What new questions do you have since we started this morning?	Instructors who have taught in the space can discuss and model their experience for those new to teaching in the space. This can be done formally (via presentation or panel) or informally (seasoned ALC instructors sit around room and share).

1:00–1:50	Course (re)design: Introduce principles related to good practices in course design. Backward or integrated design approaches help participants think more deeply about the structure and goals of their ALC course.	Learning objectives & Bloom's new taxonomy (Anderson & Krathwohl, 2001) • Introduce Bloom's taxonomy and revised taxonomy. • Present different course design approaches. • Ask participants to discuss their answers individually and in groups.	Working with an entire course in a short session might be daunting. Providing participants the opportunity to think big (and small) about a particular unit is a good way to start with the design process. Fink (2013) provided an excellent primer on integrated design that can be modified for ALCs.[1]
2:00–2:50	Managing groups: Provide participants with strategies to form and manage groups.	Session can be structured around questions related to group size, duration, formation, roles, dynamics, dysfunctions, and evaluation.	Chapter 6 of this book explores these issues and can be presented as a series of choices each instructor should explicitly make.
3:00–3:50	Design activities and assignments for ALCs: Have participants develop activities and assignments for their class in ALCs.	Faculty discuss the merits of different types of activities. Answer the following questions: • What is the purpose of the activity? • What will students be able to do/know/value at the end of the activity? • What is the description of the activity? • What are potential technologies that could support the activity?	Beichner and colleagues (2007) discussed SCALE-UP activities at North Carolina State University through Tangibles and Ponderables. This framework might be a helpful way for faculty to structure their thinking about activities for their course in an ALC. Other resources include Suskie (2009, p. 158) and Barkley, Cross, and Major (2014). Chapter 5 of this book also covers sample activities and assignments in detail.

(Continues)

Appendix 9.2: (Continued)

Day 1: Time	Schedule	Sample Activities for Participants	Notes for Facilitators
4:00–4:50	Assessing student learning in ALCs: Have participants consider methods of assessing student learning in the classroom.	Participants reflect on how they currently assess student learning and consider the following: • What is one question you want answered about assessment? • How would you differentiate between normative and summative assessment and their components? • Review good practices in assessment with examples (using rubrics, grading guides). • Discuss different types of rubrics (e.g., analytical, developmental, holistic).	This session should present different approaches to assessing student learning, from informal to formal and formative to summative. Including both low- and high-stakes assessments (and the benefits of each) is also worth considering during this time. Facilitators might have participants review the chapter on assessment (Chapter 7 of this book) prior to this session. When discussing assessment at the end of the day, consider pairing conversation with an engaging activity. Facilitators might swap this section with the early session on Day 2.

Day 2: Time	Session Topic and Goals	Sample Activities for Participants	Notes for Facilitators
8:30–10:00	Working breakfast and morning work session	Participants arrive and begin working on lesson or course components.	Facilitators are present to consult and provide feedback.

10:00–10:50	Employing technology in an ALC: Provide participants with an opportunity to receive initial exposure to and training on ALC technology and consider what technology tools work for different types of activities in ALCs.	Ask participants: • When is technology appropriate and when is it not? • How does employing technology align with course outcomes and objectives? • What are some ways to use technology in ALCs?	These sessions may include facilitation by academic technology staff. It might also be a good chance to give a short primer on room technology and a hands-on demo to participants. Be sure to acknowledge low-tech items, such as the whiteboards.
11:00–11:50	Classroom management in ALCs: Discuss classroom management issues and think about the first day/week of teaching in an ALC.	Ask participants to generate a list of tasks to complete in preparation for the first day or week. • What should I prioritize? • What supplies do I need?	Facilitators can offer some key tips (e.g., organization is vital, establish expectation, how to motivate interest in the class topic, have a tech backup, experiment, have fun).
12:00–1:00	Working lunch [or closing lunch]	Participants prepare for microteaching session.	Facilitators are present to consult and provide feedback.
1:00–4:30	Working session for participants	Participants should work on course materials from any or all of the topics discussed during the institute. Instructors' leaving this day with a clear sense of direction, perhaps unit/course outline, is a major accomplishment.	Facilitators are present to consult and provide feedback.

(*Continues*)

Appendix 9.2: (Continued)

Day 3: Time	Session Topic and Goals	Sample Activities for Participants	Notes for Facilitators
9:00–12:00	Working session for participants	This session is useful for refining ideas, making final checks on how to operate technology, and any other last-minute details.	Facilitators are present to consult and provide feedback.
1:00–4:00	Participants give microteaching lessons based on new ideas they have been exposed to and worked on during the institute. Purpose is to receive peer feedback on what participants have developed thus far.	Participants will have a set time (10–15 minutes) to present a microteaching session for a unit or lesson they have developed during the institute and for an ALC class.	A rubric for faculty to provide feedback on their peers is an excellent way to ensure these sessions are useful for presenters and audience members. A timer or a timekeeper helps keep this session on task and evenly distributed among participants.
4:00–4:30	Closing	Final thoughts and next steps are good ways to use this time.	Facilitators might want to mention existing learning communities or communities of practice related to ALCs on campus. Facilitators should have planned ways for participants to follow up and receive support after the institute concludes.

[1] A copyright-free version of Fink's Guide to Course Design is available: www.deefinkandassociates.com/GuidetoCourseDesignAug05.pdf

10

DESIGNING LEARNING
SPACES RESEARCH

M any instructors who adapt their courses for delivery in an Active
Learning Classroom (ALC) eventually wonder about the impact
of what they have done. What effects has the move to a new learning space had? Are students satisfied with the new environment? Are they
learning sufficiently well? Do the new learning activities serve all students
equally well, or do they benefit some students more than others? Are students
more engaged in ALCs than in traditional learning spaces?

Instructors who ask questions like these may wish to consider investigating the effects of their new teaching practice. Careful, systematic studies
undertaken by instructors engaged in the actual practice of teaching—often
called the scholarship of teaching and learning (SoTL)—are valuable because
their findings frequently have strong *external validity*, or generalizability,
in virtue of occurring in an authentic teaching context (Cross & Stedman,
1996). However, educational research is a specialized subfield within social
science research, built on a body of theory and existing research, with its own
techniques, tools, and practices. In order to engage productively in SoTL,
most instructors, even those with considerable research experience in their
own fields, will require some guidance to conduct a valid and reliable study
that yields information useful for advancing instructional practice. In this
chapter we provide that guidance by describing some of the main building
blocks of a successful, informative inquiry into questions concerning teaching in a new learning space. Those building blocks include the following:

- Research questions
- Quantitative and qualitative approaches to research
- Research design and methodology
- Measurement and data collection

Before we begin in earnest, we offer this brief note on terminology. For the purposes of this chapter, we will speak in terms of conducting "research," but many instructors may think of their investigations as "evaluation." *Evaluation* is usually defined as an inquiry that is limited in scope, in that its main purpose is the improvement of a particular, local program or project. By contrast, *research* seeks knowledge that is generalizable, in the sense that it is applicable to a broad range of contexts (Stufflebeam, 2001). Because of its greater aspirations, a research project is usually characterized by greater rigor, systematicity, and control over extraneous influences than are typical of an evaluation. Our intent in this chapter is to provide guidance that will be helpful to instructors conducting inquiries anywhere on the evaluation–research continuum.

Research Questions

Research questions define a research project, and they are the starting point in any investigation. Considerable time should be spent developing, refining, and clarifying them. Research questions give the project its shape, because different sorts of questions demand different types of research designs, methodologies, data collection methods, and analysis techniques. Research questions should pose a unitary query using unambiguous terminology, and they should be reasonably answerable given available resources. The meaning of these criteria will become clearer in the following examples of common errors that can lead would-be researchers to generate flawed research questions.

Asking Several Questions as One

One of the most common flaws in a research question is being compound, so that what is presented as a single question actually contains multiple separate inquiries. For instance: "Do new learning spaces inspire excited, dynamic faculty members to employ new active learning techniques that enhance student success?" This question contains several distinct strands that should be disentangled and listed as separate questions.

- Are faculty members excited to teach in new learning spaces?
- Do faculty members employ active learning techniques when they teach in new learning spaces?
- Do faculty members employ *more* active learning techniques when they teach in new learning spaces than they did before?
- Do the teaching techniques used by faculty members in new learning spaces enhance student success?

Ambiguous Terminology

Ambiguity is another common flaw in research questions. Ambiguity is often introduced into research questions through terminology that does not have a clear, single meaning. For instance, the question, "Do new learning spaces facilitate active learning techniques?" could have any one of at least three meanings, and the researchers should clarify which they intend to study.

- Do new learning spaces make it *easier for faculty members to conduct* active learning techniques?
- Do new learning spaces *result in more use of* active learning techniques?
- Are active learning techniques *more effective* when conducted in new learning spaces?

The locutions "lends itself to," "is conducive to," "promotes," "encourages," and "enhances" are similar to "facilitate" in that they could be used to mean making an activity or event more frequent, making it easier to conduct an activity or making an activity better or more effective.

Often the ambiguity is not merely terminological but also conceptual, in that the researchers themselves may not know precisely what they mean. If this sort of ambiguity is not cleared up early in a research project, it can torpedo the entire study. For example, consider the following question: "Is the student experience enriched by taking introductory science classes in new learning spaces?" Before we can answer, we must unpack the notions of *the student experience* (What experience? In class, out of class, or both? Which aspects of students' experience are relevant?) and *enrichment* (Does this mean a quantitative increase of some sort, or a qualitative improvement?). Just how these concepts are filled out depends on the researchers' intentions, but a better question might be the following: "Are students more interested in science after taking introductory science classes in new learning spaces than they were to begin with?"

Excessive Ambition

A research question should not outrun the capabilities and resources of the research team, so careful consideration of the time, funding, personnel, and skills that can be brought to bear on a research project is called for. The following plan is overly ambitious: "We will produce, test, revise, and implement a psychometrically valid and reliable measure of cognitive engagement and use this instrument in a double-blind, randomized controlled trial of the differential levels of this variable across multiple treatment conditions." A well-supported educational research group with extensive experience and expertise could accomplish this goal, but it is probably too demanding to resolve in a single study. The project of producing an instrument that validly and reliably measures cognitive engagement is difficult and time-consuming on its own. And while randomized controlled trials are common in medical research, they are nearly impossible to implement with real students in a live educational setting.

Setting Oneself Up for Failure

Education is psychologically complex, and educational outcomes are determined by a multiplicity of factors, including general academic aptitude, background knowledge, demographic features of students, and students' psychological characteristics (Pascarella & Terenzini, 2005). Given this background, researchers engaged in SoTL should not ask too much of the innovations they are introducing into their teaching, which are typically short term in nature and relatively small in the context of students' overall educational experience—a new module within a larger course, for instance, or a new approach to teaching certain topics. The effects of interventions of this sort are likely to be proximal to the intervention itself, such as changes in student content knowledge or in student attitudes or dispositions. Larger, deeper, or more distant outcomes—changes in graduation rates, for instance, or in students' general cognitive skills—are harder to achieve and probably should not form part of one's research questions.

For instance, the impact of a new, problem-based approach to teaching evolutionary theory in introductory biology courses could be sought through a question such as, "Does the new approach increase student acceptance of evolution?" rather than "Does the new approach improve 4-year graduation rates among biology majors?" or "Does the new approach improve student critical thinking skills?" The following is an example of a good research question:

> One factor associated with student engagement as measured by the National Survey of Student Engagement (NSSE) is the amount of time students meet with faculty outside of class. Does moving a large, introductory science class from a lecture hall to an active learning classroom promote increased out-of-class interaction between faculty and students?

To begin with, the first sentence sets the context for the question itself, which comes in the second sentence. By citing the NSSE and the notion of student engagement, we understand why the researchers are interested in out-of-class faculty–student interaction—because it may contribute to engagement. Additionally, the idea of *engagement* is popular, and many instructors want more of it, but its meaning is often left unclear. What sort of engagement is important? Cognitive? Affective? Interpersonal? Behavioral? This question refers to the NSSE conceptualization of engagement as a touchstone, and thus operationalizes this concept in a useful way.

However, one might still wonder what sort of interaction the researchers are interested in studying. Would it count if faculty and students are just hanging out in the hallway but not talking about class-related matters? Depending on exactly how the notion of engagement is filled out, interaction of that sort might contribute to engagement just as well as meetings that concern class material, or it might not. The researchers should probably refer to background literature on student engagement for guidance. The point is that matters like this must be addressed at the outset of a project, certainly before data collection begins, and while not every point of clarification should be built into the research question itself, the larger research plan should clear up any potential ambiguities.

Finally, note that the good research question example is fairly ambitious, in that it asks about the *promotion* of interaction, and that term suggests causation. One way to understand this would be to ask the following: Do students and faculty interact *more* now that the class is held in an ALC than they did before? Answering this question probably requires locating a comparison group, which we will discuss later in this chapter. If a comparison group is not available, the question should be changed. For instance, the researchers could change the question to one that asks about the quality and quantity of out-of-class faculty–student interaction going on now that the class meets in an ALC. It might be enough for the purposes of this investigation simply to show that faculty and students are interacting a lot, without the need for a comparison-design study that could yield causal conclusions.

Qualitative and Quantitative Approaches to Research

Many scholars draw a distinction between quantitative and qualitative approaches to empirical research. Broadly speaking, quantitative approaches focus on generating and analyzing numerical data from sources like surveys with closed-ended items, tests, and observations; qualitative approaches deal with non-numerical data such as responses to open-ended questions, audio recordings, interviews, focus groups, and videos (Trochim, 2001).

Both types of research are capable of answering important questions and providing useful information. And while almost any question can be addressed quantitatively or qualitatively, there are certain research questions that lend themselves more to a quantitative approach, and some that incline toward a more qualitative approach. The inclination for some research questions to guide a project toward quantitative and others toward qualitative approaches derives from the strengths of each family of techniques. Quantitative approaches to research excel at systematically comparing one thing with another and at measuring precisely the things being compared. Qualitative approaches are good for helping researchers understand the full context in which an educational intervention takes place and for illuminating phenomena in unexpected ways.

Quantitative Approaches

The following questions fit most naturally with quantitative methods and techniques:

- How much do student attitudes toward group work change after taking a class in a newly configured classroom?
- Do men and women respond differently to new learning spaces?
- Do ALCs have an impact on student engagement?

The first question seeks precise measurement by asking to what degree students' attitudes are altered by taking a class held in a new learning space. This question can best be answered by numerical measurement procedures and analytic techniques. Similarly, if a researcher wants to compare and understand the differences or similarities between two groups—between how men and women react to new spaces, as in the second question, or between undergraduate and graduate students or older and younger students—then the researcher will need to use precise quantitative measurement to compare these groups in a meaningful and informative way.

Finally, causal questions—questions about impact, or effects, or influences, as in the third question—almost certainly call for a quantitative approach to research design and data gathering. Answering causal questions requires not only a precise measurement but also a systematic comparison of two or more conditions or groups, as well as analytic methods that can sort through a large number of possible influences and determine which factors are relevant to the outcomes of interest and which are not. Causal questions will be discussed in much greater detail later in this chapter, along with the difference between correlation and causation.

Qualitative Approaches

Consider the following questions:

- ALCs have a physical layout that is quite different from standard lecture halls. How does this design affect the student experience? What kind of interpersonal dynamics exist in ALCs? Is it difficult for students to see or hear their fellow students or their instructor in ALCs? Does the layout alienate students from one another, or bring them closer together? Do the physical features of these spaces have any other unanticipated effects?
- What motivates instructors to teach in ALCs? How do instructors adapt their teaching strategies to the new spaces, and why do they adopt particular approaches to teaching in new learning spaces?
- Between-groups tests on survey data show that certain demographic groups of students respond more positively to ALCs than other groups. Why is this the case?

These questions are best addressed through the use of qualitative methods of data gathering and analysis. When a question asks about the context in which a phenomenon is embedded, different elements of which are crucial to understanding the phenomenon, it should be approached through qualitative methods. The first sample question fits this characterization. It inquires about several different but interconnected aspects of the physical layout of ALCs and could be answered through interviews or focus groups with ALC students and instructors.

The second question also seeks information about a complex phenomenon—instructor use of and adaptation to new learning spaces—that is best understood in the light of background about instructors themselves, the institutional context in which they work and teach, and so forth. Importantly, the number of instructors relevant to answering this question is probably relatively small, so that a more quantitative approach (e.g., asking closed-ended survey questions about different sorts of motivations and different methods of adapting to ALCs, trying to differentiate and compare groups of instructors) is inappropriate. Moreover, the researchers may not know what factors are likely to motivate faculty adaptation of their teaching to ALCs. Qualitative techniques like semi-structured interviews are excellent for exploring new phenomena, when it is not yet clear what more specific questions would be most fruitful to ask.

Finally, quantitative data often raise as many questions as they answer, as in the third question. Comparing the responses of different groups on survey questions is informative, but such comparison does not answer the question of why any noted differences exist. This exploration of differences illustrates another important role of qualitative methods, namely clarifying confusing findings that have been revealed by other techniques. One can speculate about why different groups of students react differently to ALCs, but a more systematic and reliable approach would be to hold a focus group with students from the classes surveyed, lay out the survey findings for them, and ask for their help in interpreting the data.

Mixed-Methods Approaches

At this juncture it is worth mentioning the notion of *mixed-methods research*. This phrase refers to an approach to research that integrates the quantitative and the qualitative in a comprehensive examination of a phenomenon, using each family of techniques where and when appropriate to triangulate on the object of study (Tashakkori & Teddlie, 2010). We have already hinted at some of the more common ways of integrating qualitative and quantitative methods, such as the following:

- Begin a new investigation by gathering narrative and descriptive data to create a broadly based understanding of what is under examination and to sharpen the questions that will be asked in a later stage of the research.
- Incorporate both closed- and open-ended questions into a survey so that the survey yields quantifiable information about phenomena along with understanding of background, context, and possible explanations.
- Use qualitative techniques to investigate possible interpretations of or explanations for quantitative findings that are perplexing.

Some researchers find it difficult to integrate quantitative and qualitative approaches to research in a plausible and credible way; these researchers may have theoretical commitments that work against methodological diversity (Tashakkori & Teddlie, 2010). But investigators who are working in a live educational context and whose concerns are highly practical often simply want to gather all the information they can about faculty uses of ALCs in as systematic a way as possible. For these researchers, the combination of two fruitful types of information can be very powerful.

Research Design and Methodology

The design of a study (sometimes called its *methodology*) refers to its overall structure and the important components of the research contained within that structure (Pedhazur & Schmelkin, 1991). A research design defines who or what is being studied, the framework within which the study's research questions will be addressed, the information to be gathered, whether there will be any manipulation of study conditions, and the hypothesized relationships among the matters of concern in the study. The research design used in a study should flow from the study's research questions. In what follows, we make a basic distinction between studies that focus on a single group of participants and those that involve more than one group. We also discuss what questions can be successfully addressed by each family of research designs along with characteristic problems and pitfalls of each.

Single-Group Designs

One important distinction in social science research design has to do with whether a study involves a single group or multiple groups. Learning spaces research might concern a group or groups of instructors, students, or learning spaces themselves. Studies that examine just one group are appropriate when what is being studied is a new and relatively unknown phenomenon. When that is the case, the study is likely to be exploratory and descriptive in nature, built around a set of questions such as the following: "How do faculty members adapt their teaching to a new type of learning space? What difficulties do they encounter? What benefits do they perceive?" Here, what is wanted is not a controlled experiment but a detailed narrative that provides richness of context, which other faculty members can look to for guidance. The best approach to answering this set of questions would be to use a *single-group descriptive design* by focusing on a group of faculty members who have taught in new learning environments, interviewing them about their experiences; observing some of their classes in action; and documenting those experiences using text, images, and other media. Using a detailed questionnaire to gather quantitative data would be inappropriate because the researchers probably do not know the most likely types of adaptation to new spaces, or the most common sorts of problems and benefits, on the basis of which they could construct a questionnaire. Indeed, a further outcome of the investigation might be the development of this sort of survey, informed by and built on findings of these initial investigations.

Beyond the simple description of a phenomenon, researchers are often interested in *change*. Having identified faculty attitudes toward the spaces in which they teach as a focus of interest, one might ask: "How are faculty attitudes toward new learning spaces affected as they gain experience teaching in ALCs?" One could address this question by identifying a group of faculty members scheduled to teach classes in a new learning space in a future term and gathering information about their attitudes (a) now, before they begin teaching (the baseline measure); (b) later, just after they have begun their classes; and (c) later still, after the term has concluded and they can reflect on the experience. By using this approach, often called a *pre–post measures design*, researchers can provide an illuminating account of the evolution of beliefs, reactions, perceptions, and attitudes, using data-collection methods that are quantitative, qualitative, or both.

After conducting a single-group descriptive inquiry, or simply through anecdotes, one might get the sense that not all instructors respond in the same way to new learning environments. Such a researcher could ask these questions: "Do different types of faculty members have different attitudes toward new learning spaces? Do their attitudes evolve along different trajectories?" These questions can be answered by combining demographic and background information about faculty members with data gleaned from a descriptive or pre–post measures investigation, resulting in an approach that examines the associations between different variables, or a *correlational design*. Then one can compare the beliefs, perceptions, and so forth of different sets of faculty, defined by salient characteristics—sex, for example, or age, academic discipline, tenure status, and so on. Depending on the nature of one's data, this comparison can be accomplished through statistical techniques or by constructing a series of contrasting narratives that may be based on informative instructor archetypes.

Comparison Designs

The idea of examining different groups of faculty members to answer questions about demographic differences is one illustration of the *power of comparisons* in research. If we were to discover, for instance, that tenured faculty rate the difficulty of adapting their courses to an ALC on average as a 3.91 on a 5-point difficulty scale, we would not know without further information what to do with that data point. Is 3.91 a lot or a little? Is it something to worry about or not? If we also know, however, that untenured faculty rate the difficulty of course adaptation on average as a 3.03 and that the difference between those mean scores is a statistically significant difference, this information may lead us to respond in various ways. We might direct special faculty development efforts toward tenured faculty who are scheduled to teach in ALCs. We might investigate the reasons why tenured faculty have more difficulty in adapting to ALCs: When compared to untenured faculty, do they lack technical skills, confidence, or sufficient time? Or is some other, unknown factor responsible?

Comparisons are a very common and very informative way of addressing another important type of research question regarding new learning spaces, namely questions about those spaces' impact: "Do new learning spaces encourage collaboration across disciplines? Do they increase the frequency of informal interactions between students and faculty members? Do

DESIGNING LEARNING SPACES RESEARCH

they promote student engagement with course material? Do they improve learning outcomes?" Though they differ in phrasing, these are all questions about the effects of new types of learning spaces. They all ask, in one way or another, what those spaces cause or bring about or help to happen. As we discussed in Chapter 2 and elsewhere, almost all educational outcomes of interest have multiple causes (Pascarella & Terenzini, 2005). This means both that learning spaces are very unlikely to be the *sole* cause of anything important and that they may not *directly* yield any effects they do have. In all likelihood, they work through the mediation of human perceptions, actions, responses, and so on.

Even given these caveats, it still makes sense to ask about the impact of ALCs. Questions about impact are often the first ones that come to mind when we innovate in education, because innovations are usually undertaken precisely in the hope they will have a positive impact on important features of the educational experience. In the particular case of learning spaces research, the question of impact is often associated with costs—Is the educational impact of ALCs worth the investment?—and thus it's a question many stakeholders will want addressed.

The most common, and the most effective, way of answering questions about impact is through a comparison-design study. Also known as a *multiple-groups study*, in this sort of investigation one group of participants is exposed to an innovation or intervention (the treatment group), while another group is not (the control group). If the two groups are identical in all relevant respects, then any differences found between them after the treatment period can be attributed to the innovation, because the control group tells us what the treatment group *would have been like* in the absence of the treatment. This is called *internal validity*—a study's ability to say that an observed effect is due to the treatment and not to something else (Messick, 1994).

When working in a live educational context, the two groups being compared are usually groups of students, one of which is taught using materials, technologies, techniques, or approaches different from those used with the other group. In studies of learning spaces, the groups are often classes, one of which is taught in a new or revised space while the other is taught in a traditional space. It can be difficult, however, to implement a comparison-design study in a live educational environment. Smaller schools or smaller academic departments may not offer simultaneous sections of classes taught by the same faculty members. One opportunity that is often available (but frequently overlooked) when in the planning or construction phases of learning space revision projects is that of using a current, existing class taught in a traditional learning space as one's control group, and then waiting until new spaces have been constructed and brought online to set up a treatment group. This means planning a research study while still teaching in the older-style rooms so control data can be collected.

Confounds

We said previously that in a comparison-design study, the groups being compared should be *as identical as possible in relevant respects*. But what are those respects? What are the important details to hold constant across groups? The answer is that one need not hold *everything* constant across groups—only the features relevant to the question you are investigating. Any relevant factors that differ between groups are called *confounds*. Uncontrolled confounds undermine a study's internal validity because they represent an alternative possible explanation for any differences the investigators find between the treatment and control groups.

In the case of learning spaces studies, educationally relevant features of classes being compared should be held constant. These features include the instructor, course materials, syllabus, tests and assignments, and possibly the teaching methods used in the classes. When it comes to certain factors, however, it is not obvious whether they are relevant. For instance, what about time of day that a class meets? Does that matter? Time of day may not matter intrinsically to educational outcomes, but it might matter contingently. Perhaps the faculty member in question is more or less energetic at certain times of day, or maybe certain sorts of students enroll in morning as opposed to afternoon classes. If you are interested in the effects of learning spaces on student affect or student engagement, then it would be relevant if students tend to report lower affect early in the morning or after lunch, when they tend to be sleepy. For these reasons, time of day should be held constant, if possible.

Educationally relevant features of students themselves should also be identical across groups. Students' shoe size and hair color are probably not relevant to most learning spaces research, but their age, gender, academic level, subject matter background, and general academic ability may very well be relevant. If students can be *randomly assigned* to treatment and control groups, this assignment should distribute the exogenous characteristics of students evenly between the groups, but the ability to assign students randomly is rare in a live educational environment. If students self-assign to groups, it is important that they do so without knowledge of the type of learning space the classes will be taught in. Otherwise they may engage in non-random self-selection by intentionally avoiding, or intentionally seeking out, classes taught in new learning spaces, and that self-selection may bias the study's results.

In any case it is good practice to gather background and demographic information about the students in one's study, either through surveys or by querying a student information system, to determine the comparability of groups. If treatment and control groups are found to differ in important respects, one can use appropriate statistical techniques at the data analysis stage to *control for confounds*—in other words, measuring and removing statistically any effects the differences have on the outcomes one observes.

Changing more than one feature at once

When new learning spaces are created on campus and faculty members begin teaching in those rooms, instructors quite naturally want to adapt their teaching methods to the spaces. In fact, they should do so: New learning spaces are designed to facilitate new approaches to teaching, and using the same instructional methods one has used in the past is unlikely to yield the best results.

This opportunity raises the question of whether it is possible to alter more than one feature of one's treatment group compared to the control and still assess the impact of the new learning space. The answer is that it is certainly possible, as long as care is taken in drawing conclusions from the study. If an instructor moves from a traditional classroom to an ALC and implements a variety of new teaching techniques at the same time, or introduces new educational technologies to the class, or establishes an online presence for the course that did not exist before, any differences observed between the control and treatment groups must be attributed to the *combination* of differences as a whole. The investigator cannot identify the effects of any individual difference or change in isolation.

Novelty

One important confound that often affects studies of new learning spaces is the novelty of those spaces. The physical space itself, and the design, layout, and technological affordances of ALCs are frequently new to the faculty teaching in those spaces and to the students enrolled in courses held in them, and some research indicates that people respond differently to novel situations than to familiar ones (Clark & Sugrue, 1991).

Comparing an ALC to a newly constructed but traditional-format classroom can eliminate one source of the "novelty effect," but the novelty of ALCs' design and layout remains. The only way to address this confound is through a series of studies that track student and faculty responses to new learning spaces over time, as those spaces become more familiar. Preliminary research along these lines at the University of Minnesota provides some reason to think that the improved student perceptions of their learning environment associated with ALCs is *not* a function of novelty (see Chapter 2).

No comparison, no problem?

Is it possible to assess impact *without* a comparison design? For example, suppose we just ask an experienced instructor who has moved from a traditional classroom to an ALC whether the move has made a difference. And suppose she reports that she has taught this class for 10 years and has never seen her students respond in this or that way. Is her testimony evidence of change brought about by the new learning space?

To answer this question, we should remember that there are different types and degrees of evidence one can have about impact, and that some evidence is almost always better than none at all. Furthermore, social science research *never* yields certainty. Error can never be eliminated entirely, no matter how rigorously controlled a study is. The important questions are, how much evidence is enough, and of what sort, for the purposes and audience of a given study? Instructor testimony does provide *some* evidence of change, even though human perception and memory are subject to many sources of bias and inaccuracy. Testimony may be sufficient for certain purposes—to inspire other faculty to give new learning spaces a try, for instance. But it may not be sufficient for other purposes, such as guiding institutional decisions about new classroom construction on campus. Thus, in selecting a research design, knowing your audience or stakeholder can help determine your methodology.

Measurement and Data Collection

Faulty research questions are probably the most common weakness in educational research conducted by nonspecialists; problems with *measurement* run a close second. Often, the measures in a study—whatever the investigators use to gather data—are an afterthought and a significant source of error in the study. Even something as simple as a basic survey of student attitudes can be done well or badly, which can make a large difference to the amount of evidence provided by the study's conclusions. Some measurement work requires a good deal of special expertise (e.g., factor analysis, item response theory, reliability testing), but other important work is within the reach of non-specialists (e.g., basic survey design, think-aloud testing, inter-rater reliability training and testing). Some effort to ensure the quality of one's measurement should be part of any investigation of new learning spaces.

Types of Measures

Any investigation of new learning spaces, even purely qualitative studies, will gather information that could be called "data," and even if no attempt is made at quantifying the information collected, that data gathering can be understood as measurement. There are many ways of collecting data, each of which has advantages and disadvantages. All of these methods can be found in the learning spaces research described in Chapter 2.

Interviews

Simply speaking with people in a focused and intentional way can yield very useful information. Interviews excel at painting a richly contextualized portrait of a phenomenon from one person's point of view, and they can range from tightly structured (using a predetermined set of questions in a specified order—an interview protocol—with each interviewee) to unstructured (a free-flowing conversation the direction of which is determined organically as the interview proceeds). Interviews generate large amounts of detailed data, which can be challenging to analyze.

Focus groups

Sometimes thought of as a sub-class of interviews, focus groups involve speaking with several people in a group setting to generate detailed information from a variety of points of view. The interplay of perspectives can be quite revealing, particularly if the participants feel free to express both agreement and disagreement. Focus groups require skill to conduct successfully because the group conversation must be guided and managed in a deft, tactful manner (Krueger & Casey, 2014).

Surveys and questionnaires

Surveys are collections of questions that are usually delivered on paper or online to participants in a study. Due to the ease of constructing and implementing surveys, they are probably the most common measure used in educational research in general and in learning spaces research in particular. However, it is very easy to construct a survey that does not yield useful information because the questions are ambiguous, are badly worded or selected, or have bias and error built into the response scales. Many high-quality guides to survey design and implementation are available, such as Dillman, Smyth, and Christian's (2014) *Internet, Phone, and Mixed Mode Surveys*. Another important method for improving survey design is the *think-aloud technique*, in which a few potential survey-takers are recruited to respond to a draft survey while speaking their thoughts aloud in the presence of a researcher who can use the feedback to improve the validity of the survey.

Tests, assignments, and other performance measures

Information about student learning is often provided by assignments associated with a class or by standardized tests and other measures of student performance. When well constructed, tests can yield important information about outcomes of great educational interest. Like surveys, however, tests developed in an informal way are often unreliable or lacking in other properties (e.g., consistency over time) necessary for them to produce data useful for educational studies (Thorndike, 2005). In some disciplines (e.g., physics or chemistry), standardized measures of student learning exist that are tested and reliable. These measures can be very useful, but they generally apply only at lower class levels. *Class grades* are usually compiled from a variety of assignments and are often used as indicators of student learning, but attention should be paid to their reliability and to the fact that they often have a distribution concentrated in a small area of the available scale.

Observations

Sometimes the phenomena one is interested in studying can be observed directly, such as the type and frequency of learning activities that occur in a class, the way an instructor moves through a classroom, or some aspects of group interaction at round tables in ALCs. When possible, observation has the advantage of providing large quantities of data that are not subject to the same biases that afflict self-reported data, although observers must be well trained and aware of the biases they bring to the task. Data collected by technical means, through people's interaction with digital technology of various sorts, can be thought of as a subtype of observations. Many new learning spaces have the means to track instructor use of the various technologies in the classrooms, and these data can be revealing as part of a well-constructed research project.

Learning activities

Several common questions about ALCs have to do with the learning activities that occur in those classrooms. Do faculty members use student-centered learning activities more frequently in ALCs, compared to traditional classrooms? What is the proportion of time spent in lecture as opposed to student-centered activities in ALCs? While these are good research questions, it should be noted that it is not easy to measure with any precision either the frequency or duration of non-lecture learning activities. *Self-report measures* like surveys, interviews, and focus groups rely on the perceptions and memory of students or faculty members, who are typically thinking about course content while in class rather than mentally keeping track of types of learning activities. In addition, the terminology used to describe non-lecture activities is specialized, diverse, and non-standardized, making it difficult to be sure that survey respondents will all understand what you mean by, for example, *cooperative learning, collaborative learning*, or *active learning*.

Though they are time-consuming, observations are probably the best method of measuring different types of classroom learning activities; recent work on the Reformed Teaching Observation Protocol (RTOP) and the Classroom Observation Protocol for Undergraduate STEM (COPUS) shows promise in creating validated, reliable observation instruments (Amrein-Beardsley & Osborn Popp, 2012; M. K. Smith, Jones, Gilbert, & Wieman, 2013). In addition, the University of California, Davis Educational Effectiveness Hub (cee.ucdavis.edu) has developed the Generalized Observation and Reflection Platform (GORP; gorp.ucdavis.edu), which can accommodate existing and new custom protocols in a visually intuitive online platform.

Duration

The question of how long various activities, practices, and events last is a frequent matter of concern in the study of education in general and of ALCs in particular. Questions of duration can include the following: How long did particular in-class activities last? How much time do students spend on-task, and how much off-task? How much time do students spend preparing for class, or studying for a test? Measuring duration presents special difficulties. The chief difficulty is that the most obvious measure, retrospective self-report, is fraught with well-known problems that arise from the fact that human memory is a complex process of active construction (Schacter, 2002). If students are asked, for instance, how long they spent studying for last week's exam, and then asked the same question on the following day, their answers often vary wildly (Dewey, 2004).

Again, direct observation is the most reliable way to measure duration, but not everything of interest can be observed. For example, whether student behavior is on-task or off-task is determined in part by the interior states of student attention and cognition that an observer cannot verify. Finally, sometimes the available data on duration do not map seamlessly onto the categories of interest in a study. An ALC may track the duration of an instructor's projecting from a laptop onto the main projection screen, or how long a video signal from student tables is projected to the whole class, but those quantities may bear little relationship to the quantity of time the class spent actually focusing on those materials.

Learning outcomes

For many faculty, administrators, and other stakeholders, the question of paramount importance about ALCs is not how students react to or perceive the new spaces, or whether instructors find them easier or more enjoyable to teach in, but whether those spaces improve learning outcomes. Studying the impact of ALCs on learning outcomes is not intrinsically more difficult than studying their impact on anything else, but it does require a clear, coherent conceptualization of the learning outcomes themselves (see Chapter 8) as well as some way of measuring those outcomes.

One approach that is probably best avoided is using self-report measures of learning. Simply asking students whether and how much they have learned tends to be unreliable unless the questions are very carefully constructed, and even under the best of circumstances, self-reports are correlated to only a moderate degree with more objective measures of learning (Benton, Duchon, & Pallett, 2013).

A better option is to use student grades as a measure and to examine whether holding a class in an ALC improves student grades as compared to a control class. Studies with this structure were described in Chapter 2. Grades are a very convenient measure and are institutionally important, but one should take care to remove from class grades any components unlikely to have been influenced by the space in which the class was held—credit awarded for online work, for instance, or points from a lab section that was not held in an ALC. One should also ensure that grades in the class under study are distributed broadly enough for any effects of the new learning space to be visible, and that the class is not being graded "on the curve," which is in any case not the best policy for classes held in ALCs (see Chapter 7). For these and other reasons, gaining access to the entire grade book or spread-sheet is preferable to a final grade reported to the registrar.

Sometimes a class contains performance measures that are an improvement on overall grades as measures of learning, such as a cumulative final exam or a capstone project. Scholars in some disciplines (e.g., physics, chemistry, biology) either have created or are in the process of creating standardized instruments designed to measure learning outcomes in certain sorts of classes. Using instruments of this sort is an excellent idea because they have already been tested for reliability and validity (Hestenes, Wells, & Swackhamer, 1992). Another excellent approach to studying learning outcomes, which is not often conducted but can be extremely valuable, is to examine not only the immediate impact of ALCs on learning outcomes but also their effect on *retention* of learning over time. This examination can be done by using a sequence of measurements and tracking students' trajectories over the series: a pre-class measure of learning, a post-class measure, and then a later follow-up measure. A very convenient way to study retention is by looking at the impact of a class held in an ALC on student learning in a successor class taken by a large subset of students in the original class.

A final way of investigating student learning is to examine variables that mediate between teaching and learning outcomes. A large body of educational theory and empirical evidence indicates that such variables as cognitive engagement, prompt and frequent feedback on performance, student–content interaction, and the adoption of student-centered teaching techniques have a positive impact on student learning outcomes (Bernard et al., 2009; Chickering & Gamson, 1987). One could therefore study the impact of ALCs on student learning *indirectly* by asking whether teaching in ALCs results in conditions that we have reason to believe are conducive to the promotion of student learning.

Conclusion

The purpose of this chapter has been to highlight the basic building blocks of educational research projects that are focused on new learning spaces. Our goal in this chapter is to help faculty members and other interested stakeholders make informed decisions about whether to begin SoTL projects of their own and how to approach such projects.

Inevitably, much has been left out of this brief introduction to designing SoTL research for reasons of space and complexity. For instance, we have not discussed qualitative or quantitative data analysis or the role of institutional review boards in the research process, even though both are crucial to a successful study. We have mentioned in only a cursory way the issues surrounding developing reliable and valid instruments to measure variables of interest. Many resources exist to guide instructors and staff who wish to investigate these topics more extensively, including books, online repositories, and courses. In addition, many institutions of higher education are adding staff to their faculty support units who have expertise in educational research and who can collaborate with instructors to study new learning spaces. We want to emphasize, however, that there is value in any thoughtful, systematic investigation undertaken by faculty and staff working in a live educational context, even if that investigation does not have the complexity, rigor, and polish of a professional research study. Some evidence is better than no evidence at all.

11

FUTURE DIRECTIONS

Universities don't simply deliver content or distribute information; they bestow epistemic author-
ity. And they do so by sustaining intellectual practices and their standards of excellence and goods.
They create knowledge by forming people into distinct communities. Research universities have
been organized around the premise that knowledge is not just an inert object to be efficiently
distributed. It is rather an activity that one engages in—and into which one is cultivated.

—Chad Wellmon[1]

As we have argued, the advent of Active Learning Classrooms (ALCs) in the past decades has reinvigorated undergraduate learning by facilitating particular activities that are difficult to orchestrate in traditional classrooms with fixed-row seating oriented to a single focal point. The layout of these new spaces suggests students will collaborate and discuss—two activities essential to developing discerning intellects within a disciplinary community. It disrupts what Merrow (2006) called the nonaggression pact between students and instructors that tolerated passive behavior, and it does so by changing expectations of what might take place in the classroom and what happens in college.

We have suggested that to be effective in these rooms, an instructor must "teach the room," teach students how to function under these new conditions. On one level, these are operational directives—how to attract attention, how to function well in a group, how to be heard. On another level, teaching the room also means vesting students with a sense of what it means to pursue, create, agree upon, and transmit knowledge. We want them to develop high-level transferable skills and evidence-based reasoning as well as the ability to view a problem from multiple perspectives. For many students, this combination of high expectations and active learning may initially be uncomfortable. The sense that the path toward developing a scholarly self must be exercised and developed, at least partly, through a cooperative framework may seem contradictory. But the evidence for cooperative learning, for active learning, for learning in the ALCs all points in the same direction, so teaching the room also means helping students understand how learning happens and the rationale for organizing a class in this manner.

Future Directions for Research

In the early chapters of this book, we outlined the current state of research on ALCs, but there are still many questions to explore. For instance, there are what we might term *Goldilocks questions*: What is the right amount of student exposure to an ALC in order to fully participate in the room's benefits? That is, is there a lower limit or threshold of time a student should spend in an ALC to benefit from the experience? Especially with the rise in hybrid courses, we can imagine meeting in an ALC episodically: once a week, once a month, twice a semester. What amount of time in the room is enough to gain the advantages the room confers? Conversely, can a student spend a surfeit of time in an ALC, whereby it becomes unproductive for her learning or wasteful of university resources? That is, is there an upper limit of productive time that a student might spend in an ALC? Will ALCs produce diminishing returns after a student has taken a certain number of courses that meet in those rooms? And related to these questions, if time in ALCs must be rationed due to demand for the space, when would a student benefit the most from the experience—at the start, in the middle, or at the end of the curriculum?

In regard to the mechanisms by which ALCs operate, it would be valuable to know how the social context of learning might vary across populations. Are the effects of social context different, for example, in a so-called minority–majority school? Does social context play a different role in non-STEM courses, in courses with smaller class sizes, or in upper-division and graduate-level courses?

In our experience, many people have expressed curiosity on a number of unanswered questions. For instance, we've often been asked what the long-term impact of the ALCs might be. Does exposure to ALCs affect retention in school or in the discipline? Might they impact developmental outcomes over a student's undergraduate or graduate career or their time-to-degree? Another set of questions cluster around the impact of particular technologies. Which technologies—moveable seating, tables, whiteboards, wireless microphones, projection screens, and so on—are essential to see the learning gains we measure in fully equipped rooms? Yet another set of concerns asks about the group experience: What are the best ways to create student groups—randomly, through student self-selection, or by distribution of student characteristics (and if so, what characteristics and what distribution)? How long should student groups last, and what sort of projects should they undertake? Finally, as newer versions of ALCs become prevalent, in general, how do they compare? For example, are tables on tiers with a fixed focal point more conducive to a blend of lecture and active learning than a standard room filled with tables and no central focal point? Are rooms that offer great flexibility of arrangements of furniture and technology the best environment for supporting multiple teaching techniques? Do ALCs with proximate informal spaces present a significant advantage for conducting group work?

Future Directions for Space

After decades of small changes, current classroom design seems to be evolving rapidly. Adam Finkelstein (2015) from McGill University recently suggested that in addition to new ALCs, we will likely see redesigned science laboratories (see Images 11.1 and 11.2) and active lecture halls. We are already seeing examples of the latter with Iowa State University's LeBaron Hall Auditorium (Twetten, 2006) and Oregon State University's 600-person "Teaching-In-The-Round" Large Arena Classroom in the Learning Innovation Center (University of Oregon Academic Extension, 2015; see Image 11.3). In addition, we're beginning to see ALCs that are designed to remotely connect to another ALC. This allows tables of students at one site to interact with those at another, such as the classrooms in the College of Pharmacy at the University of Minnesota's Duluth and Twin Cities campuses. Broadly speaking, this type of design may eventually open the door to new approaches for connecting distant students to ALCs. All of these flexible classroom designs—along with several others—are built to encourage a combination of active learning and lecture approaches and signal new directions for learning spaces.

Whether they are ALCs, laboratories, or lecture halls, these new spaces suggest student-centered pedagogical approaches in their design and arrangement. As we rebuild our classrooms, we are also rewriting the educational contract and disavowing the nonaggression pact between instructors and students. We are signaling the importance of participation to learning, and with the tables that give students space to work and discuss we confer respect on students' abilities to grapple with new ideas in new ways. As they cycle through learning independently, in small groups, in large teams, and as a class, they gain a sense of what they can accomplish individually and together as they develop scholarly habits of mind. This new educational contract, of

Image 11.1 Using a digital microscope to project a prepared slide, Frank Williams identifies microanatomy features in an animal sciences histology course at the University of Minnesota.

Image 11.2 The veterinary sciences active learning wet lab at the University of Minnesota.

Image 11.3 The circular design of the 600-seat arena classroom at Oregon State University reduces the distance between the instructor and student to only eight rows or 30 feet and features 360-degree projection areas. This classroom-in-the-round is part of the Learning Innovation Center (LInC) that also includes a 72-seat active learning studio, and a 228-seat parliament classroom designed to replicate a debate-style seating arrangement.

Note. Photo by Steve Maylone and courtesy Bora Architects.

course, is not built solely on the backs of students. How an instructor organizes the student experience is imperative. As we warned at the start of this book, *this could be great, or this could be a real disaster.* So much of what happens in ALCs depends on thoughtful consideration of the opportunities for learning these rooms present.

Note

1. Jaschik, S. (2015, May 8). Organizing enlightenment. *Inside Higher Ed*. Retrieved from www.insidehighered.com. The idea of epistemic authority and how individuals develop trust in authority beyond themselves, including moral communities, is fully argued in Linda Trinkaus Zagzebseki's, *Epistemic authority: A theory of trust, authority, and autonomy in belief*. New York, NY: Oxford University Press, 2012.

REFERENCES

ACT. (1998). *Prediction research summary tables.* Iowa City, IA: Author.

ACT. (2007). *The ACT technical manual.* Iowa City, IA: Author.

Ahmad, S., & Rao, C. (2012). Common goals, uncommon settings: The impact of physical environment on teaching and learning English for communication. *Developing Country Studies, 2*(9), 45–56. Retrieved from http://www.iiste.org/Journals/index.php/DCS

Alexandrin, J. R., Schreiber, I. L., & Henry, E. (2008). Why not disclose? In J. L. Higbee & E. Goff (Eds.), *Pedagogy and student services for institutional transformation: Implementing universal design in higher education* (pp. 377–392). Minneapolis, MN: Regents of the University of Minnesota.

Alvarado, C., Dominguez, A., Rodriguez, R., & Zavala, G. (2012). Expectancy violation in physics and mathematics classes in a student-centered classroom. In S. Rebello, P. Engelhardt, & C. Singh (Eds.), *AIP conference proceedings* (Vol. 1413, pp. 103–106). Omaha, NE: American Institute of Physics. doi:10.1063/1.3680004

Ambrose, S. A., Bridges, M. W., DiPietro, M., Lovett, M. C., & Norman, M. K. (2010). *How learning works: Seven research-based principles for smart teaching.* San Francisco, CA: Jossey-Bass.

Amedeo, D., Golledge, R. G., & Stimson, R. G. (2009). *Person-environment-behavior research: Investigating activities and experiences in spaces and environments.* New York, NY: Guilford Press.

Americans With Disabilities Act of 1990, Pub. L. No. 101-336, 104 Stat. 328 (1990).

Amrein-Beardsley, A., & Osborn Popp, S. E. (2012). Peer observations among faculty in a college of education: Investigating the summative and formative uses of the Reformed Teaching Observation Protocol (RTOP). *Educational Assessment, Evaluation and Accountability, 24*(1), 5–24. doi:10.1007/s11092-011-9135-1

Anderson, L. W., & Krathwohl, D. R. (2001). *A taxonomy for learning, teaching, and assessing: A revision of Bloom's taxonomy of educational objectives.* Boston, MA: Allyn & Bacon.

Andrade, M. S. (2006). International students in English-speaking universities. *Journal of Research in International Education, 5*(2), 131–154. doi:10.1177/1475240906065589

Anson, R., & Goodman, J. A. (2014). A peer assessment system to improve student team experiences. *Journal of Education for Business, 89*(1), 27–34. doi:10.1080/08832323.2012.754735

Arendale, D. R. (2004). Pathways of persistence: A review of postsecondary peer cooperative learning programs. In I. M. Duranczyk, J. L. Higbee, & D. B. Lundell

(Eds.), *Best practices for access and retention in higher education* (pp. 27–40). Minneapolis, MN: University of Minnesota. Retrieved from http://www.cehd.umn.edu/crdeul/pdf/monograph/5-a.pdf

Atir, S., Rosenzweig, E., & Dunning, D. (2015). When knowledge knows no bounds: Self-perceived expertise predicts claims of impossible knowledge. *Psychological Science, 26*(8), 1295–1303. doi:10.1177/0956797615588195

Austin, A. E., & Sorcinelli, M. D. (2013). The future of faculty development: Where are we going? *New Directions for Teaching and Learning: The Breadth of Current Faculty Development: Practitioners' Perspectives, 2013*(133), 85–97. doi:10.1002/tl.20048

Bacon, D. R., Stewart, K. A., & Silver, W. S. (1999). Lessons from the best and worst student team experiences: How a teacher can make the difference. *Journal of Management Education, 23*(5), 467–488. doi:10.1177/105256299902300503

Baepler, P., & Walker, J. D. (2014). Active learning classrooms and educational alliances: Changing relationships to improve learning. In P. Baepler, D. C. Brooks, & J. D. Walker (Eds.), *New Directions for Teaching and Learning: Active Learning Spaces, 2014*(137), 27–40. doi:10.1002/tl.20083

Baepler, P., Walker, J. D., & Driessen, M. (2014). It's not about seat time: Blending, flipping, and efficiency in active learning classrooms. *Computers & Education, 78*, 227–236. doi:10.1016/j.compedu.2014.06.006

Barkley, E. F., Cross, K. P., & Major, C. H. (2014). *Collaborative learning techniques: A handbook for college faculty* (2nd ed.). San Francisco, CA: Jossey-Bass.

Barr, T. F., Dixon, A. L., & Gassenheimer, J. B. (2005). Exploring the "lone wolf" phenomenon in student teams. *Journal of Marketing Education, 27*(1), 81–90. doi:10.1177/0273475304273459

Barrows, H. S. (1986). A taxonomy of problem-based learning methods. *Medical Education, 20*, 481–486. doi:10.1111/j.1365-2923.1986.tb01386.x

Beichner, R. J. (2014). History and evolution of active learning spaces. *New Directions for Teaching and Learning: Active Learning Spaces, 2014*(137), 9–16. doi:10.1002/tl.20081

Beichner, R. J., Bernold, L., Burniston, E., Dail, P., Felder, R., Gastineau, J., . . . Risley, J. (1999). Case study of the physics component of an integrated curriculum. *American Journal of Physics, 67*(S1), S16–S24. doi:10.1119/1.19075

Beichner, R. J., Saul, J. M., Abbott, D. S., Morse, J. J., Deardorff, D. L., Allain, R. J., . . . Risley, J. S. (2007). The student-centered activities for large enrollment undergraduate programs (SCALE-UP) project. In E. F. Redish & P. J. Cooney (Eds.), *Reviews in PER: Research-based reform of university physics* (Vol. 1, pp. 2–39). College Park, MD: American Association of Physics Teachers. Retrieved from http://www.compadre.org/per/per_reviews/volume1.cfm

Beigi, M., & Shirmohammadi, M. (2012). Attitudes toward teamwork: Are Iranian university students ready for the workplace? *Team Performance Management: An International Journal, 18*(5/6), 295–311. doi:10.1108/13527591211251087

Bennett, S. (2007). First questions for designing higher education learning spaces. *Journal of Academic Librarianship, 33*(1), 14–26. doi:10.1016/j.acalib.2006.08.015

Benson, T. A., Cohen, A. L., Buskist, W., Gurung, R. A., Cann, A., Marek, P., . . . Long, H. E. (2005). Faculty forum. *Teaching of Psychology, 32*(4), 237–270. doi:10.1207/s15328023top3204_8

Benton, S. L., & Cashin, W. E. (2014). Student ratings of instruction in college and university courses. In M. B. Paulsen (Ed.), *Higher education: Handbook of theory and research* (Vol. 29, pp. 279–326). Dordrecht, Netherlands: Springer.

Benton, S. L., Duchon, D., & Pallett, W. H. (2013). Validity of student self-reported ratings of learning. *Assessment & Evaluation in Higher Education, 38*(4), 377–388. doi:10.1080/02602938.2011.636799

Bernard, R. M., Abrami, P. C., Borokhovski, E., Wade, C. A., Tamim, R. M., Surkes, M. A., & Bethel, E. C. (2009). A meta-analysis of three types of interaction treatments in distance education. *Review of Educational Research, 79*(3), 1243–1289. doi:10.3102/0034654309333844

Billson, J. M., & Tiberius, R. G. (1991). Effective social arrangements for teaching and learning. *New Directions for Teaching and Learning, 1991*(45), 87–109. doi:10.1002/tl.37219914510

Bligh, B., & Pearhouse, I. (2011). Doing learning space evaluations. In A. Boddington & J. Boys (Eds.), *Re-shaping learning: A critical reader—The future of learning spaces in post-compulsory education* (pp. 3–18). London: Sense.

Boettcher, J. V., & Conrad, R. M. (2010). *The online teaching survival guide: Simple and practical pedagogical tips.* San Francisco, CA: Jossey-Bass.

Braxton, J., Bray, N., & Berger, J. (2000). Faculty teaching skills and their influences on the college student departure process. *Journal of College Student Development, 41*(2), 215–227. Retrieved from https://muse.jhu.edu/journals/journal_of_college_student_development/

Braxton, J. M., Jones, W. A., Hirschy, A. S., & Hartley, H. V., III. (2008). The role of active learning in college student persistence. *New Directions for Teaching and Learning: The Role of the Classroom in College Student Persistence, 2008*(115), 71–83. doi:10.1002/tl.326

Braxton, M., & Sullivan, A. S. (2000). The influence of active learning on the college student departure process: Toward a revision of Tinto's theory. *Journal of higher education, 71*(5), 569–590.

Britton, J. (1990). Research currents: Second thoughts on learning. In M. Brubacher, R. Payne, & K. Richett (Eds.), *Perspectives on small group learning: Theory and practice* (pp. 3–11). Oakville, Ontario: Rubicon.

Brookfield, S. D., & Preskill, S. (1999). *Discussion as a way of teaching: Tools and techniques for democratic classrooms.* San Francisco, CA: Jossey-Bass.

Brooks, D. C. (2011). Space matters: The impact of formal learning environments on student learning. *British Journal of Educational Technology, 42*(5), 719–726. doi:10.1111/j.1467-8535.2010.01098.x

Brooks, D. C. (2012). Space and consequences: The impact of different formal learning spaces on instructor and student behavior. *Journal of Learning Spaces, 1*(2). Retrieved from http://libjournal.uncg.edu/ojs/index.php/jls/article/view/285/275

Brooks, D. C., & Solheim, C. (2014). Pedagogy matters, too: The impact of adapting teaching approaches to formal learning environments on student learning. *New Directions for Teaching and Learning: Active Learning Spaces, 2014*(137), 53–61. doi:10.1002/tl.20085

Brubacher, M., Payne, R., & Rickett, K. (Eds). (1990). *Perspectives on small group learning: Theory and practice.* Oakvale, Ontario: Rubicon.

Bruff, D. (2009). *Teaching with classroom response systems: Creating active learning environments.* San Francisco, CA: Jossey-Bass.

Bruffee, K. A. (1993). *Collaborative learning: Higher education, interdependence, and the authority of knowledge.* Baltimore, MD: Johns Hopkins University Press.

Bruffee, K. A. (1995). Sharing our toys: Cooperative learning versus collaborative learning. *Change: The Magazine of Higher Learning, 27*(1), 12–18. doi:10.1080/00091383.1995.9937722

Buskist, W., & Saville, B. K. (2001). Creating positive emotional contexts for enhancing teaching and learning. *APS Observer, 13*(3), 12–13, 19. Retrieved from http://www.socialpsychology.org/rapport.htm

Buurma, R. S. (2014). Victorian literature & Victorian informatics syllabus. Retrieved from http://rachelsagnerbuurma.org/uncategorized/vic_info-draft-syllabus/

Byers, T., Imms, W., & Hartnell-Young, E. (2014). Making the case for space: The effect of learning spaces on teaching and learning. *Curriculum and Teaching, 29*(1), 5–19. doi:10.7459/ct/29.1.02

Cabrera, A. F., Colbeck, C. L., & Terenzini, P. T. (2001). Developing performance indicators for assessing classroom teaching practices and student learning: The case for engineering. *Research in Higher Education, 42*(3), 327–352. doi:10.1023/A:1018874023323

Carr, N., & Fraser, K. (2014). Factors that shape pedagogical practices in next generation learning spaces. In K. Fraser (Ed.), *The future of learning and teaching in next generation learning spaces: International perspectives on higher education research* (Vol. 12, pp. 175–198). Bingley, UK: Emerald Group.

Chickering, A., & Gamson, Z. (1987). Seven principles for good practice in undergraduate education. *AAHE Bulletin, 39*(7), 3–7. Retrieved from http://www.aahea.org/articles/sevenprinciples1987.htm

Choi, S. M., Guerin, D. A., Kim, H. Y., Brigham, J. K., & Bauer, T. (2013–14). Indoor environmental quality of classrooms and student outcomes: A path analysis approach. *Journal of Learning Spaces, 2*(2). Retrieved from http://libjournal.uncg.edu/jls

The Chronicle of Higher Education. (2015). *Almanac of higher education.* Retrieved from http://chronicle.com/section/Almanac-of-Higher-Education/883?cid=megamenu

Clark, R. E., & Sugrue, B. M. (1991). Media in teaching. In M. C. Wittrock (Ed.), *Handbook of research on teaching* (3rd ed., pp. 464–478). New York, NY: Macmillan.

Cohen, E. G. (1994). Restructuring the classroom: Conditions for productive small groups. *Review of Educational Research, 64*(1), 1–35. doi:10.3102/00346543064001001

Cotner, S., Baepler, P., & Kellerman, A. (2008). Scratch this! The IF-AT as a technique for stimulating group discussion and exposing misconceptions. *Journal of College Science Teaching, 37*(4), 34–39. Retrieved from http://www.nsta.org/college/

Cotner, S., Loper, J., Walker, J. D., & Brooks, D. C. (2013). It's not you, it's the room: Are high-tech, active learning classrooms worth it? *Journal of College Science Teaching, 42*(6), 82–88. Retrieved from http://www.nsta.org/college/

Cox, M. D. (2004). Introduction to faculty learning communities. *New Directions for Teaching and Learning, 2004*(97), 5–23. doi:10.1002/tl.129

Cross, K. P., & Stedman, M. H. (1996). *Classroom research: Implementing the scholarship of teaching.* San Francisco, CA: Jossey-Bass.

Crouch, C. H., & Mazur, E. (2001). Peer instruction: Ten years of experience and results. *American Journal of Physics, 69*(9), 970–977. doi:10.1119/1.1374249

Crutchfield, T. N., & Klamon, K. (2014). Assessing the dimensions and outcomes of an effective teammate. *Journal of Education for Business, 89*(6), 285–291. doi:10.1080/08832323.2014.885873

Cuseo, J. (1992). Cooperative & collaborative learning in higher education: A proposed taxonomy. *Cooperative Learning and College Teaching, 2*(2), 2–5.

Cuseo, J. B. (2002). *Organizing to collaborate: A taxonomy of higher education practices for promoting interdependence within the classroom, across the campus, and beyond the college.* Stillwater, OK: New Forums Press.

Dahlstrom, E., & Bichsel, J. (2014). *ECAR study of undergraduate students and information technology, 2014.* Louisville, CO: EDUCAUSE Center for Analysis and Research. Retrieved from https://net.educause.edu/ir/library/pdf/ss14/ERS1406.pdf

Dahlstrom, E., & Brooks, D. C. (2014). *ECAR study of faculty and information technology, 2014.* Louisville, CO: EDUCAUSE Center for Analysis and Research. Retrieved from http://net.educause.edu/ir/library/pdf/ers1407/ers1407.pdf

Dallimore, E. J., Hertenstein, J. H., & Platt, M. B. (2012). Impact of cold-calling on student voluntary participation. *Journal of Management Education, 37*(3), 305–341. doi:10.1177/1052562912446067

Davidson, N., & Major, C. H. (2014). Boundary crossings: Cooperative learning, collaborative learning, and problem-based learning. *Journal on Excellence in College Teaching, 25*(3&4), 7–55. Retrieved from http://celt.muohio.edu/ject/

Davidson, N., Major, C. H., & Michaelsen, L. K. (2014). Small-group learning in higher education—cooperative, collaborative, problem-based, and team-based learning: An introduction by the guest editors. *Journal on Excellence in College Teaching, 25*(3/4), 1–6. Retrieved from http://celt.muohio.edu/ject/

Davidson, N., & Worsham, T. (1992). *Enhancing thinking through cooperative learning.* New York, NY: Teachers College Press.

Davis, B. G. (2009). *Tools for teaching.* San Francisco, CA: Jossey-Bass.

DeBeck, G., & Demaree, D. (2012). Teaching assistant–student interactions in a modified SCALE-UP classroom. *2011 Physics Education Research Conference,* 167–170. doi:10.1063/1.3680021

Demski, J. (2012, June 3). Tech flex. *Campus Technology*. Retrieved from http://campustechnology.com/Articles/2012/06/03/Tech-Flex.aspx

Deslauriers, L., Schelew, E., & Wieman, C. (2011). Improved learning in a large-enrollment physics class. *Science, 332*(6031), 862–864. doi:10.1126/science.1202043

Dewey, J. (1997). *Democracy and education. An introduction to the philosophy of education*. New York, NY: Free Press. (Original work published 1916)

Dewey, R. A. (2004). *Psychology: An introduction*. Boston, MA: Wadsworth.

Dillman, D. A., Smyth, J. D., & Christian, L. M. (2014). *Internet, phone, mail, and mixed-mode surveys: The tailored design method* (4th ed.). Hoboken, NJ: John Wiley & Sons.

Dori, Y. J., & Belcher, J. (2005). How does technology-enabled active learning affect undergraduate students' understanding of electromagnetism concepts? *Journal of the Learning Sciences, 14*(2), 243–279. doi:10.1207/s15327809jls1402_3

Dori, Y. J., Belcher, J., Besette, M., Danziger, M., McKinney, A., & Hult, E. (2003). Technology for active learning. *Materials Today, 6*(12), 44–49. doi:10.1016/S1369-7021(03)01225-2

Eberlein, T., Kampmeier, J., Minderhout, V., Moog, R. S., Platt, T., Varma-Nelson, P., & White, H. B. (2008). Pedagogies of engagement in science: A comparison of PBL, POGIL, and PLTL. *Biochemistry and Molecular Biology Education, 36*(4), 262–273. doi:10.1002/bmb.20204

EDUCAUSE Learning Initiative. (2012). *7 things you should know about flipped classrooms*. Retrieved from https://net.educause.edu/ir/library/pdf/eli7081.pdf

Eggleston, T. J., & Smith, G. E. (2002). Parting ways: Ending your course. *American Psychological Society Observer, 15*(3). Retrieved from http://www.psychologicalscience.org/index.php/publications/observer

Endo, J. J., & Harpel, R. L. (1982). The effect of student–faculty interaction on students' educational outcomes. *Research in Higher Education, 16*, 115–135. doi:10.1007/BF00973505.

Erdle, S., Murray, H. G., & Rushton, J. P. (1985). Personality, classroom behavior, and student ratings of college teaching effectiveness: A path analysis. *Journal of Educational Psychology, 77*(4), 394–407. doi:10.1037/0022-0663.77.4.394

Felder, R. M., & Brent, R. (2001). Effective strategies for cooperative learning. *Journal of Cooperation and Collaboration in College Teaching, 10*(2), 69–75. Retrieved from http://opened.uoguelph.ca/TSS/educational_development/periodicals.aspx

Felder, R. M., & Brent, R. (2007). Cooperative learning. In P. A. Mabrouk (Ed.), *Active learning: Models from the analytical sciences: ACS Symposium series* (Vol. 970, pp. 34–53). Washington, DC: American Chemical Society. Retrieved from http://www4.ncsu.edu/unity/lockers/users/f/felder/public/Papers/CLChapter.pdf

Fink, L. D. (2013). *Creating significant learning experiences*. San Francisco, CA: Jossey-Bass.

Finkelstein, A. (2015, August). *Next generation active learning classrooms*. Session presented at the National Forum on Active Learning Classrooms, Minneapolis, MN.

Florman, J. C. (2014). TILE at Iowa: Adoption and adaptation. *New Directions for Teaching and Learning: Active Learning Spaces, 2014*(137), 77–84. doi:10.1002/tl.20088

Fraser, K. (Ed.). (2014). *The future of learning and teaching in next generation learning spaces: International perspectives on higher education research* (Vol. 12). Bingley, UK: Emerald Group.

Freeman, S., Eddy, S. L., McDonough, M., Smith, M. K., Okoroafor, N., Jordt, H., & Wenderoth, M. P. (2014). Active learning increases student performance in science, engineering, and mathematics. *Proceedings of the National Academy of Sciences, 111*(23), 8410–8415. doi:10.1073/pnas.1319030111

Fried, C. (2008). In-class laptop use and its effects on student learning. *Computers & Education, 50*(3), 906–914. doi:10.1016/j.compedu.2006.09.006

Gaffney, J. D. H., Gaffney, A. L. H., & Beichner, R. J. (2010). Do they see it coming? Using expectancy violation to gauge the success of pedagogical reforms. *Physical Review Special Topics: Physics Education Research, 6*(1), 1–16. doi:10.1103/physrevstper.6.010102

Germany, L. (2014). Learning space evaluations: Timing, team, techniques. In K. Fraser (Ed.), *The future of learning and teaching in next generation learning spaces: International perspectives on higher education research* (Vol. 12, pp. 267–288). Bingley, UK: Emerald Group.

Gierdowski, D. (2013). Studying learning spaces: A review of selected empirical studies. In R. G. Carpenter (Ed.), *Cases on higher education spaces: Innovation, collaboration, and technology* (pp. 14–39). Hershey, PA: IGI Global. doi:10.4018/978-1-4666-2673-7.ch002

Gillespie, K. J., Robertson, D. L., & Associates. (2010). *A guide to faculty development* (2nd ed.). San Francisco, CA: Jossey-Bass.

Giuliodori, M. J., Lujan, H. L., & DiCarlo, S. E. (2008). Collaborative group testing benefits high- and low-performing students. *Advances in Physiology Education, 32*(4), 274–278. doi:10.1152/advan.00101.2007

Goodsell, A. M., Maher, M., Tinto, V., & Associates. (Eds.). (1992). *Collaborative learning: A sourcebook for higher education*. University Park, PA: National Center on Postsecondary Teaching, Learning, and Assessment.

Granitz, N. A., Koernig, S. K., & Harich, K. R. (2009). Now it's personal: Antecedents and outcomes of rapport between business faculty and their students. *Journal of Marketing Education, 31*(1), 52–65. doi:10.1177/0273475308326408

Haak, D. C., HilleRisLambers, J., Pitre, E., & Freeman, S. (2011). Increased structure and active learning reduce the achievement gap in introductory biology. *Science, 332*(6034), 1213–1216. doi:10.1126/science.1204820

Hall, D., & Buzwell, S. (2012). The problem of free-riding in group projects: Looking beyond social loafing as reason for non-contribution. *Active Learning in Higher Education, 14*(1), 37–49. doi:10.1177/1469787412467123

Hart Research Associates. (2015). Falling short? College learning and career success. Washington, DC: Association of American Colleges and Universities. Retrieved from https://www.aacu.org/sites/default/files/files/LEAP/2015employerstudentsurvey.pdf

Harvey, E. J., & Kenyon, M. C. (2013). Classroom seating considerations for 21st century students and faculty. *Journal of Learning Spaces, 2*(1). Retrieved from http://libjournal.uncg.edu/jls/article/view/578

Henshaw, R. G., Edwards, P. M., & Bagley, E. J. (2011). Use of swivel desks and aisle space to promote interaction in mid-sized college classrooms. *Journal of Learning Spaces, 1*(1). Retrieved from http://libjournal.uncg.edu/jls/article/view/277

Hestenes, D., Wells, M., & Swackhamer, G. (1992). Force concept inventory. *Physics Teacher, 30,* 141–151. doi:10.1119/1.2343497

Hill, M. C., & Epps, K. K. (2010). The impact of physical classroom environment on student satisfaction and student evaluation of teaching in the university environment. *Academy of Educational Leadership Journal, 14*(4), 65–79. Retrieved from http://www.alliedacademies.org/affiliate-academies-ael.php

Hillyard, C., Gillespie, D., & Littig, P. (2010). University students' attitudes about learning in small groups after frequent participation. *Active Learning in Higher Education, 11*(1), 9–20. doi:10.1177/1469787409355867

Institute of International Education. (2014). *Open doors report.* Retrieved from http://www.iie.org/Research-and-Publications/Open-Doors

Johnson, D. W., & Johnson, R. T. (2009). An educational psychology success story: Social interdependence theory and cooperative learning. *Educational Researcher, 38*(5), 365–379. doi:10.3102/0013189X09339057

Johnson, D. W., Johnson, R. T., & Smith, K. A. (2006). *Active learning: Cooperation in the college classroom* (2nd ed.). Edina, MN: Interaction Book Co.

Johnson, D. W., Johnson, R. T., & Smith, K. A. (2013). Cooperative learning: Improving university instruction by basing practice on validated theory. *Journal on Excellence in University Teaching, 25*(3/4), 85–118. Retrieved from http://celt .miamioh.edu/ject/fetch.php?id=594

Junco, R. (2012). In-class multitasking and academic performance. *Computers in Human Behavior, 28*(6), 2236–2243. doi:10.1016/j.chb.2012.060.

Kagan, S. (1992). *Cooperative learning.* San Juan Capistrano, CA: Resources for Teachers.

Kapitanoff, S. H. (2009). Collaborative testing: Cognitive and interpersonal processes related to enhanced test performance. *Active Learning in Higher Education, 10*(1), 56–70. doi:10.1177/1469787408100195

Kiewra, K. A. (1985). Investigating notetaking and review: A depth of processing alternative. *Educational Psychologist, 20,* 23–32. doi:10.1207/s15326985ep2001_4

Kim, H. S. (2002). We talk, therefore we think? A cultural analysis of the effect of talking on thinking. *Journal of Personality and Social Psychology, 83*(4), 828–842. doi:10.1037/0022-3514.83.4.828

Kim, H. S. (2008). Culture and the cognitive and neuroendocrine responses to speech. *Journal of Personality and Social Psychology, 94*(1), 32–47. doi:10.1037/0022-3514.94.1.32

Krueger, R. A., & Casey, M. A. (2014). *Focus groups: A practical guide for applied research.* Thousand Oaks, CA: SAGE.

Lackney, J. A. (1999). A history of the studio-based learning model. Retrieved from the Mississippi State University Educational Design Institute at http://www.edi .msstate.edu/work/pdf/history_studio_based_learning.pdf

Larson, C. O., & Dansereau, D. F. (1986). Cooperative learning in dyads. *Journal of Reading, 29*(6), 516–520. Retrieved from http://www.jstor.org/journal/jread

Lasry, N., Charles, E., & Whittaker, C. (2014). When teacher-centered instructors are assigned to student-centered classrooms. *Physical Review Special Topics: Physics Education Research, 10*(010116), 1–9. doi:10.1103/physrevstper.10.010116

Latane, B., Williams, K., & Harkins, S. (1979). Many hands make light the work: The causes and consequences of social loafing. *Journal of Personality and Social Psychology, 37*(6), 822–832. doi:10.1037/0022-3514.37.6.822

Levi, D. (2013). *Group dynamics for teams.* Thousand Oaks, CA: SAGE.

Ling, P., & Fraser, K. (2014). Pedagogies for next generation learning spaces: Theory, context, action. In K. Fraser (Ed.), *The future of learning and teaching in next generation learning spaces: International perspectives on higher education research* (Vol. 12, pp. 65–84). Bingley, UK: Emerald Group.

Loes, C. N., An, B. P., Saichaie, K., & Pascarella, E. T. (in press). Does collaborative learning influence persistence to the second year of college? *Journal of Higher Education.*

Loes, C. N., & Pascarella, E. T. (2015). The benefits of good teaching extend beyond course achievement. *Journal of the Scholarship of Teaching and Learning, 15*(2), 1–13. doi:10.14434/josotl.v15i2.13167

Loughry, M. L., Ohland, M. L., & Woehr, D. J. (2014). Assessing teamwork skills for assurance of learning using CATME Team Tools. *Journal of Marketing Education, 36*(1), 5–19. doi:10.1177/0273475313499023

Lyon, D. C., & Lagowski, J. J. (2008). Effectiveness of facilitating small-group learning in large lecture classes. *Journal of Chemical Education, 85*(11), 1571–1576. doi:10.1021/ed085p1571

Matthes, D. (2015, August). *Assignments that maximize the value of round tables and white boards.* Interactive session presented at the 2015 National Forum on Active Learning Classrooms, Minneapolis, MN.

Mazur, E. (1996). *Peer instruction: A user's manual.* Upper Saddle River, NJ: Prentice Hall.

Mazur, E. (2009). Farewell, lecture? *Science, 323*(5910), 50–51. doi:10.1126/science.1168927

McKeachie, W., & Svinicki, M. (2014). *McKeachie's teaching tips* (14th ed.). Boston, MA: Cengage Learning.

Merrow, J. (2006). My college education: Look at the whole elephant. *Change: The Magazine of Higher Learning, 38*(3), 8–15. doi:10.3200/CHNG.38.3.8-15

Messick, S. (1994). The interplay of evidence and consequences in validation of performance assessment. *Educational Researcher, 23*(2), 13–23. doi:10.3102/0013189X023002013

Meyers, S. A. (2008). Working alliances in college classrooms. *Teaching of Psychology, 34*, 29–32. doi:10.1080/00986280701818490

Michael, J. (2006). Where's the evidence that active learning works? *Advances in Physiology Education. 30*, 159–167. doi:10.1152/advan.00053.2006

Michaelsen, L. K., Knight, A. B., & Fink, L. D. (Eds.). (2004). *Team-based learning: A transformative use of small groups in college teaching.* Sterling, VA: Stylus.

Millis, B. J., & Cottell, P. G. (1998). *Cooperative learning for higher education faculty.* Phoenix, AZ: Oryx Press.

Moog, R. (2014). Process-oriented guided-inquiry learning. In M. McDaniel, R. Frey, S. Fitzpatrick, & H. L. Roediger (Eds.), *Integrating cognitive science with innovative teaching in STEM disciplines.* St. Louis, MO: Washington University Libraries. Retrieved from http://openscholarship.wustl.edu/circle_book/

Moore, D. A., & Healy, P. J. (2008). The trouble with overconfidence. *Psychological Review, 115*(2), 502. doi:10.1037/0033-295X.115.2.502

Moreno, A., Ovalle, D. A., & Vicari, R. M. (2012). A genetic algorithm approach for group formation in collaborative learning considering multiple student characteristics. *Computers & Education, 58*(1), 560–569. doi:10.1016/j.compedu.2011.09.011

Morrone, A. S., Ouimet, J. A., Siering, G., & Arthur, I. T. (2014). Coffeehouse as classroom: Examination of a new style of active learning classroom. *New Directions for Teaching and Learning: Active Learning Spaces, 2014*(137), 41–51. doi:10.1002/tl.20084

Muthyala, R. S., & Wei, W. (2013). Does space matter? Impact of classroom space on student learning in an organic-first curriculum. *Journal of Chemical Education, 90*, 45–50. doi:10.1021/ed3002122

National Association of Colleges and Employers. (2014). *Job outlook 2015.* Bethlehem, PA: Author. Retrieved from http://www.naceweb.org/surveys/job-outlook.aspx

National Center for Education Statistics. (2013). *Digest of education statistics* (No. NCES 2014-015). Washington, DC: U.S. Department of Education.

Nilson, L. B. (2010). *Teaching at its best: A research-based resource for college instructors.* San Francisco, CA: Jossey-Bass.

Noble, J., & Sawyer, R. (2002). *Predicting different levels of academic success in college using high school GPA and ACT composite score.* Iowa City, IA: ACT.

Oakley, B. (2002). It takes two to tango: How "good" students enable problematic behavior in teams. *Journal of Student Centered Learning, 1*(1), 19–27. Retrieved from http://cat.xula.edu/journals/

Oakley, B., Felder, R. M., Brent, R., & Elhajj, I. (2004). Turning student groups into effective teams. *Journal of Student Centered Learning, 2*(1), 9–34. Retrieved from http://cat.xula.edu/journals/

Oliver-Hoyo, M. T. (2011). Lesson learned from the implementation and assessment of student-centered methodologies. *Journal of Technology and Science Education, 1*(1), 2–11. doi:10.3926/jotse.2011.6

Padgett, R. D., Goodman, K. M., Johnson, M. P., Saichaie, K., Umbach, P. D., & Pascarella, E. T. (2010). The impact of college student socialization, social class, and race on need for cognition. *New Directions for Institutional Research, 2010*(145), 99–111.

Palinscar, A. S., & Brown, A. L. (1984). Reciprocal teaching of comprehension-fostering and comprehension-monitoring activities. *Cognition and Instruction, 1*(2), 117–175. doi:10.1207/s1532690xci0102_1

Pandey, C., & Kapitanoff, S. H. (2011). The influence of anxiety and quality of interaction on collaborative test performance. *Active Learning in Higher Education, 12*(3), 163–174. doi:10.1177/1469787411415077

Pascarella, E. T., & Terenzini, P. T. (2005). *How college affects students: A third decade of research* (Vol. 2). San Francisco, CA: Jossey-Bass.

Pedalty, M. (2008). Making a statement. In J. L. Higbee & E. Goff (Eds.), *Pedagogy and student services for institutional transformation: Implementing universal design in higher education* (pp. 79–85). Minneapolis, MN: Center for Research on Developmental Education and Urban Literacy, University of Minnesota. Retrieved from http://www.cehd.umn.edu/passit/docs/pass-it-book.pdf

Pedhazur, E. J., & Schmelkin, L. P. (1991). *Measurement, design, and analysis: An integrated approach.* Hillsdale, NJ: Lawrence Erlbaum.

Petersen, C. I., & Gorman, K. S. (2014). Strategies to address common challenges when teaching in an active learning classroom. *New Directions for Teaching and Learning, 2014*(137), 63–70. doi:10.1002/tl.20086

Picciano, A. G., & Dziuban, C. D. (Eds.). (2007). *Blended learning: Research perspectives.* Newburyport, MA: Sloan-C.

Picciano, A. G., Dziuban, C. D., & Graham, C. R. (Eds.). (2013). *Blended learning: Research perspectives* (Vol. 2). New York, NY: Routledge.

Piontek, M. E. (2008). Best practices for designing and grading exams. *CRLT Occasional Papers, 24*, 1–12. Retrieved from http://www.crlt.umich.edu/resources/occasional

President's Council of Advisors on Science and Technology. (2012). Report to the President: *Engage to excel: Producing one million additional college graduates with degrees in science, technology, engineering, and mathematics.* Washington, DC: Executive Office of the President. Retrieved from https://www.whitehouse.gov/sites/default/files/microsites/ostp/pcast-executive-report-final_2-13-12.pdf

Prince, M. (2004). Does active learning work? A review of the research. *Journal of Engineering Education, 93*(3), 223–231. doi:10.1002/j.2168-9830.2004.tb00809.x

Rao, S. P., Collins, H. L., & DiCarlo, S. E. (2002). Collaborative testing enhances student learning. *Advances in Physiology Education, 26*(1), 37–41. doi:10.1152/advan.00032.2001

Ridenour, J., Feldman, G., Teodorescu, R., Medsker, L., & Benmouna, N. (2013). Is conceptual understanding compromised by a problem-solving emphasis in an introductory physics course? *AIP Conference Proceedings, 1513*(338). doi:10.1063/1.4789721

Rieger, G. W., & Heiner, C. E. (2014). Examinations that support collaborative learning: The students' perspective. *Journal of College Science Teaching, 43*(4), 41–47. doi:10.2505/4/jcst14_043_04_41

Robertson, G. (2013). Teaching to the space: Students' perceptions of learning following their teachers' participation in a programme of collaborative professional development supporting teaching in the Collaborative Learning Forum. *Research and Development in Higher Education: The Place of Learning and Teaching, 36,*

404–413. Retrieved from http://www.herdsa.org.au/wp-content/uploads/confer
ence/2013/HERDSA_2013_ROBERTSON.pdf

Ruiz, N. G. (2014). *Brookings Metro Immigration Facts Series: Vol. 15. The geography
of foreign students in U.S. higher education: Origins and destinations.* Retrieved from
http://www.brookings.edu/research/interactives/2014/geography-of-foreign-
students#/M10420

Salter, D., Thomson, D. L., Fox, B., & Lam, J. (2013). Use and evaluation of a
technology-rich experimental classroom. *Higher Education Research & Development, 32*(5), 805–819. doi:10.1080/07294360.2013.777033

Sana, F., Weston, T., & Cepeda, N. J. (2013). Laptop multitasking hinders classroom learning for both users and nearby peers. *Computers & Education, 62,*
24–31. doi:10.1016/j.compedu.2012.10.003

Sandall, L., Mamo, M., Speth, C., Lee, D., & Kettler, T. (2014). Student perception
of metacognitive activities in entry-level science courses. *Natural Sciences Education, 43*(1), 25–32. doi:10.4195/nse2013.06.0021

Savin-Baden, M., & Major, C. H. (2004). *Foundations of problem-based learning.* Buckingham, UK: Society for Research in Higher Education and Open
University Press.

Savin-Baden, M., McFarland, L., & Savin-Baden, J. (2008). Learning spaces,
agency and notions of improvement: What influences thinking and practices about teaching and learning in higher education? An interpretive meta-
ethnography. *London Review of Education, 6*(3), 211–227. doi:10.1080/14748
460802489355

Schacter, D. L. (2002). *The seven sins of memory: How the mind forgets and remembers.*
New York, NY: Houghton Mifflin.

Scott, S. S., McGuire, J. M., & Shaw, S. F. (2003). Universal design for instruction.
Remedial and Special Education, 24(6), 369–379. doi:10.1177/0741932503024
0060801

Slavin, R. (1990). *Cooperative learning: Theory, research, and practice.* Englewood
Cliffs, NJ: Prentice Hall.

Slavin, R. E. (1996). Research on cooperative learning and achievement: What
we know, what we need to know. *Contemporary Educational Psychology, 21*(1),
43–69. doi:10.1006/ceps.1996.0004

Smith, K. A. (2004). *Teamwork and project management* (2nd ed.). New York, NY:
McGraw-Hill.

Smith, K. A., Sheppard, S. D., Johnson, D. W., & Johnson, R. T. (2005). Pedagogies of engagement: Classroom-based practices. *Journal of Engineering Education,
94*(1), 87–101. Retrieved from http://www.engr.wisc.edu/services/elc/Pedago
gies_of_student_engagement_Smith.pdf

Smith, M. K., Jones, F. H. M., Gilbert, S. L., & Wieman, C. L. (2013). The classroom observation protocol for undergraduate STEM (COPUS): A new instrument to characterize university STEM classroom practices. *CBE-Life Sciences
Education, 12*(4), 618–627. doi:10.1187/cbe.13-08-0154

Smith, M. K., Wood, W. B., Adams, W. K., Wieman, C., Knight, J. K., Guild, N., & Su, T. T. (2009). Why peer discussion improves student performance on in-class concept questions. *Science, 323*(5910), 122–124. doi:10.1126/science.1165919

Sorcinelli, M. D., Austin, A. E., Eddy, P., & Beach, A. (2006). *Creating the future of faculty development: Learning from the past, understanding the present.* Bolton, MA: Anker Press.

Springer, L., Stanne, M. E., & Donovan, S. S. (1999). Effects of small-group learning on undergraduates in science, mathematics, engineering, and technology: A meta-analysis. *Review of Educational Research, 69*, 21–51. doi:10.3102/00346543069001021

Strobel, J., & Van Barneveld, A. (2009). When is PBL more effective? A meta-synthesis of meta-analyses comparing PBL to conventional classrooms. *Interdisciplinary Journal of Problem-Based Learning, 3*(1), 4–58. doi:10.7771/1541-5015.1046

Stufflebeam, D. L. (2001). *Evaluation models: New directions for evaluation.* San Francisco, CA: Jossey-Bass.

Sukhai, M. A., Mohler, C. E., & Smith, F. (2014). *Understanding accessibility in "practical space" learning environments across disciplines.* Toronto, Ontario: Council of Ontario Universities. Retrieved from http://www.accessiblecampus.ca/wp-content/uploads/2014/07/Understanding-Accessibility-in-Practical-Space-Learning-Environments-Across-Disciplines.pdf

Suskie, L. (2009). *Assessing student learning: A common sense guide.* San Francisco, CA: Jossey-Bass.

Svinicki, M., & McKeachie, W. J. (2011). *McKeachie's teaching tips: Strategies, research, and theory for college and university teachers* (13th ed.). Belmont, CA: Wadsworth.

Taneja, A., Fiore, V., & Fischer, B. (2015). Cyber-slacking in the classroom: Potential for digital distraction in the new age. *Computers & Education, 82*, 141–151. doi:10.1016/j.compedu.2014.11.009

Tashakkori, A., & Teddlie, C. (2010). *SAGE handbook of mixed methods in social & behavioral research.* Thousand Oaks, CA: SAGE.

Terenzini, P. T., Cabrera, A. F., Colbeck, C. L., Parente, J. M., & Bjorkland, S. A. (2001). Collaborative learning vs. lecture/discussion: Students' reported learning gains. *Journal of Engineering Education, 90*(1), 123–130. doi:10.1002/j.2168-9830.2001.tb00579.x

Thorndike, R. M. (2005). *Measurement and evaluation in psychology and education.* Upper Saddle River, NJ: Pearson Education.

Tiberius, R. G., & Billson, J. M. (1991). The social context of teaching and learning. *New Directions for Teaching and Learning: College Teaching From Theory to Practice, 1991*(45), 67–86. doi:10.1002/tl.37219914509

Tinto, V. (1997). Classrooms as communities: Exploring the educational character of student persistence. *Journal of Higher Education 68*(6), 599–623. doi:10.2307/2959965

Tinto, V., Goodsell, A., & Russo, P. (1993). Collaborative learning and new college students. *Cooperative Learning and College Teaching, 3*(3), 9–10.

Titsworth, B. S., & Kiewra, K. A. (2004). Spoken organizational lecture cues and student notetaking as facilitators of student learning. *Contemporary Educational Psychology, 29*, 447–461. doi:10.1016/j.cedpsych.2003.12.001

Tomcho, T. J., & Foels, R. (2012). Meta-analysis of group learning activities: Empirically based teaching recommendations. *Teaching of Psychology, 39*(3), 159–169. doi:10.1177/0098628312450414

Trochim, W. M. K. (2001). *Research methods knowledge base.* Mason, OH: Thomson Learning.

Tuckman, B. W. (1965). Developmental sequence in small groups. *Psychological Bulletin, 63*(6), 384–399. doi:10.1037/h0022100

Tuckman, B. W., & Jensen, M. A. C. (1977). Stages of small-group development revisited. *Group & Organization Management, 2*(4), 419–427. doi:10.1177/105960117700200404

Twetten, J. (2006). Iowa State University: LeBaron Hall Auditorium. In D. G. Oblinger (Ed.), *Learning spaces* (Vol. 2). Washington, DC: EDUCAUSE. Retrieved from http://www.educause.edu/research-and-publications/books/learning-spaces/chapter-22-iowa-state-university-lebaron-hall-auditorium

University of Oregon Academic Extension. (2015, May 29). Universal classroom design [Web log post]. Retrieved from http://blogs.uoregon.edu/introreport/2015/05/29/universal-classroom-design/

VanBergeijk, E., Klin, A., & Volkmar, F. (2008). Supporting more able students on the autism spectrum: College and beyond. *Journal of Autism and Developmental Disorders, 38*, 1359–1370. doi:10.1007/s10803-007-0524-8

Van Horne, S., Murniati, C., Gaffney, J. D., & Jesse, M. (2012). Promoting active learning in technology-infused TILE classrooms at the University of Iowa. *Journal of Learning Spaces, 1*(2). Retrieved from http://libjournal.uncg.edu/jls

Van Horne, S., Murniati, C. T., Saichaie, K., Jesse, M., Florman, J. C., & Ingram, B. F. (2014). Using qualitative research to assess teaching and learning in technology-infused TILE classrooms. *New Directions for Teaching and Learning: Active Learning Spaces, 2014*(137), 17–26. doi:10.1002/tl.20082

Walker, J. D., Baepler, P., Brooks, D. C., & Saichaie, K. (2012). *Role-differentiated responses to active learning classrooms: The University of Minnesota.* Washington, DC: EDUCAUSE. Retrieved from http://www.educause.edu/library/resources/role-differentiated-responses-active-learning-classrooms-university-minnesota

Walker, J. D., Brooks, D. C., & Baepler, P. (2011). Pedagogy and space: Empirical research in new learning environments. *EDUCAUSE Quarterly, 34*(4). Retrieved from http://www.educause.edu/ero/article/pedagogy-and-space-empirical-research-new-learning-environments

Weaver, B. (2009). Collaborating with users to design learning spaces: Playing nicely in the sandbox. *EDUCAUSE Quarterly, 32*(1). Retrieved from http://er.educause.edu/articles/2009/3/collaborating-with-users-to-design-learning-spaces-playing-nicely-in-the-sandbox

Weimer, M. (2013). *Learner-centered teaching: Five key changes to practice* (2nd ed). San Francisco, CA: John Wiley & Sons.

Weimer, M., & Lenze, L. (1997). Instructional interventions: Review of the literature on efforts to improve instruction. In R. Perry & J. Smart (Eds.), *Effective teaching in higher education: Research and practice* (pp. 154–168). New York, NY: Agathon Press.

Wenger, E. (1999). *Communities of practice: Learning, meaning, and identity.* Cambridge, MA: Cambridge University Press.

Whiteside, A., Brooks, D. C., & Walker, J. D. (2010). Making the case for space: Three years of empirical research on formal and informal learning environments. *EDUCAUSE Quarterly, 33*(3). Retrieved from http://www.educause.edu/ero/article/making-case-space-three-years-empirical-research-learning-environments

Wick, S., Decker, M., Matthes, D., & Wright, R. (2013). Students propose genetic solutions to societal problems. *Science, 341*(6153), 1467–1468. doi:10.1126/science.1230002

Wilson, J. H., Ryan, R. G., & Pugh, J. L. (2010). Professor–student rapport scale predicts student outcomes. *Teaching of Psychology, 37*(4), 246–251. doi:10.1080/00986283.2010.510976

Wilson, J. M. (1994). The CUPLE physics studio. *Physics Teacher, 32*(9), 518–523. doi:10.1119/1.2344100

Wilson, J. M., & Jennings, W. C. (2000). Studio courses: How information technology is changing the way we teach, on campus and off. *Proceedings of the IEEE, 88*(1), 72–80. doi:10.1109/5.811603

Wolf, L. E. (2001). College students with ADHD and other hidden disabilities. *Annals of the New York Academy of Sciences, 931,* 385–395. doi:10.1111/j.1749-6632.2001.tb05792.x

Zafar, B. (2011). How do college students form expectations? *Journal of Labor Economics, 29*(2), 301–348. doi:10.1086/658091

ABOUT THE AUTHORS

Paul Baepler serves as a research fellow in the Center for Educational Innovation (CEI) at the University of Minnesota. His role is to investigate the efficacy of educational innovations in the classroom and elsewhere in higher education. Baepler earned his PhD in American literature and his book, *White Slaves, African Masters* (University of Chicago Press, 1999), explores the little-known Barbary captivity narrative. His work has appeared in a variety of journals including *Computers and Education, Journal of College Science Teaching, EDUCAUSE Quarterly, The Journal of Faculty Development,* and *The New England Quarterly.* Along with Brooks and Walker of this volume, he coedited the Active Learning Spaces volume of *New Directions for Teaching and Learning.* Previously, he worked at the Center for Teaching and Learning and the Digital Media Center, and he is the faculty director for test preparation in the College of Continuing Education.

D. Christopher Brooks has served as a senior research fellow for the EDUCAUSE Center for Analysis and Research (ECAR; www.educause .edu/ecar) since December 2013. Prior to joining ECAR, Brooks served as a research associate in the Office of Information Technology at the University of Minnesota where he researched the impact of educational technologies and Active Learning Classrooms on teaching practices and learning outcomes, completion rates and the impact of massive open online courses on student learning, and evaluating blended learning environments. His research appears in a range of scholarly journals including the *British Journal of Educational Technology, EDUCAUSE Quarterly, International Journal for the Scholarship of Teaching and Learning, Journal of College Science Teaching, Evolution, Journal of Political Science Education,* and *Social Science Quarterly,* and in the edited volume *Blended Learning: Research Perspectives,* Vol. 2. His coedited "Active Learning Spaces" volume of *New Directions for Teaching and Learning* was published 2014. Brooks earned his PhD in political science from Indiana University in 2002. He has taught courses in comparative politics and political theory at Indiana University–Purdue University Fort Wayne, St. Olaf College, and the University of Minnesota.

Christina I. Petersen is an education program specialist in the Center for Educational Innovation at the University of Minnesota. She works with colleges, departments, and individuals from multiple disciplines to develop curriculum and courses that incorporate evidence-based pedagogical practices to foster student learning. Her own research interests include influences on faculty attitudes toward student-centered teaching approaches and factors that lead to effective student team functioning. At the University of Minnesota, she has taught courses in higher education pedagogy, neuropharmacology, and scientific presentation skills courses, many of these in active learning classrooms. Petersen also served as a research assistant professor in the anesthesiology department at Vanderbilt University where she studied molecular mechanisms of cardiac arrhythmia. Petersen has published in *Nature Neuroscience, Proceedings of the National Academies of Science,* and *New Directions in Teaching and Learning.* She earned a PhD in pharmacology from Vanderbilt University in 1999.

Kem Saichaie is the associate director of learning and teaching support in the Center for Educational Effectiveness at the University of California, Davis (UC Davis). He provides leadership to support the teaching community at UC Davis and promotes the integration of research-based practices into traditional, blended, hybrid, and online learning spaces. Additionally, Saichaie is leading the strategic instructional support and assessment initiatives associated with active learning classrooms at UC Davis. Saichaie led similar efforts as the director of educational technology at the University of Massachusetts–Amherst (UMass). He has been involved with the faculty development and assessment efforts related to ALCs at the University of Iowa and the University of Minnesota and also taught courses in ALCs at the University of Iowa, UC Davis, and UMass. Saichaie has published in a number of venues including *The Journal of Higher Education, International Journal for the Scholarship of Teaching and Learning, Medical Teacher, New Directions in Teaching and Learning* (Learning Spaces volume), *New Directions in Institutional Research,* and EDUCAUSE's Seeking Evidence of Impact series. Saichaie earned a PhD higher education and student affairs from the University of Iowa in 2011.

J. D. Walker is a research associate in the Center for Educational Innovation (CEI) at the University of Minnesota, where his work focuses on investigating the impact of digital technologies and other educational innovations on student learning outcomes in higher education, as well as on student engagement and the faculty teaching experience. In collaboration with CEI and faculty colleagues, he has conducted studies of the effectiveness of new, technology-enhanced classroom spaces; flipped and blended-format classes; multimedia and mobile technologies; classes delivered as massive open online courses; and the social context of teaching and learning. Walker earned his PhD in philosophy from the University of North Carolina at Chapel Hill in 1996, and he taught as a faculty member at the University of Minnesota-Duluth, the University of Pennsylvania, and Franklin and Marshall College. He earned an MA degree in quantitative methods in education from the Department of Educational Psychology at the University of Minnesota in 2010.

Baepler, Paul, 36, 63
Beichner, Robert, 196
    on criterion-referenced grading, 162
    on grade curving avoidance,
        142–43
    on group size, 133
    on outcomes and objectives in
        groups, 126
    on ponderable course time, 12
    SCALE-UP approach, 12–14
    on socialization and student success,
        13–14
    on tangible course time, 12
Belcher, John, 12, 14–15
BIOL. *See* Biology class
Biology (BIOL) class, at University of
    Minnesota, 26–27
blended setting, group work in, 141
blending. *See* flipping and blending
Boyd, Diane, 193
brown-bag series, for instructors, 7
Bruininks Hall. *See* Robert H.
    Bruininks Hall
Bryant, William Cullen, 83
Buurma, Rachel Sagner, 68

calendar of activities, in genetic
    engineering proposal project,
    97–103
CATME. *See* Comprehensive
    Assessment of Team Member
    Effectiveness
causal questions, in quantitative
    research, 216
central focal point, visual distraction
    minimization and, 175, 177
circuit-training exam preparation, 165
class discussion. *See also* structured
    discussions and debates
    in genetic engineering proposal
        project, 115–17
    small group, for skill development,
        73, 92
    whole-, 163–64, 179

Classroom Observation Protocol for
    Undergraduate STEM (COPUS),
    227
class-specific examples, to reduce
    student resistance, 63–64
class time flow management, 58
Clemson University, in ALC history, 12
clicker use
    for auditory distractions, 179–80
    quizzes and questions, 159–60
    verbal communication reliance on,
        182–83
closed captioning, 171, 179
closing group activities, 123, 144–45
    group accomplishments and peer
        reflection, 145
    thank-a-group member, 145
Coastal Carolina University SCALE-UP
    initiative, 14
collaborations, for instructor support,
    197
collaborative exams
    for final exam, 154–55
    learning enhanced through, 154
    two-stage, 155–56
collaborative learning, ix, 16, 123. *See
    also* cooperative learning
collaborative quizzes, 158–59
colleague observation, for instructors, 54
community of practice (CoP)
    consultant approach, 196n2
community partners semester-long
    project, 76–78
comparison designs, in research,
    220–22
complex course content presentation
    copy of slides and notes, 184
    introductory outline, 185
    material confusion polling, 185
    time organization help, 185
    UDL principle on, 184
Comprehensive Assessment of Team
    Member Effectiveness (CATME),
    130

off-task laptop use, 174–77
  seating for, 177
  smart phones use and, 176
visual impairments, 171, 174–78

WebAIM, 186
weighting grades, to promote group
  work, 141–42
Wellmon, Chad, 230
whole-class discussions
  for auditory distractions
    minimization, 179
  for instructor feedback, 163–64

Wick, Sue, 11, 58
Williams, Frank, 54, 233
wireless Internet, in ALC, 10
workshops, for instructors
  formal, 189
  informal events, 188–89
  sample descriptions, 199–203
  standalone workshop topics, 7

"Your Own Devices Policy," of Buurma,
  68

zero-sum grading approach, 162

student-motivating system of grading. A major advance in our thinking about how we grade and how students learn."—**Barbara Walvoord**, *Professor Emerita, University of Notre Dame*

Engaging in the Scholarship of Teaching and Learning
A Guide to the Process, and How to Develop a Project from Start to Finish
Cathy Bishop-Clark and Beth Dietz-Uhler
Foreword by Craig E. Nelson

"Bishop-Clark and Dietz-Uhler have made a unique contribution in the present volume. It is an exceptionally fine, straightforward and brief guide for faculty looking at their first scholarship of teaching and learning (SOTL) project. For most such readers, it will probably seem to be the most helpful of the [available] guides. And, although it is written with the novice in mind, many of us with more experience also will benefit from reading through it.

"I anticipate that this book will lead many more faculty members to see their teaching as an opportunity to engage in SOTL. And, even though it is clearly an effective guide for individual thinking, it will be even more effective when used as the focus of a faculty learning community or by a less formal group of faculty working together. Indeed, the core structure and especially the worksheets will help groups to stay focused and productive. However used, it will help teachers use SOTL as a way to improve their students' learning and to foster more advanced learning outcomes while simultaneously enhancing the faculty members' own professional development and careers. I hope you find it as interesting and helpful as I did."—*Craig E. Nelson, Emeritus Professor of Biology, Indiana University, and Founding President, International Society for the Scholarship of Teaching and Learning*

Sty/us

22883 Quicksilver Drive
Sterling, VA 20166-2102

Subscribe to our e-mail alerts: www.Styluspub.com

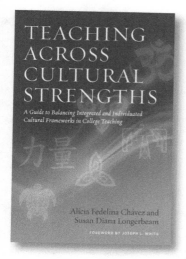

Teaching Across Cultural Strengths

A Guide to Balancing Integrated and Individuated Cultural Frameworks in College Teaching

Alicia Fedelina Chávez and Susan Diana Longerbeam

Foreword by Joseph L. White

"*Teaching Across Cultural Strengths* is a shining star in a night sky of relative darkness on inclusive teaching in the academy. Through their practical yet creative approach, Chávez and Longerbeam make a pivotal impact on the ways culture plays out between and among students and teacher in postsecondary education. Its contribution to students of color and women's learning is substantial, with clear application to these groups as well as others in all academic disciplines. In fact, by placing primary emphasis on culture, this book could bring about a movement to reform the relationship between student and teacher in higher education producing optimal learning in every field. The work presented by these authors can significantly transform teaching on any college campus with a progressive view of learning. Faculty in every academic discipline concerned about student learning and how it occurs through their teaching will find this book practical and insightful. Student affairs educators responsible for professional development, or with deep concern for out-of-class learning, will find this imperative reading to assist students in their learning, growth, and development. Chávez and Longerbeam get high praise for illuminating the place of culture in post-secondary learning."—*Florence M. Guido*, *Professor, University of Northern Colorado*

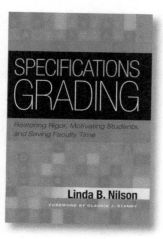

Specifications Grading

Restoring Rigor, Motivating Students, and Saving Faculty Time

Linda B. Nilson

Foreword by Claudia J. Stanny

"What a ridiculously simple yet profound plan for achieving what Nilson purports. Imagine, students demonstrating mastery of skill for a grade! Students taking back ownership of their progress! Students becoming our clients rather than our customers! Specs grading, get ready to sashay in and partner up with the outcomes that grades should really reflect." —*Carol Washburn*, *Senior Instructional Designer, Manager, Teaching & Learning, Center for Instructional Development & Distance Education, University of Pittsburgh*

"This book will change your life! Every instructor should buy it now. Nilson shows us how to make grading easier, more logical, and more consonant with research on learning and motivation. A practical, time-saving,

(Continues on previous page)

Clickers in the Classroom
Using Classroom Response Systems to Increase Student Learning
Edited by David S. Goldstein and Peter D. Wallis
Foreword by James Rehm

"A significant contribution to enhance active learning in the classroom."—*Patrick Blessinger*, *Executive Director and Chief Research Scientist, Higher Education Teaching and Learning Association*

The research demonstrates that, integrated purposefully in courses, the use of clickers aligns with what neuroscience tells us about the formation of memory and the development of learning. In addition, they elicit contributions from otherwise reticent students and enhance collaboration, even in large lecture courses; foster more honest responses to discussion prompts; increase students' engagement and satisfaction with the classroom environment; and provide an instantaneous method of formative assessment.

This book presents a brief history of the development of classroom response systems (CRSs or clickers) and a survey of empirical research to provide a context for current best practices, and then presents seven chapters providing authentic, effective examples of the use of clickers across a wide range of academic disciplines, demonstrating how they can be effective in helping students to recognize their misconceptions and grasp fundamental concepts.

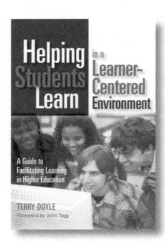

Helping Students Learn in a Learner-Centered Environment
A Guide to Facilitating Learning in Higher Education
Terry Doyle
Foreword by John Tagg

"I see this book as a great read for experienced faculty who want to figure out a new way to construct a less lecture-based classroom environment, and for new faculty who need tips on how to teach well in a learner-centered environment. I have been teaching for 20 years and have been a faculty developer for the past 10 and, even with all of that experience, I still learned several things in reading this book."—*Todd Zakrajsek*, *Director of the Faculty Center for Innovative Teaching at Central Michigan University*

(Continues on previous page)